# NORMALCY NEVER AGAIN

"Dr. Lewis T. Tait Jr. and Dr. Christian Van Gorder's *Normalcy Never Again* shakes us out of our status quo, calling us to a prophetic antiracist future for all God's children."

**—PETER GOODWIN HELTZEL,**
visiting researcher, Boston University School of Theology

"This book is a brilliant exposition on racist oppression—of how the powerful have often beleaguered the weak in empire. The religious claim that we are all children of God irrespective of differences exposes the very hypocrisy of the many religious elites who support oppressors or silently approve of oppression. From the age of slavery and the continued persecution of Africans in America to the present cries of the 'Black Lives Matter" Movement, the racist-oppressive treatment of many is a dark stigma on American democracy and its claim to offer liberty and justice for all."

**—MUHAMMAD SHAFIQ,**
professor and executive director, Hickey Center for Interfaith Studies
and Dialogue, Nazareth College, Rochester, New York

"In their important book, Van Gorder and Tait stress that racist oppression, like all other forms of evil, is fundamentally an assault against human dignity and an affront to all with open and humane hearts. The painful experience of the African Slave Trade, far from being a buried past, is a crime in search of a just and equitable resolution, its wounds ever so fresh. As such it is part of that growing catalogue of great crimes that stretches from the genocide of the Armenians in the Ottoman Empire to the killing fields of Cambodia, from Auschwitz to Rwanda to Bosnia. Written in an engaging style, the central message of the book is a resolute and inspiring manifesto for solidarity, for justice, and for human rights."

**—ARTYOM TONOYAN,**
professor of global and international studies, Hamline University,
St. Paul, Minnesota

"This book is part a cry of agony and part a map of how to chart a way out of this agony. The agony it describes is not natural but born of the racist construction of the Black body in the United States. This agony is vividly captured in the catalogue of dehumanization that has marked the lives of Black people in the US for centuries. Steeped in Afrocentric wisdom, the book provides a vision that does not only seek to alleviate this pain, but also to create a more humane world. All those who work to create a more just world will benefit from reading this book."

**—DAVID TONGHOU NGONG,**

professor of religion and theology, Stillman College

# Normalcy Never Again

*Racist-Oppression and Today's Justice Movement*

## A. CHRISTIAN VAN GORDER
## & LEWIS T. TAIT JR.

WIPF & STOCK · Eugene, Oregon

NORMALCY NEVER AGAIN
Racist-Oppression and Today's Justice Movement

Wipf & Stock
An Imprint of Wipf and Stock Publishers
199 W. 8th Ave., Suite 3
Eugene, OR 97401

www.wipfandstock.com

PAPERBACK ISBN: 979-8-3852-0914-9
HARDCOVER ISBN: 979-8-3852-0915-6
EBOOK ISBN: 979-8-3852-0916-3

03/26/25

An African wisdom proverb explains: "A person who doesn't thank others doesn't thank the Creator." The way one says "thanks" in Twi is, *Me Da Ase;* literally - "I will lie at your feet." Wyatt, Felix, Lewis T. Tait Sr. and Peter, Maria, and Erika Lutsch made us. We dedicate this book to our ancestors. Speak through us: What do we need to say?

We also honor the lives of four little girls: Miss Addie Mae Collins, 14; Miss Denise McNair, 11; Miss Carole Robertson, 14; Miss Cynthia Wesley, 14. Rest in Power.

*Almighty Savior, whose heavy cross was laid upon the stalwart shoulders of Simon the Cyrenian, a son of Africa in that sad hour of your agony and mortal weakness regard with your favor this race still struggling beneath the cross of injustice, oppression, and wrong laid upon us.*

**—Reverend Gregory Alexander McGuire, 1923**

# Contents

# Dizzying Tensions

## GREAT GRANDFATHER

*It is our duty to fight for our freedom.*
*It is our duty to win.*
*We must love each other and support each other.*
*We have nothing to lose but our chains.*

**—Assata Shakur**

Wyatt Tate, great-grandfather, was born in 1842 in the Crimson Tide State of Alabama. He was murdered in 1892 by police who branded him a "Black Desperado" just as they'd call me (Tait) a "thug." Black lives didn't matter in 1892. Wyatt Tate began as a slave — "stamped from the beginning." Tate came into this world without honor – a disrespected Black.

The year they shot Tate, he bought a horse about to be slaughtered. But my great-grandfather, a horse whisperer, named it "Prince" and spoke life into it. He knew words that would help a battered Prince became strong again. Soon, the horse was performing stunts: Wyatt could call Prince from anywhere, and it would come to him. Covetously, a White saw Prince and asked Wyatt to sell it — never expecting to hear "no." In the Empire South, when White folks asked Blacks for anything, they assumed they'd always get what they wanted.

Wyatt Tate depended on Prince for transport, and farm work. He had no intention of selling his horse. Maybe the White couldn't imagine how great-grandfather came to own such a majestic animal. So, the White did what his dead ancestors had always done before — he stole it — the same way White so-called "Christians" stole everything from us: Thieves.

When great-grandfather returned from a business trip, his horse was gone. In a few days, he found Prince in a White woman's yard, called the horse, and it came to him. At that moment, Wyatt noticed Prince had fresh whip-scars all over its back.

Days later, police-officer William Ikner came to Tate's homesTXd and tried to re-capture Prince from great-grandfather. Instead, a well-placed bullet stopped Officer Ikner's heart. Tate was forced to say hurried goodbyes to his wife and brothers, J.C., his son, and granddad Felix, and flee into Alabama's steaming swamplands. Wyatt Tate survived for two weeks before the dogs picked up his scent. He stood his ground and waited: When police-man, J.D. Foster was in sight, Tate shot him dead. Tate then killed another human-hunter, Carey Willis, and wounded bounty-hunter James Dunklin before taking a bullet to his heart.

Newspaper headlines in Monroeville, Alabama, that week in 1894 read: "Wyatt Tate Kept Posse at Bay." They ran a picture of great-granddad with the caption: "Negro Desperado Pursued to a Swamp – Reinforce-ments Sent." The article reported: "Reliable information has just reached from Monroe County that young Murdock Fountain shot and killed Wyatt Tate last night while attempting to arrest him. . . . Wyatt Tate is the Negro Desperado of Monroe County who, weeks ago, wantonly killed Constable Ikner and Sheriff J.D. Foster. The Governor and relatives of Sheriff Foster had offered rewards, amounting to about $600 to be paid to Mr. Fountain."[1]

A decade later (1905), *The Mobile Register*, reported it was great grand-uncle J.C.'s turn: "Brother of Wyatt Tate Killed: When the Deputy Sheriff came to the Theodore Turpentine Company camp near Mobile looking for J.C. Tate, the officer was attempting to execute a warrant for Tate's arrest when Tate wounded the sheriff's assistant. . . . Tate was known in the neighborhood as a 'bad Negro' going constantly armed and had, on other occasions, defied arrest."[2] Grandfather Felix (or F.W.) cared for great-grandmother and two sisters until marrying grandmother. They brought my father into the world - their first child, the Rev. Lewis T. Tait, Sr.

## HEALING THREE-FIFTHS AMERICA

*I can bear no longer what I have borne.*

**—Martin Prosser**

Clay Cane said, in America, African Americans "existed in identities that were not valued."3 A lot of folks feel undervalued, commodified, erased, unseen, unheard, and unloved.

Time to shift the narrative: Time to gain a clear-eyed awareness of un-derlying systemic realities — racist-oppression. Racist-oppression doesn't only identify points of difference ("racism") it weaponizes and incentivizes it in structural ways. While prejudices have always existed, the more recent concept of "racism" is overburdened with a myriad of meanings. We need a new term because "racism," which began as a replacement for "prejudice," has lost any shared meaning. It is a word used so often it invites a pro-grammed response: Like a mosquito, it is often swatted away. "Racism" is "one of the most contentious words in America. For the dominant caste, the word is radioactive – resented, feared, denied, lobbed-back to anyone who dares to suggest it. Resistance to the word often derails any discussion of the underlying behavior it is meant to describe, thus eroding it of meaning."[4] We will use the term "racist-oppression" to stress the intersections between all other forms of oppression, including xenophobia, sexism, and homophobia. All of these fears are cradled inside the myth of White supremacy. "White supremacy" – now, that's a term which is self-explanatory.

When we uncover the control mechanisms of Empire's insatiable greed, we can begin to address social inequities. Those who love America must admit America's always been a business pretending to be a country: Greed is the gospel mission of Empire.[5] Confederate leader, the one-eyed-Jefferson Davis, boasted: "This government wasn't founded by negroes for negroes. It was founded by white men for white men. The "inequality of the white and black races" was " stamped from the beginning"[6] The Confederacy lost the battle but won the war.[7] Be clear: The Empire system isn't defective: It's a finely-tuned machine working as designed. Racist- oppression is not an unwanted flaw: It's the glue holding America together. The plan was never to have Whites do dirty jobs for little or no pay.

Healing looks like justice. Christ Jesus asks a woman in the Gospels: "Do you want healing?" Some folks are so accustomed to sickness that they cannot imagine health. Healer-prophets like Jesus remind us of that acts of violence only lead to cle of more violence. Some folks say America needs prayer: What America needs is an exorcism from legions of demons.

What does healing look like? It looks like justice and equity. There's a West African (Akkan) wisdom-word, "Sankofa," which teaches we should recapture what's been stolen. The Yoruba people shout to enemies: "Bole-kaja!" which means "Come on! Let's fight!" We're not timid. We know who we are. Because we have Sankofa power, we take control of our own spaces based on our own interests. No one else can define us with their imposed, constructed identities.

In Empire, "normal" has been the "witchcraft" of psycho-pathological Whiteness.[8] White power, "nurtured to perfection in unwholesome ways," is the myth that Whites are superior.[9] The religion of Whiteness is a diaboli-cal economic organizing-scheme "justified by religious convictions."[10] It is a virus, James Baldwin explains, "that makes the sufferer think the symptom is the cause."[11] Oceans of paralyzing manipulation are invested into propping up White supremacy. In contrast, a *Sankofa* path leads us out of hatred and into heart and spirit health.

"Racism" is an excuse for Empire's structural caste system that asserts myths of inferiority based on skin color. It claims that those from other "castes" deserve economic domination. Caste functions to intensify the greed-power-drive. Acquiring more motivates the need to exploit others. Whites impose one standard of ethics on themselves and another on others. Empire thrives on violence while posing to be civilized. In Empire, "caste becomes the underlying grammar we encode as children as when learning our native language. . . . Race is the visible agent of the unseen force of caste. Caste is the bones and "race" is the skin. Race is what we can see . . . Caste is fixed and rigid. Race is fluid and superficial, subject to periodic redefinition to meet the needs of the dominant caste."[12]

Empire thrives on fear, hatred, greed, and division. The first step is to realize what we have accepted as normality is not normal. In 2021, President Biden called for a return to normalcy. Some folks talk about a "new normal" but that's not what we need. Dr. King's "I Have A Dream Speech" originally had the working-title: "Normalcy Never Again!?"[13] That's why we chose this title for this book. Before Dr. King concluded his sermon, he said America's "normalcy" was bankrupt. He said: "Return-to-sender" needs to be stamped on the "bad-check" of false promises. Dr. King's message for America was, and still is, "Normalcy Never Again!"

Four millennia ago, heart-healers of ancient *Kemet* — modern Egypt — shared seven wisdom principles called *Ma'at* — truth, justice, harmony, balance, order, reciprocity, and propriety. These qualities are love-making creative powers that foster healthy self-image. *Ma'at* overcomes webs of disease with health, breaks webs of dysfunctional chaos with harmony, and conquers oppression with durable foundations such as order, propriety, reciprocity, and balance.

James Baldwin wrote: "The only thing White people have that Black people need or should want is power - and no one holds power forever." In what Maya Angelo calls "these yet to be United States" power-sharing is what justice looks like. Angel Kyodo Williams declares: "Injustice has a flavor, a smell. It chokes the breath and burns the gut. It rises through the body like poison, like fire."[14] For many, the question is: "In what way am I going to die today?"[15] Folks carry anxieties about potential violence into a future that feels unsafe. Larry Ward teaches: "America's racial-karma invites us to be attentive to our heart's conditioning . . . and heal our compromised social imagination."[16]

Everybody knows there's one experience of "liberty and justice" for some but a different standard for others. Ask the parents of Mr. Trayvon Martin and Master Tamir Rice, the families of Ms. Breonna Taylor and Ms. Sandra Bland, the orphans of Ms. Sonji Taylor, Mr. George Perry Floyd, Mr. Philando Castille, Mr. Freddie Gray about what is "normal" in Empire. But there's a way out of this miasma. Soul- healing wisdom — *Ma'at* — offers a path. African wisdom is a life- rope we can use to escape the quicksand. Buddhist art often shows lotus flowers blossoming out of mud. Similarly, trauma can be healed through spirit-health. Healthy relationships can flourish even in this capitalistic religious Empire of twisting, fun-house, halls of distorted mirrors.

Maybe you just want to escape: Understandable. Freedom-searchers once found freedom in Canada: Not perfect, but that still works. There's freer-air in Barbados or Accra or Aruba, and it's less icy and fever-inducing. Or you can stay in Empire where our mothers and fathers died. We built this: We can rebuild it. You will still need a refuge, an "elsewhere," even if you stay, because we'll always need safe harbors. James Baldwin claims there's "no salvation without love, the wheel in the middle of the wheel. . . . Love is a mighty fortress."[17] Get free!

Dr. John W. Kinney observes we are surrounded by a wickedness beyond evil. Audrey Lourde expounds: "Caring for myself isn't self-indulgence it's self-preservation and that's an act of political warfare."[18] White-negativity is individualized, while Black-negativity is corporatized.[19] There's no point in thinking "we-can-all-get-along if we act White" (assimilation), or oppressing bullies (with guns) will leave-us-alone if we leave them alone (segregation). Reject Empire's efforts to "programmatically strip" us of our "cultural identity and brainwash" us into accepting a mindset that we are weak, powerless, or inferior.[20]

Empire is a chained lion with decomposing teeth. It offers nothing on the menu except injustice. But dissemblers aren't going to give up their power anytime soon. Their system is performing exactly as it is designed to work. What's different now is that we are no longer fooled. Now, our focus must be on ourselves. Now is no time to marinate in bitterness. We have to be our own abolitionists: No one's coming to save us. General Harriet, Sojourner, Dr. King, and Minister Malcolm are all gone. We have to turn "Nat Turner" and "Fannie Lou Hamer" into verbs.

Are we saying Mother Africa's wisdom offers us an "Underground Railway" out of insanity? Yes. Oppression will move in as a permanent resident as long as we accept its permanence. Healing *Ma'at* is for everyone. Whatever you want to call your path of harmony, health, truth (*kweli* in Swahili), justice, balance, order, reciprocity, and propriety is fine. If you want to call your wisdom-medicine Christianity, Islam, Buddhism, Rastafarianism, or whatever — it's all good. Join us on a path following a North Star out of this oppressing "Dismal Swamp."

White supremacy myths have no power other than the power we give them. It will fail because, as Texans say, it's "all-hat-and-no-cattle." Fabricated Whiteness delivers no-liberation. It liberates no one — especially Whites. Whiteness is a demonic ethno-religion that suffocates life and brainwashes "Whites" with lies about their place in the world. It manufactures atrophied souls and cannibalizes itself. It is a "normal" that must be renounced. Normalcy never again!

There's nothing new under the sun: What's called "normal" now has been going on since jump-street. We can turn to our lineages — African or non-African — to find workable solutions to problems. Dominators scheme in shadows and — like all vampires — cannot survive in the pure light of day. Ugly demons — pushed out of shadowy, sunken-places — will spit toxic venom. Today's furies of evil confirm that their time is running out: Their days are numbered.

Knowledge about what's "normal" for Empire — an accurate diagnosis — leads to solutions. Having only half the equation means having only half the answers. The problem is that capitalism — established mostly by violence — is the language of America. It's even in the word — "America" — an anagram for "I-Am-Race." D.L. Hugley says: "Everything's about race because, in America, it's always been about race here. The places we could work and live, the places we could eat, the places we could go to school."[21] So, what's our solution? We are!

Tait is Black — Van Gorder is White. We both agree it's in everyone's interest to level the playing-field while there's still a playing-field to level. Wizard-oppressors who've always held power are being outed. Changing demographics are shifting social dynamics. Malcolm X foresaw what would happen when racists discern the "handwriting-on-the-wall" about their fall. The threat of losing control "informs everything else about how Whites view present society."[22]

Unless this yet-to-be United States becomes united, we will continue to spiral down towards a fascist-apartheid state (e.g., "The Handmaids Tale"). America was shredded by a Civil War before Blacks (and strategic-partners) fought against slavery and then, the neo-slavery, which led to a civil rights movement. America's now being shredded by injustice and will only be rescued by a human rights and justice movement. Dr. King said: "It was normalcy in Birmingham that led to the murder on Sunday morning of four beautiful, unoffending, innocent girls. . . . it is normalcy all over the country which leaves Blacks perishing on a lonely island of poverty in the midst of a vast ocean of material prosperity. The only normalcy that we will settle for is the normalcy that recognizes the dignity and worth of all of God's children."[23]

## "A HORRIBLE REPTILE"

*Oh! be warned! A horrible reptile is coiled up in your nation's bosom; the venomous creature is nursing at the tender breast of your republic; for the love of God, tear away, and fling from you the hideous monster, and let the weight of twenty-millions crush and destroy it forever!*

### —Fredrick Douglass

An African (Ewe) healing-wisdom proverb warns: "As long as a snake is loose in the house one should not sit casually making conversation." In 2020, Black Lives Matter (BLM) protests erupted after the public lynching of Mr. George Perry Floyd. BLM began in 2013, when three organizers, Opal Tometi, Alex Garza, and Patrice Khan-Cullors, created a Black-centered political-will building project. In the spirit of Ella Baker, Diana Nash, Septima Poinsettia Clark, Dorothy Haight, and Joann Robinson, women are piloting this warship through muddy waters. BLM was not founded as a church-based movement, and preachers were conspicuously absent when it began. On the other hand, there will always be a place for ego-free preachers like Rev. Kelly Miller Smith (TN) who, as a civil rights fighter, "pastored from below" — and offering requested, practical support to front-line protestors.

A death-centered Empire holds a "monopoly on violence: Police, prisons, military and the courts."[24] Violence is fear-generating and life-controlling. In 1856, Mr. Dred Scott appealed to slaveocracy-justice but was told that the Constitution saw him as only "three-fifths of a person."[25] At this, William Lloyd Garrison called our Constitution — and its ten protections of slavery — "A covenant with death and agreement with hell."[26] Until today, this "three-fifths" designation (Article 1, section 2c, clause 3) of the Constitution, has never been directly rescinded. With its "broad and powerful architecture of false assumptions," Black Americans officially remain a separate, degraded people.[27] Capitalist oppression eats us up and spews us out. Thickets of laws have set in motion a "fantastic system of evasions, denials, and justifications."[28] Laws hardwire the ethno-religion of Whiteness. Scriptwriters of our caste-system set actors in assigned roles and limit their lines. Those playing stereotypical roles are "without the tools to defend ourselves come to fulfill the roles the dominant culture tells us to play. We can end up acting out self-denigrating behaviors by which we exploit one another for material gain, distorted admiration, and the appearance of power."[29] Normalcy never again!

When the Constitution's three-fifths designation was penned, Jefferson, Washington, Madison (and others) knew England was already confronting the evils of commodifying humans. Even opponents of slavery — such as John Adams or Ben Franklin — made a three-fifths bargain with the devils of White supremacy.[30] Today, only America honors enslavers on its currency and has its national capital named after an enslaver. Only America has a "National Anthem" written by an enslaver, Francis-Scott Key (who bought his first human in 1800). This is the same anthem that has inspired billionaire-sports team owners to flog any who knelt in protest against police brutality. Francis-Scott Key was a racist who said Africans were "a distinct and inferior race of people, which all experience proves to be the greatest evil that afflicts a community."[31] Key initiated a host of racist proposals while holding political-office. When writing the anthem (1814) he was on a British ship while fleeing slaves in small boats were desperately seeking to board in hopes of gaining their freedom.

James Baldwin wrote, instead of "drowning" in history, we have to learn "how to use it."[32] The foundations for oppression require an erasure of memory. Empire oppression happens in a geography of stolen land. White supremacy launched a genocide of millions of uprooted Turtle Islanders, not just "ideas" — but real women and men — to clear space. A death-dealing slaveocracy was created to preserve enslavers; if England had won the Revolutionary War, the British abolition of slavery would have made irrelevant the main cause of the Civil War.

These facts are hard to swallow because so much American education is miseducation. Truth-tellers are scorned as anti-patriots who "cancel-culture" in the service of "political correctness." No: Those floating in a lazy-river of privileged ignorance choose fantasy-over-fact. So-called "political correctness" is an effort to foster civility after centuries where women, Blacks, Asians, First Nations, Same-Gender-Loving, Jews, Catholics, Spanish-speakers, Muslims, and immigrants have been silenced by White supremacist ahistorical exceptionalism.[33] Amazingly, "the conceit of American virtue survives the shooting of schoolchildren in Connecticut and the killing of millions of civilians from Vietnam and Iraq."[34] Now's the time to take the oppressor's knee off our necks and demand a reckoning of Empire's "moral monsters."[35] Normalcy never again!

## JIGSAW PUZZLE

*The problem of the 20th Century is the problem of the color-line - the relation of the darker to the lighter races of men in Asia and Africa, in America, and the islands of the sea.*

**—Dr. William Edward Burghardt Dubois,** *Souls of Black Folk***, 1903**

Ours is an arranged marriage. A concocted, contrived past explains a perplexing present. To think of it another way: What rapist asks those they rape about their "relationship"? Those guilty of rape often fabricate narratives that those raped bear responsibility for their rape. The rapist shouldn't tell those raped to move-on as if nothing has happened to their bodies and souls.

How can racist oppressors — who've displaced entire cultures from Africa, attempted to erase languages, arts, and music, and assassinated spiritualities to enslave Africans for more than three- centuries in forced "plantation" prison camps — preach "reconciliation?" The old plantation cannot be remodeled: It must be burned to the ground with cotton-fields scorched. Normalcy never again means rejecting the lies that inequities will be fixed by folks who really have no intention of dismantling their own privilege or giving up their own power and spaces of comfort and ease.

The Civil Rights Movement began a generation ago: After only a generation of less-horrific conduct, some claim we should all get-along. We can hear it now: "I never owned slaves. My ancestors never had slaves. Am I accountable for slavery? Why are you so angry? How dare you call me a racist?" But if wealth is inherited, how is debt not also inherited? Unresolved problems remain unresolved until they are resolved. We live in different countries in the same country. Maybe it's not "your fault" that you don't understand justice issues: But it is your problem.

Some folks say, "that's just the way it is" and feel no motivation to work for change.[36] But anyone should be able to understand why we are angry. James Cone calls African Americans a "blues-people." You can't sweep the blues under the rug. Trying to react to every trigger of anger can burn a person out. But, at the same time, we also cannot become triggered and conditioned to respond with sadness to every act of injustice. Today, injustice, inequity, police brutality, unemployment, crime, and confusion rock our world. Those who oppress us can police our actions but cannot control our hearts. Exploitative-dominators should never be called saints.

If you don't know what's killing you, you might die from it unless you begin to see things with sharp clarity. The good news is we can translate our anger into healing paths of wisdom-activism (*Ma'at*). Musician Gil-Scott

Heron said he often wanted to scream with rage — instead (and for as long as he could), he wrote and sang solution-songs with clarity and hopeful energy.

Anger is a constant fact because there's so much to be angry about. We have to guard our souls, spirits, bodies, and minds so we can move forward — with righteous passion. Constructive energies can anchor us in the storms, and Mother Africa's healing wisdom can protect us with peace in chaos. Dissonant noises need not invade our centering-strength. We're better than their hot mess: Instead of an intake of an oily, fatty diet of fast food and pablum, our heritage-table is lavishly spread with fresh, healthy, natural, nutritious food grown in rich, deep soil.

An African proverb imparts: "Someone who loves the children of others also shows love to themselves." A reliable way forward is Mother Africa's vision of *Ubuntu* — defining what matters in terms of interrelationships. *Ubuntu* teaches: "I am because we are!" With healed hearts, we can collaborate with healthy folks to build healthy communities. Sometimes, Empire feels like a jigsaw puzzle with pieces lost under-the-rug. Advocating for an *Ubuntu* justice-making community is a healing way away from the Empire's "every man for himself" mentality. An *Ubuntu* vision — caring for each other connects us together with our loving Creator.

## A COMPLEX PATRIOTISM

*"Who invented the N@#*? I didn't invent him. Whites invented him. If I am not the N@#*, and if it's true that your invention reveals you, then who is the N@#*? . . . What Whites have to do is try and find out in their own hearts why it is necessary to have a N@#* in the first place, because I'm not a N@#*. I'm a man. But if you think I'm a N@#*, it means you need it."*

**—James Baldwin**

Frederick Douglass wrote: "We shall neither die here in America, nor be driven out, but we shall go with these people either as a testimony against them or as evidence in their favor throughout their generations."[37] While we must co-exist, we must also reject illusions of inclusion. We reject vague "We-are-the-World" fuzzy platitudes that ignore systemic oppression.

Who is a patriot? The difference between shallow nationalism — blind-allegiance to a country — and sturdy patriotism is that a patriot "wants the nation to live up to its ideals" instead of accepting mediocrity. Some folks love to sing a National Anthem, penned by a slave-owning oppressor, as their symbol of unity – but listen to the third verse – it blatantly promotes slavery![38]

Patriotism is more complex than flying a flag. Indeed, it can be a "struggle waving a flag."[39] Tiffany Cross shares: "Our blood stripes the American flag red, staining the white backdrop. Yet that white backdrop dominates so much. Black folks have saved this nation many times fighting for the very system designed for our demise. We're not just participants in the American experiment. We're every bit as much its architects and framers."[40] This is our land because our tears and blood have watered this soil. We reject our constant "thingification." Hanif Abdurraqib says: "Trying to push our shoulder against one of the millions of doors America built to keep us out. And we are all here, we, unlikely patriots."[41]

Black patriotism blends righteous anger and biblical hope. Hope springs from the power of noble ideals such as democracy, equity, and equality. Theodore Johnson claims: "For Black Americans, loving country and criticizing it have always been inseparable – something other Americans have often struggled to understand."[42] Our spirits are "sewn into the fabric of America."[43] We know what America can become because we know what it's not. Since we actually built this nation, our love-investment makes sense. The truth about this dungeon-cave is that it's not a place to nurture misplaced fantasies. Richard Wright said Black Americans were "negative Americans" because we're the "only Americans who [have to] say, 'I want to be an American.'"[44] We're "forever strangers" inside our own country.[45]

What Black Americans cannot forget — Whites refuse to remember. Dr. King thought: "The oceans of history are made turbulent by the ever-rising tides of hate. History is cluttered with the wreckage of nations and individuals that have pursued a self-defeating path of hate."[46]

History's traumas cannot be unlived. But they need not be constantly re-experienced. "Amnesia" is a medical condition describing mental forgetfulness. Whites, understandably, want to gloss over the details of America's past. Memory is an enemy — not a friend — to the oppressor. Our history doesn't burden us because it was horrible — it burdens us because it's still happening. However, discomfort can also push us towards healing in the same way an open wound demands cleaning for healing to happen. No one cares about the promise of America more than those who cherish an ancient *Sankofa* wisdom. A "new normalcy" for America's brightest future must include social equitability and full inclusion for all. Normalcy never again!

## CONJURING DARK

*You made the earth as you wished to alone, all people's, herds, and flocks, all on one earth, which walk on legs or on high that fly on wings, the lands of Khor and Kush and the lands of Egypt. You set every man in place and supply his needs. . . . Their tongues differ in speech and their characters likewise. Their skins are distinct, for you distinguish the people.*

**—Hymn of the Sun—God Aten, ca.1330 B.C.E.**

Felix von Luschan wrote: "There are no other savages in Africa than some Whites acting crazily."[47] The wisdom of Africa provides solid "stepping-stones" of guidance across mirky swamps covered in fog. Those before us have gathered wisdom path-stones across harsh deserts. We relish all of the world's wisdom — all of the world's art, music, religions, and philosophies — because these belong to everyone. We don't seek to own what we cannot own. We're midstream among those who are secure and only put up with those deformed into cold self-isolations. We're secure because we know who and where we're from — Mother Africa.

Enslavers wrote about "discovering" Africa, but — in fact — they've yet to discover Africa. Oppressors saw Africans as either hapless victims or tribal primitives. Racist-oppressors built museums with exhibits where bought-and-sold African "performers" dressed in animal skins to embody the myth of Mother Africa's backward-savagery. All these efforts revealed that they were the savages.[48]

Dominators devised tales of a King Kong gorilla and a Tarzan swinging in trees with apes. Tyrannizers stumbled upon Zimbabwe's *Mosokye-yi Onye* ("Water-that-Thunders") and arrogantly renamed that holy place *Victoria Falls*. Hiding their own crimes, European colonizers fabricated smug myths about a "dark Continent" that never actually existed.

Curses from racist-oppressors sought to muffle their own nagging self-hatred. Colonial dominators envied Africa's granite community-strengths, alluring beauties, graceful smiles, and robust brightness. Even today, those who try to subjugate us hate us because they hate themselves. Bullies fear spiritual energy like rats fear light. Torturers, caged in cynicisms, tried to enslave us in cages but could never own our hearts. Even now, we accept every soul who accepts us on our terms. Africans know who a primitive savage is and, also, who is freely arrayed in resplendent expressions of mature confidence and steadying wisdom.

## EXPLOITING AFRICA

*"Whose Christianity should we teach in the schools? Which scriptures should guide our public policy? Should we go with Leviticus which suggests that slavery is all right while eating shellfish is an abomination? How about Deuteronomy which suggests stoning your child if he strays from the faith? Or should we just stick to the Sermon on the Mount – a passage so radical that it's doubtful that our Defense Department would survive its application?"*

**—Barack Obama**

Black lives didn't matter when Africans met White missionaries promoting their White Jesus and criticized Black spiritualities while forcing Africans to work for invaders for trinkets so that they could steal the wealthy natural resources of a vast and rich continent.

In 1871, explorer-missionary David Livingstone vanished for four years into the "heart of Africa." Journalist Henry Stanley hurried to find the famous Scotsman while reporting about Mother Africa as a cabal of lecherous, polygamous cannibals craving human sacrifices. Stanley pleaded for Whites to send missionaries of religion and Empire ("Christ and Civilization") to save the Dark Continent's ungodly pagans. He looked down on all Africans as childish savages who were "beastly, mysterious, heathenish, libidinous, evil, lazy and smelly."[49]

America's post-Civil War policy towards Africa began with repatriating slaves to Liberia, which became a warehouse for unwanted Africans. Many returnees served as missionaries, with a colonial-mindset promoting a colonial-agenda, in places with colonial names like "Nigeria."[50] A colonial-mind provides its own self-imposed cages and chains.

Beginning in 1884 and drinking pricey whiskey-on-ice around a horseshoe-shaped mahogany table above a garden courtyard, representatives of fifteen European nations spent a few winter months in Berlin carving up Africa like vultures' feasting on a corpse. Rivers, mountains, cities, and empty spaces on a map of Africa were traded like playing cards in a game. Britain, for example, "gave" Africa's Portuguese colonies to Germany (1898). Belgium was "gifted" Rwanda (1885). When Belgium took control of Rwanda, the Hutu and Tutsi shared intercultural harmony with each other with little intercultural animosity. But the Belgians elevated the 15% minority Tutsi over the Hutu majority in a divide-and-conquer strategy to foster divisions between people. In a genocide (1994), the colonial-era construction of a mental cement wall of differences between these two cultural identities led to the mass-killings of over a million people.

By 1900, America had become a colonizing power. Theodore Roosevelt, quoting an African proverb, preached Empire should "walk softly and carry a big stick." Roosevelt dismissed Africans (1895) as "A perfectly stupid race who can never rise to a very high plane, the Negro has been kept down as much by lack of intellectual development as anything else."[51] This kind of Whiteness rhetoric from one of the "four Mt. Rushmore greats" shows that none of them merit to become carved into ancient, cherished, sacred Oglala Lakota-Nation Black Hills granite.

America matched Europe in weaponizing imperialism to promote the myth of Whiteness. Exploiters showed no concern at all for African sovereignty. Colonizers assumed the world's language should be English and that European cultural norms were universally valid. Rudyard Kipling paternalistically told the colonized to "Take up the White man's burden."

A wisdom proverb from Mother Africa shows: "The hunt will always glorify the deeds of the hunter until the Lion tells the story." In the "Belgian" Congo, America was the first country to recognize King Leopold's dystopian realm and the last to withdraw recognition after ten million Congolese had been mutilated and massacred. Belgian profit-driven incentives mandated police would be paid handsomely for each severed hand cut from an "uncooperative" Congolese villager. Belgians began cutting-off anyone's hand available in order to exceed quotas and receive cash-rewards. The European definition of civilizing Africans meant cutting-off their hands for cash. As mountains of severed hands piled high , Europeans scurried to hide the awful truth.[52]

Colonialism (land appropriation) always advances through crisis. It is modeled on slavery and is another method of slavery. Colonialism weaponizes the systematic control of economic, educational, and spiritual abuse to teach the oppressed to accept their inferiority. Speaking of European colonizers, Marimba Ani explains, "wherever they have been they have destroyed along their road, taking, taking, taking."[53] Colonialism erases truths with lies: Those who believe these lies find themselves falling into an ever-downward spiraling cycle: Self-soul genocide.

But there was also an actual genocide: An example of European hatred for Africans came when Ethiopia was thrown to Italian fascist-wolves in the 1930s to appease Generalissimo Benito Mussolini's ravenous cravings for glory. As Ethiopian King Haile Selassie (Prince Ras Tafari) sought justice at the League of Nations, America did nothing. In contrast, Ethiopia's plight enchanted the intelligentsia of the African Diaspora: Many donated funds for Ethiopia's military defense. Italian fascist colonialism was ferociously merciless. One European reported: Italians "began to slaughter at midnight and continued through the next day. Ethiopians were killed indiscriminately, burnt alive in their huts, and shot as they escaped. Italians chased people down and ran them over or tied their feet to the tailgates of trucks to drag them to death. People were beaten, women were scourged, men emasculated, and children crushed underfoot. Throats were cut. People were disemboweled and left to die or hung and stabbed to death."[54]

After World War II, America and Europe sought to re-colonize Africa by systematically pillaging her natural resources while also using Africa as their chemical and nuclear trash-can — dumping tons of their toxic waste into the continent. Africa also became the destination for expired (or banned) pharmaceuticals and pesticides. Debt — the oldest weapon of exploitation — was used by imperialists to create a "debt-crisis" across Africa. In South Africa, "Apartheid" policies were supported worldwide as corporations grew rich. African despots became pawns for the CIA, who steered bribes to dictators in exchange for misdeeds, including the assassination of the Congo's first Prime Minister, husband and father, Patrice Lumumba (1961). The CIA also propped up despot Mobutu Suseke who continued King Leopold's rape of that once-rich nation.

The hellish violence at the broken heart of the Congo has overflown today into Sudan, Rwanda, Uganda, and nearby Zimbabwe. Today, the Congo is a haunted hellscape where battles have resulted in over five million Congolese dying since 2000. Lawless leaders of Uganda's *Lord's Resistance*, known for abdicating children to become killers, found safe-haven in the Congo. Rebels terrorize the Sudanese by smuggling weapons across the Congolese border. All this has happened as some of those oppressed were trained to become ruthless oppressors.

## NOT ALL SKIN FOLK ARE KIN FOLK

*What about White-supremacy's hate-children? I'm sorry but they're to me as contemptible as White people who hate Black people and even more problematic." Those from the "school of self-hatred" spread self-doubts in others about the rich heritages of their own ancestors; willing to dispute and "shoot the African nose off the Sphinx" are "Samboites" because they are part of a "self-hate spectrum that "blaspheme" by promoting "myth-ridden opinions about Blackness."*

**—David Hunter, *I Hate Black People Who Hate Black People***

House-lackey Peter Prioleau warned enslavers that Denmark Vesey was plotting a rebellion (1822). His betrayal led to his own release from slavery and the execution of dozens of patriots. South Carolina awarded Prioleau a yearly pension that he used to buy seven slaves.[55] Another turncoat, William

O'Neal, was an FBI-plant at Chicago's Black Panther Party who set-up Mr. Fred Hampton's murder.[56] Every society has sunken-soul sycophants and underling-minions who take the Judas-Iscariot-path of betraying their own.[57] "One of the most insidious symptoms of *Post Traumatic Slave Syndrome* is the adoption of the slave master's value system."[58]

We must fight against "racist-adjacent" Black grifters; addicted to White. Our ancestors taught us to pity those who hate themselves and have fallen into buried places.[59] These inducers of nauseousness have lost their compass and forgotten their grandmother's songs. They're all about self-promotion to grab a few extra scraps of cornbread. A few Blacks performing Blackness in blackface, to avoid being penalized for Blackness, have participated in an anti-Black agenda. They serve those who will use them up and throw them away. These ventriloquized parrots crave the love of their abusers and seek acceptance from supremacists who'll never accept them. As Public Enemy's Chuck D (Carlton Douglas Ridenhour) raps: "Every brother ain't a brother."

When a White-demon enters a Black-grifter's body, possession-oppression operates with efficiency as a "psychological condition achieving self-perpetrating motion by its own internal dynamics."[60] To suggest some Blacks haven't been granted "White privilege" — haven't won a pass into Massa's house — is to ignore a key stratagem of White supremacy — the use of "Black representatives" to do their bidding. To say that anti-Black grifters haven't been given limited power by oppressors ignores that (three of six) Black police-officers murdered Mr. Freddy Gray.[61] The term "Uncle Tom" (from a character in *Uncle Tom's Cabin*) speaks of grifters who've bargained away the rich legacies of heritage-pride for a pot of cold and tasteless porridge.

Who deformed these "Caesar-Pleasers?" This personality disorder of self-harm is self- imposed. They've strip-mined Mother Africa's wisdom from out of their bones. They crave imagined streets-of-gold instead of stony-the-road-we-trod. Just like R-and-B stars whose careers are washed-up decide to begin singing gospel, these opportunists are going for the shorter line to attention and the easier way to status. Even though prodigals have lost their way, elders stand ready to guide these soul-swindlers out of their lonely, hot cotton-patches. Mother Africa's fierce wisdom-love for all her offspring is always stronger than their timid fear of her healing name.

O.J. Simpson said: "I'm not Black. I'm O.J."[62] Yet, being Black became urgent all in a minute when O.J. needed to dodge a murder-rap — just like a rich White guy. Self-erasure happens out of an insatiable craving for currency. Money, "America's love language,"[63] is the Faustian reward for Anglo-conformity (the illusion of inclusion). When Michael Jordan was asked about politics, he said "no comment" because: "Republicans buy shoes too."[64] Corporatist Tiger Woods decided he wasn't Black but "Cablanasian": "What the hell is a Cablanasian? Here was "Tiger Woods telling America that its favorite bedtime story – the Black athlete breaking barriers to entry wasn't the story after all."[65] Reggie Williams explains, "to address people who believe they are White is to interact with devotees of a social-political ideology that functions as a religion. Yet, one does not need to be White to be a devotee of Whiteness. Whiteness has its converts who are people of color persuaded by it as a financially incentivized anthropology to embrace its hierarchy of human worth."[66] They love the Money-god.

The anti-Black elite often advance careers by "minimizing or erasing racism" and "attacking special programs" geared toward the Black community.[67] One of Empire's most galvanizing grifters has been Supreme Court Justice Clarence Thomas. In college, Thomas marched in rallies and ardently fawned over Minister Malcolm X.[68] Before assuming Thurgood Marshall's Supreme Court seat, Thomas's chances seemed doomed over a cascade of sexual-misconduct charges until he said critics were staging a "high-tech lynching": language which struck a deep memory-chord.[69] Thomas has often questioned the very existence of discrimination while voicing views such as: "It'd be just as insane for blacks to expect relief from the federal government for years of discrimination as it would be for a mugger to nurse his victim back to health."[70] Thomas even mocked his sister as a welfare-recipient.[71] In his autobiography, Thomas wrote that Blacks are self-destroying "damaged people" in need of moral reformation.[72]

Black-Judases find nefarious ways to advance their agendas at the expense of Black communities. Booker T. Washington cracked "darky-jokes" to warm up apprehensive White crowds to enlist financial support. Some in the Black political establishment have used "their perches to articulate the worst stereotypes of Blacks in order to shift blame away from their own incompetence."[73] "Black-identity amputation" happens when grifters shape-shift into disembodied abstractions.[74] This isn't new: Minister Malcolm said: "If the slave master were sick, the "House Negro" would say, "*Massa, we sick!*" While the "Field Negro," who knew himself and the nature of his oppressor, would defiantly shout, "I hope you die!"[75] Both black and white snakes deliver toxic poisons.

# Beyond Oppression

## DRUM-MAJOR INSTINCT

*"The drum . . . is charged with evocative power. The drum is not only a musical instrument, but also a sacred object and even the tangible form of divinity. It is endowed with a mysterious power, a sort of life-force, which however, has been incomprehensible to many missionaries and early travelers, who ordered its suppression and influence by forbidding its use."*

**—Drums of Passion, Babatunde Olatunji**

There's power in controlling your own story with your own voice. A wisdom-proverb from Mother Africa says: "One must touch a drum before it will speak." The drum is the heartbeat of a traditional African village. They are works of beautiful craftsmanship that can summon ancestral spirits. Drums also play an integral role in cultural ceremonies and life transitions. Even making a drum was an act of worship: Offerings were often made to the spirits of the trees from which the drums were carved. As a boy, I'd (Tait) travel with Dad to revivals in South Carolina. Before he preached, I'd drum in the testimony time. Then, when Dad finished preaching, I'd return to the drums to serve as a conduit for the Creator as folks shouted, spoke in tongues or "fell-out" in the Spirit. When I was drumming, I was echoing the beats of the universe. And through the drums, the Creator freed folks to dance into healing. Worshipers may have come weighed down that day but were lifted up into joyful encouragement by the drums. Music can release waves of healing energy.

There's an internal mechanism within our hearts beating out life's rhythms. If our hearts were turned off — even for a few minutes — we'd die. I've been where the drumming was so intense that everyone fell into a trance. Drums unify our focus and resonate deep into souls and spirits. When Africans were cargo through the Middle Passage, they took courage, beating the drum by the hour, unleashing vibration-waves of sound still echoing across cold oceans. Pounding the drum kept spirits afloat. When racist oppressors aimed at breaking our backs in steaming cotton fields, our ancestors lifted up the rhythm of chant and drums that danced with words and wordlessness. Steady drumming and singing took possession of this cold, hard, and rocky land.

Drum authority — the swaying rhythm — and charming beauty of Black-lit faces mystified our ancestors' crippled, soul-disfigured kidnappers, creeping along in ugly inner-worlds, fearful of our drums. Oppressors dreaded us getting united by the beat of the drum. Since enslavers lived in immoral secrecy, they assumed our drums were building communication-bridges out of bondage. Music can destroy obnoxious malignancies. Uncle Charlie feared we would fly rebellious across hateful skies. Ole Massa and Ole Miss weren't free inside and didn't want us to have any other "gods" besides their wickedness. Maybe our drums might've awakened them from hollow places. When the Irish beat the *peobroch, the* Scots the *bodhran,* the Dutch *de Scotjes, the* Germans the *trommels,* or when the French played *tambours,* weren't they feeling more human?

Across the Melenated Diaspora, drums are social glue echoing our heartbeats. Spiritual traditions pulse with drums. Drums take us home again: You hear Mother Africa's laugh in the *golpe* of Venezuela, the *tamborito* of Panama, the *guaguanco* of Brazil, the Afro-Cuban *mambo* (Kongolese *mambe,* "song") and the Barbadian *bomba.* Even the folk phrase: "Give me some skin" speaks of hands caressing drums. Zora Neale Hurston said we carry a "drum in our skin."[76] Dr. King asked friends and family at his funeral to: "Say I was a drum-major for justice. Say I was a drum-major for peace. I was a drum-major for righteousness. And all the other shallow-things won't matter. I won't have any money to leave behind. I won't have the fine and luxurious things of life to leave behind. But I just want to leave a committed life behind."[77]

## MOTHERLAND

*What is Africa to me? / Copper sun or scarlet sea, jungle-star, or jungle-trek / Strong bronzed men or regal black / Women from whom my loins I sprang when birds of Eden sang? / One three centuries removed from the scenes his father loved / Spicy grove, cinnamon tree, / What is Africa to me?*

**—Countee Cullen, *Heritage***

Africa is the birthplace of humanity. Now called "Egypt," Kemet is the mother of religion and philosophy. Romans named her "Libya." Greeks called her *Aethiopia* ("burnt faces") or Cush. Later she was named "Africa" based on a colony near Carthage (Tunis) with that name.

One West African name for the continent is *Akebulan*, "Land of the Spiritual People." The designation "Africa" comes from the Arabic, *Ifriqiya*. In earliest times, most called her *Bilad al-Sudan, Land of the Blacks*. We should all call her "Mother" because (anthropologists confirm) humanity — 4.4 million years ago — began in Africa. *Denkneshi* (Amharic for "beautiful") is our first-known ancestor unearthed in Ethiopia's Rift Valley. Cain Hope Felder noted Genesis claims the Garden of Eden is in Africa, bounded by the "Gihon" (Blue Nile) and the "Pishon" (White Nile) meaning, based on the Bible, all of us came from the clay of Mother Africa. Around 70,000 BCE, people began leaving Africa, and around 100,000 BCE, language was first invented in Africa, and around 50,000 BCE, music was first invented in Africa.

Countee Cullen mused: "What is Africa to me?" A businessperson may not realize many business principles have roots in Africa. What has become "normal" has now pushed us away from our African foundations. African-centered worldviews are independent of the approval of non-Africans. The truths of the world's wisdom will never be confined by one heritage. The Creator's multifaceted greatness merits a prismatic mosaic of cultures expressing divine image.

## BEYOND OPPRESSION

*Afrocentricity is simple. If you examine the phenomena concerning African people, you must give them agency. If you don't you are imposing Eurocentrism on them.*

**—Molefi Asante**

Today, racist-oppressors ask us to "step-out-of-the-car" and surrender our bodies to their unstable capriciousness. Before, when racist-dominators first began capturing our ancestors, they brought 240 Africans — on August 6, 1444, into the wheezing confusion of Lagos, Portugal. Prince Henry held the first slave-auction in that "Age of (unjust) Conquest." Survival sometimes looks falsely like meek surrender when profane evil meets holy persistence.

The Portuguese built an impregnable slave-castle ("Elmina") in Ghana for their satanic alchemy of turning flesh into gold. The Spanish, and then, the English and Dutch, joined this wicked business of thieving people's lives. In 1502, Spanish businessmen brought the first captured Africans to

"Hispaniola" (Caribbean). The first enslaved — twenty Angolans — came to Jamestown, VA, in August 1619: Covid-1619. Empire begins in 1619.

Myths of African inferiority test the limits of what folks "can be made to believe about themselves."[78] In Europe, a new concept emerged that humanity had distinct "races" of people — just as there are distinct categories of plants and animals. Pseudo-scientific bio-racism began in the Spanish Inquisition when it was preached that not all humans were created equal.[79] Pope Nicholas V issued the "Doctrine of Discovery" (1452) which justified colonialization, genocide, and slavery. The Pope claimed God decreed the degradation of Africans and the First Nations for financial gain. Enslavement-religion kept Europeans away from empathy and towards moral indifference — justifying exploitation with money-loving Eurocentric-Christianity.

Toni Morrison writes the prime function of "racism" is to distract us from oppression.[80] Business brands, for example, distract us with public-relations campaigns for justice while not operating equitable workplaces. We need brutal clarity to confront pervasive mediocrity. The term "race" in terms of people originated with Francois Bernier (1620–1688) who began lumping folks into categories. Swedish botanist Carl von Linne (nee Carolus Linnaeus, 1707–1778) saw a correlation between a person's outward appearance and their intelligence.[81] The notion some groups are better than others was never scientific: "grouping people made it easier to control them, dehumanize them, and ultimately to justify the entire colonial mind."[82] Johann Friedrich Blumenback (1752–1840) taught *Caucasians* (a term he coined) were the "most beautiful, closest to representing God's image, and the original humans."[83] Comte Joseph Arthur de Gobineau (1816-1882) tried to prove that Africans were inferior to Europeans.[84] Louis Agassiz, Josiah Nott, and George Glidden wrote (*Types of Mankind,*1854) that Blacks had a distinctive knee-joint and long-heel after centuries of being a "submissive knee-bender."[85]

Exploiting dominators have nothing we want and no food we crave. If you come, not as a taker, but as a giver — full of love, joy, and peace — you're welcome to sit at our table. Our ancestors are more alive than zombicidal takers in love with imposing themselves on others. Our ancestors are close: We're resting in the cool shade of their beauty. We have thought-leaders and motivation-makers, such as Marimba Ani, Kimberle W. Crenshaw, Patricia Hill Collins, Clenora Hudson-Weems, John Henrik Clarke, Angela Davis, Maulana Karenga, Nai'im Akbar, Cain Hope Felder, Mozella Mitchell, Chancellor Williams, Asa Hilliard III, Yosef ben-Jochannan, Molefe Kete Asante, Ibrahim Kendi, and others. They teach a fresh approach that rejects fixating on racist-oppression. Afrocentricity discards supremacist Eurocentricity and re-centers us by affirming our agency. An African-centered approach doesn't exclude other cultures. Afrocentricity embodies the wisdom and synergies of Africa. It is not romanticized-Blackness or mythical obfuscation. Each person has to understand who they are before they can have healthy relationships with others. Heart-healing and spirit-liberation are processes, that involve both an ending and a beginning. African healing wisdom is our arsenal of capability that alleviates toxic imbalance. It is a retrieval of a sacred home. It unmasks that which is against us and empowers that which is for us. The task of each of us is to see this world with fresh clarity and secure confidence.

Must you be of African ancestry to embrace a healing African wisdom worldview? No. Humanity begins in Africa. African spiritual wisdom is as universally applicable as Confucian-Taoist, Buddhist, Jewish, Christian, or Muslim wisdom, offering creative angles of insight.

Experiences of oppression are anything but monolithic. In Empire, oppression is often demarcated by random factors such as wealth, hair texture, skin color, religion, gender, and sexual orientation. What is certain, however, for any African in Empire is that they'll face marginalization. Frantz Fanon said that anyone of African-descent entering a majorative European society enters a domination zone where "Black" is a monolithic label. Each of us carries the "particular privileges of our individual lives" even as we experience a constructed, limiting social-identity shaped by "race, gender, class, citizenship, sexuality, disability, and other features."[86] As James Baldwin advises us, "complexity is our only safety."[87]

Africa is a multivalent context with layers of non-categories: There are no Black folks in Africa: "Africans are not Black. They are Igbo and Yoruba, Ewe, Akan, Ndebele. They are not Black. They are just themselves, and that is who we are. What we take as gospel in American-dream culture is alien to them. They do not become Black until they go to America or the U.K. It is then that they become Black."[88]

Worldwide, there are over a billion folks of African-descent. The lives of almost fifty million Melenated North Americans are as varied as the experiences of 850 million resident Africans, and millions of Afro-Brazilians or Afro-Caribbean. More than 100 million of African-descent living outside Africa have variant views on the rich legacies of our Motherland.[89]

Critics of an African-centered worldview assume it claims (as does Eurocentricity) the superiority of all-things-African. In fact, Africa's wisdom traditions have never taught that others are inferior. Whether one is Dutch, Irish, Colombian, Cuban, Mandingo, Igbo, Ashanti, Yoruba, or Xhosa, we're all children of one Creator. An African re-orientation is a healing resource for growth, not a weapon to denigrate others. Celebrations of *Juneteenth* or

*Kwanzaa* are not negations, but revelries of inclusion. Critics who dismiss Afrocentricity as "identity-politics" embody the truth of the Arab proverb: "The thief believes everyone steals."

White supremacists are panicky about any African-centered agenda that moves beyond rhetorical empowerment to actual power which might threaten their dominance. Fearful insecurity is at the heart of racist-oppression. Marimba Ani explains Europeans have long celebrated justice while acting unjustly and have "talked equality" while promoting inequality.[90] For White supremacists, once power is gained, it must be preserved. They prefer a past-forgetful, universalist approach that blurs inconvenient truths into a *We-Are-The-World-Kumbayah*-stew.

A perfect example of reactive fear comes in the "All Lives Matter" response to #blacklivesmatter (BLM). Where was the "All Lives Matter" crowd from 1619–2013 (when the BLM movement began)? Marc Lamont Hill writes: "When Black people were stolen and enslaved, White people could have abolished the project of slavery by saying, wait, no, all lives matter."[91] The same folks who clamor "All Lives Matter" also shout "Blue Lives Matter" in reference to the police. This raises an obvious question: If both "All Lives Matter" and "Blue Lives Matter," the point of tension is actually not the word "Lives" or "Matter" but "Black." The genius of the modest phrase "Black Lives Matter" exposes that, in Empire, Black lives have never mattered. The inclusive path to "all-lives-matter" first goes through "Black lives matter."

Afrocentricity is a healing wisdom that empowers us to go beyond oppressors' exploitative agendas, espousing African inferiority. Mother Africa is a vast continent of queens and kings, scholars, poets, philosophers, healers, scientists, theologians, businesspeople, artists, and leaders who defeat labels and trapping categories to offer liberation. It is home for world-builders, dreamers, workers, protectors, soldiers, and lovers: The cradle of all human civilization.

## "KNOW THYSELF"

*The spell of Africa is upon me. The ancient witchery of her medicine is burning in my drowsy, dreamy blood. This is not a country, it is a world, a Universe of itself and for itself, a thing Different, Immense, Menacing, and Alluring. It is a great black bosom where the Spirit longs to die . . . Africa is the Spiritual Frontier of Humankind.*

**—Dr. William Edward Burghardt DuBois**

Long before European racist-oppressors appropriated African philosophy, ancestors carved into ancient Kemetic temple door-frames the axiom: "Know

Thyself." The greatest privilege any of us should seek, according to African wisdom, is to be ourselves in all of our fullness. African philosophy teaches that none will ever be powerful if isolated from knowledge of self. "Know Thyself" is the process of self-discovery which is self-empowerment. False, fixed identities imposed by others that try to define us will confine us, defeat our promise, and limit our possibilities. James Baldwin reasoned: "One can only face in others what one can face in oneself." As slave songs constantly declare in so many ways, we are loved and chosen by our Creator.[92]

The truth about "Know Thyself!" means "I exist." "Know Thyself!" is stronger than "Stay in Your Place!" Knowing who we really are with radical self-acceptance, is our strongest weapon against oppression. In Alex Haley's *Roots,* the kidnapped prisoner-of-war Mandinka Kunta Kinte is thrashed until he renounces his name and takes a prisoner-name ("Toby"). Dominators want to define us and break the authority of "Know Thyself!" Do not "go through the gates of other people's definitions."[93] The oppressor knows Kinte's true-name is an affirmation that he belongs to himself. Kidnapped Africans were forcibly tied with malformed masters (in ugly clothes). Exploiters sought to erase Mother Africa's culture as well as our memory of self. Even today, some receive the names and curses of others. Even today, some accept mind-oppression instead of spirit-freedom while losing control of their own narrative.[94]

One Black Texas couple (1970s) named their child "Miss" so that anyone who spoke to her would use a title of respect.[95] Dignity comes from living out: "Know Thyself!" Even now, shadows of enslavement have kept many from knowing if we're Nuba, Ibo, Yoruba, Asante, Shango, Ewe, Ogun, Xhona, Oshun, or Obatala. Fortunately, our ancestries are coming to the light through modern technologies. An example of technology's vindicating power comes from the story of Miss Sally Hemings, a child-captive of her pedophile owner, Thomas Jefferson, who exploited her sexually for decades. What a President denied on his "sacred honor" has now been exposed through DNA-testing, and the scars of a fourteen-year-old girl, trapped in his grimy basement, are revealed after two long centuries.[96]

## BLACK HILARITY (AND COOKING!) HEALS

*As humans our limitations rest only in our ignorance. We're ignorant of who we are and what we can do. We have a need to gain a consciousness and only in consciousness is our true human capacity opened to us.*

**—Nai'im Akbar**

Gratitude fosters the rule of the many instead of the few: We stand in a line of flourishing souls overcoming unimaginable obstacles. "Third-world prophet and natural mystic," Bob Marley sings: "We're the survivors / The Black survivors / Like Daniel out the lion's den, survivors / Like Shadrach, Mesech, and Abednego / Thrown to the fire but never get burned."[97] Alicia Garza encourages: "We're the survivors of White supremacy. The survivors of whips and chains, and failing schools, and crumbling neighborhoods."[98] Our resilient strength is our super-power.

What isn't healthy is to ignore wounding legacies. [99] Humor — such as shared by comedians Moms Mabley, Richard Pryor, Chris Rock, Flip Wilson, Dave Chappell, Donald Glover, Jourdon Anderson, Eddie Murphy, D.L. Hugley, George Wallace, and others — are examples of using laughter as a weapon for empowerment.[100] "It's a myth we cannot go back to Africa. Start telling jokes with kids in the village and you're back in a minute."[101] A tradition of trickster-tales uses wit to outwit dimwits. One slave captured for eating one of the master's swine responded: "Yes suh Massa, you got less pig now but you sho got more N@#*."[102] Humor is both balm and weapon: "Laughing is an underground-railroad for those of us lucky enough to ride its tracks . . . Black hilarity heals." Sister Akiba taught: "The vehicle through which we have mushed you in your savage face for murdering us because you are a land-thieving lazy-ass who believed that something called God told you to kidnap, dehumanize, and torture other people into doing your fucking farming, child-care, and nation-building."[103] Normalcy never again!

Creative artistic expressions, food, and — most of all — family and friends, provide restoring springs. Cooking, after a long day, can be a healing resource away from the stresses of daily combat. Faith is another resource that empowers many. We're not defeated: Gratitude empowers us. Elders taught us to sing "we've come this far by faith, leaning on" the Creator. Elders gave us their *Imani* (belief) in our Creator.

## SANKOFA POWER

*Out of Africa, always something new.*

**—Pliny the Elder, 23—79 C.E.**

*Sankofa* is a potent word from the West African Akkan language that means to "retrieve" or "return" and "recover" while we move forward. The way out — is back through.[104] *Sankofa* is a deep-dive into knowledge based on critical examination and patient investigation. Our spirits can fly across a cold North Atlantic and retrieve what's been stolen: our certain names. This is not a call to return to "some fantastical elsewhere."[105] *Sankofa* means going back to Africa, and to the mission of its healing wisdom, beyond the holds of dark cargo ships where we were captured warriors. Rejecting the twisted logic of oppression, *Sankofa* frees embodied hearts, forges therapeutic self-definitions, and gives us tools to empower our youth. *Sankofa* confronts crippled, sunken-place spirituality. In African traditions, science is embodied spirituality and spirituality is embodied science.[106] *Sankofa* awakens embodied songs from the stupor of imposed deceptions. *Sankofa* healing wisdom rejects the isolating self-incarceration of the cynically un-ethnic, the bland un-cultural, the materialist un-spiritual, and the blindly anti-social. *Sankofa* doesn't essentialize: It prismatizes. *Sankofa* has no time for the dull lull of "master-slave dialectics."[107]

We've lost something wandering in this strange land: We've lost knowing the richness of our heritages. Minister Malcolm X was taught: "Africa was a jungle, a wild place, where people were savage cannibals who ran naked through a countryside overrun with dangerous animals. Such an image of Africa was so hateful to Blacks that some of us have refused to identify with Mother Africa. . . . You cannot hate the roots of a tree and not hate the tree itself."[108]

We need to "fetch" our own healing: With our ancestors guiding us we can build soaring arches of spirit- wholeness. Our gratitude can take us beyond oppressing cargo ships and cotton fields and into inner-stability. The cost of ingratitude brings the internalizations our racist-oppressors want us to experience when they sink their sharp vampire-fangs into our necks. But zombie clumsiness is not our portion. Ancestors guide us towards positive routes of escape out of bondage that they've cut through swamps: They've sacrificed for us. We're leaning against their strong backs and feeling their muscular hands on our shoulders. No form of oppression could dim our ancestor's bright radiance or brilliant intensity — our people.

The blessings of gratitude sanction us to watch, fight, and pray against deceptions. Our greatest fight has always been — not with those malformed ghosts — but, as Minister Malcolm said — with finding courage to be ourselves. The brute forces of dead-ocean monsters are not nearly as dangerous as a lack of resolve to keep sharing our truth. We fight an "astute and agile guerrilla warfare" against our racist-oppressors.[109] Our Creator offers us a path of creative self-determination; leading to balance and wholeness. We've replaced naivety with *Sankofa* wisdom. Givers are not tempted to imitate flaccid takers. We refuse to squander even a moment towards their embodied emptiness: They have nothing at all to offer us.

The blessing of our gratitude is fierce love: In the movie *Hurricane,* boxer Rueben "Hurricane" Carter proclaimed: "Hate brought me here [prison], but love's gonna break me out!" Quicksand bottomless, snake-pits of exhaustion, betrayal, abuse, rape, torture, theft, injustice, and death are not our portion. The Creator's love, alive in our spirits, and renovating our will, transforms dark places into warm spaces. We carry Mother Africa's tropical sunlight and our ancestor's hotness into frigid caves. With our children beside us, healing wisdom melts the ice of this place. We etch creative patterns — innovative designs — into thick ice.

The blessing of gratitude is ability. Our bright eyes affirm that we bless the Creator that we're wonderfully made. We've chosen an ever upward life-path that converts dissonance into consonance. Our cultural dexterity makes us able to "actualize ourselves in this society."[110]

A fruit of gratitude is creativity: The uplifting power of creativity flips ugliness into beauty. Creative spirituality tosses despair into the dumpster. Dancing warms cold spaces: Dehumanization is met with creativity's humanizing authority. Music, gospel-songs, holler-songs, work-songs, preaching, proverbs, storytelling, quilt-making, wood-working, and a hundred other flourishings translate frustrations into art. Robert Palmer, speaking of the Blues, wrote: "How much history can be transmitted by pressure on a guitar string? The thought of generations, the history of every person who's ever felt the blues come down like showers of rain."[111] We got this.

The cost of ingratitude is uncertainty: "Since the world of the contemporary African has been shaped by racist ideologies formulated long ago, it is necessary to understand the deep investments paid into White supremacy, in order to correctly interpret current events and formulate meaningful plans for the future."[112] Creative beauty overflows into vigorous lives.

The cost of ingratitude is confusion. Attacked from all sides, we still have a pathway forward. *Sankofa* gives us back our names and helps us recover what's been stolen across time and space. Racist-oppressors rely on mythical fictions, ephemeral ghosts, and robotic demons to stock their twisted and fabled realms. Racist-oppressors see Black folks as a flat and manageable category of exotic otherness. *Sankofa,* in response, is a steady, calming, clarifying initiative-taking resource for soul and spirit healing; not just reactive to an Empire opposing our dignity.

# Flashes of Clairvoyance

*What is that we are after? We want to be Americans, full-fledged Americans with all the rights of other citizens. But is that all? Do we simply want to be Americans? Occasionally through all of us there flashes some clairvoyance, some clear idea, of what America really is. We who are dark can see America in a way that White Americans do not.*

**—Dr. William Edward Burghardt Dubois**

## TURTLE ISLAND

*From here, in the name of the Holy Trinity one could send as many slaves from Africa as one could sell . . . one could send 40 million if there were enough ships to bring them here.*

**—Christopher Columbus, on his third voyage to the Caribbean, 1498**

Long before Europeans came to what First Nations called "Turtle Island" with their enslaving, money-loving religion of expansion to begin butchering locals and spreading disease, indigenous First Nations had raised great civilizations. They built wealthy communities that were careful not to deplete the treasures of nature but to leave them for future generations. From the land, shared by all, they received food, medicine, and inspiration. For the First Nations, the odd concept of "owning" the land was as bizarre as the idea of "owning" the wind and the rain.

Ivan Van Sertima traces encounters between Africans and Turtle Islanders to be predating Christopher Columbus. One of the first Euro-conquistadors, Columbus, launched a race-war against 50 million Turtle Islanders; resident in these lands "for about 19,000 years."[113] MapEuropean map-makers, ignoring the First Nations, named the "New World" for

Amerigo Vespucci — a slave-owner.[114] Yes, even our continent is named after a White, male, enslaving businessman!

"Dishonest words are the food of rotten spirits."[115] Europeans justified their maltreatment of Turtle Islanders by declaring that they were inferior barbarians. Indigenous cultures could be slaughtered without guilt before God because the savages would not conform to Euro-Christianity. But, it was mostly European diseases, however, that slayed over twelve million souls. Today, only three-million First Americans remain, mostly in poverty. Before Columbus and other invaders, there was nothing "White" or "Christian" or "Capitalist" about "America."

Divide-and-conquer strategies have always been weaponized against both African and Indigenous cultures. The Declaration of Independence actually describes the First Nations as "merciless Indian Savages." Whites sent Blacks westward as "Buffalo soldiers", and many of the "Indian-killers" at Wounded Knee were Black troops commissioned by Whites to kill Lakota.

White supremacists exiled First Nations survivors to remote camps in unwanted lands. Broken treaties litter a tragic history: In the Dakota's Black Hills, for example, Whites honored treaties until they found gold when trespassing. The Supreme Court ruled that Whites did not need to give back the stolen land. While admitting injustice, the Empire's solution was devious: The Oglala Lakota Sioux were not getting any of their land back. How about nine million small, green pictures of slave-master George Washington instead? No deal? No.

There are "565 Federally recognized tribes and 326 reservations occupying over 56 million acres or four percent of the entire country.[116] Profound problems remain unaddressed in these communities. Today, The Pine Ridge Indian Reservation is the poorest county in America.[117] First Nations women, often referred to with the pejorative insult "squaw," are some of the most highly raped and abused women in the world.[118] Many reservations are used as toxic-waste dumps. In one instance, over two hundred tons of radioactive mill-tailings were dumped into the Cheyenne River, the water-source of the Pine Ridge Reservation. Dump sites with nuclear-waste on the same river (around Igloo, SD) are left untouched: "too expensive to clean up." Since these sites were opened there's been an "increase in the number of still-births, . . . cleft palates, and cancer deaths since 1970."[119] The basic human rights and needs of the First Nations are ignored.

George E. ("Tink") Tinker of the Osage (*wazhwaze*) explains every First Nations action, even the choice of dress, should "both physically and symbolically . . . mimic the balancing of the cosmic energies of sky and earth. And doing things this way reminds us constantly of who we are, each of us."[120] Elder Tinker reminds the First Nations that the crass promise of capitalistic money-serving rarely translates into cultural, moral, or spiritual-wisdom power.


## THE SOUTHERN CRUCIBLE

*Every time I saw a White man, I was afraid of being carried away—Slavery is next to hell.*

**—Harriet Tubman**


*Hypocrites and concubines/ living among the swine / They run to God with lips and tongue/ but leave their hearts behind. / Heaven! Heaven! Everyone talkin' 'bout heaven ain't goin' there!*

**—Spiritual**


"I, who am Black, would love her, but she spits on my face / I, who am Black, would give her many rare gifts but she turns her back on me / So, now I seek the North – the cold faced North," wrote Langston Hughes writing about Black America's Great Migration (1916-1945).[121]

Today, a majority of African Americans still live in the South, a "Land where my Father's died / Land of the Pilgrims (from Africa) Pride."[122] Do Euro-Southerners stop on highways and realize they're traversing roads probably built during slavery or neo-slavery? Do they realize their food probably came from fields cleared by captives? Facing history can divide us when ignored or heal us when confronted. James Baldwin wrote that bipolar Euro-Southerners had: "Two entirely antithetical doctrines, two legends, two histories . . . on the one hand, the proud citizen of a free society and on the other has not yet dared to free itself of the necessity of naked and brutal oppression. He's part of a country that boasts that it has never lost a war, but he's also the representative of a conquered nation."[123]

Euro-Southern society was slave-society. Exploitative Whiteness, what Baldwin called "the Southern Way," began in the North. By 1720, one out of every seven New York City residents was enslaved with Wall Street being a major slave-market.[124] New England Puritans first provided Protestant justification for enslavement. In 1641, Massachusetts enacted perpetual-slavery laws (as opposed to indentured servitude).[125] Similar laws were not set in Virginia until 1661 (Maryland, 1663).[126] Puritans preached enslaving Africans was a "Christian mission."

Dr. King felt the racist-oppression he faced in Chicago was harsher than in the South. While post-Civil War America demanded Euro-Southerners enlist Black representatives (the first Black governor of Louisiana was P.B.S. Pinchback) there were no Black Americans in state-offices North of the Mason-Dixon line until AME Pastor Benjamin J. Arnett joined the Ohio legislature in 1885. The first Afro-Northerner was elected to a federal office in 1929.[127]

After the Civil War, the Southland, ruled by mobs, was both integrated and segregated. Euro-Southerners claimed "Black friends" and having "polite" relationships. Lynched and lyncher often knew each other's names and families. White supremacists "*loved*" their Negroes" while hating Blacks in general. The Euro-South disproves the notion that racist-oppression vanishes if Blacks and Whites live together. Whenever Whites lived in majority- Black areas, they often felt they "lived in grave danger of being attacked by Blacks as if surrounded by wild animals."[128]

Many Afro-Southerners voted with their feet to go North. "The South may be a land of flowers for Anglo-Saxons," one woman illuminated, "but for the Negro – at her touch, the flowers fold their petals and wither away, and she finds herself with bleeding hands grasping prickly thorns."[129] Blacks despised the hypocrisy of White "Christians" and knew the myth of the Southern gentleman was a farce.[130] One exile noted: "White folks and Blacks go in-and-out the same doors up there." Another alleged: "I suppose the worst place there is better than the best place here."[131] Nina Simone said it straight: "Mississippi Goddamn!" In 2020, trying to move from the "Noose-South" to the "New South" the State of Mississippi (and NASCAR) lowered the Confederate flag. Even then, many Whites declined to acknowledge its history as a symbol used by the KKK to endorse "a certain attitude toward the Negro."[132] Mississippi's Governor announced that many "people of goodwill" loved the Confederate Battle-flag.[133] Seriously? Confederate flag- worshippers may not be serial killers, but they're also not "people of goodwill."[134] The Governor said Mississippi's history was "complicated and imperfect." Indeed: Mississippi is the state that gets first prize in almost every contest you probably don't want to win. It's the poorest state with the poorest qualities of health and education, the highest obesity and, in a not-to-distant past, the most lynchings.

Mississippi's Governor also said historical statues should not be taken down. Generally true, but statues of slave-owners and traitors are not usually put up in the first place. What definition of civility allows folks to be taunted by marble-racist-oppressors at tax-payer expense? We *should* honor our ancestors, just the right ones. D.L. Hugley observed: "All over America, we go to schools named after people who hated us and barbecue-in-parks with statues of people who hated us."[135] Where are the statues for Viola Liuzzo, Andrew Goodman, and James Cheney and other anti-racists?[136]

Why not raise statues for Levi Coffin, William Garrison, or Elijah Love-joy.[137] Why not name schools after Maya Angelo instead of Jefferson Davis Elementary.[138]

The campus of the University of Mississippi (Ole Miss) has a statue of James Meredith, the Black student it took 30,000 armed soldiers to protect from Whites. Erected during Mr. Meredith's lifetime, he wasn't invited to speak at the dedication ceremony. It was not until 2024 that a statue in Fort Mill (SC) honoring ten Black slaves forced to fight for the Confederacy was finally removed. Beneath this statue of a Mammy holding a White baby, the plaque read: "Dedicated to the Faithful Slaves who, loyal to a sacred trust, toiled for the support of the army, with matchless devotion and with sterling fidelity guarded our defenseless homes, women, and children, during the struggle for the principles of our Confederate States of America."[139] Wow!

The South is America's most dramatic region because it's full of actors, White and Black.[140] Dr. King predicted, "one day the South will recognize its real heroes." Yet, in Stone Mountain, GA, it will take tons of dynamite to destroy the huge idol-carvings of Robert E. Lee, Stonewall Jackson, and J.E.B. Stuart.[141] One proof that "New Southerners" have stopped fighting the Civil War would be if, today, Stone Mountain would become a site for an anti-Klan museum with a bell evoking MLK's speech about ringing bells of freedom. The New South, replacing the Noose South, must constantly heed the wisdom of John M. Perkins, founder of Jackson, Mississippi's great *Voice of Calvary Ministry*: "You don't give people dignity. You affirm it."[142]

## THE GOD-FACADE

*My view of Christianity is such that I think no man can consistently profess it without throwing the whole weight of his being against the monstrous system of injustice that lies at the foundation of all our society.*

**—Harriet Beecher Stowe**

Religion and politics are married in Empire with religion being the prime vehicle the status quo uses to dominate society. Enslavers were identified as "Christian" even as they jammed ships (with names like "The Jesus") full of the enslaved. Among "Christians," only a few groups — notably Mennonites and Quakers — rejected the heresy that slavery was God's Will.[143]

Whiteyanity, a socio-religion fixed in violence, celebrates the lynching of Jesus while also valorizing Christian supremacy. Disdain for adherents of other religions (and "liberal" Christians) is common and "heathen" became the Whiteyanity version of the "N-word." Racist-oppressors have long used religion to throw shovels-of-dirt against the caskets of souls buried alive with judgmentalism. Blacks knew Euro-Christians were hypocrites but, as one said: "Of course, I don't hate them: There are probably some good White folks – mighty few though."[144]

An example of religion marginalizing Africans is found in so-called "humanitarian" efforts where heathens were objectified by-products of spiritual colonialism. Some Southerners supported buying slaves as a form of missions, winning them to the White Jesus. Other enslavers claimed they were "kind" to their property. Missionaries claimed, "Christianity would make slaves more docile."[145] Some missions prepared Africans for colonialism. DuBois said the "cloak of Christian mission enterprise" hid centuries of oppressive African exploitation.[146]

Africans who became Christians would have their Black souls "purified white as snow" while still enslaved. White enslavers quoted St. Paul: "Slaves obey your masters."[147] In 1830, the *Southern Catechism of the Episcopal Church*, for enslavers to manipulate captives, asked:

> Q: Who gave you a master and a mistress? / A: God gave them to me.
>
> Q: Who says that you must obey them? / A: God says that I must.
>
> Q: What book tells you these things? / A: The Bible.
>
> Q: How does God do all His work? / A: He always does it right.
>
> Q: Does God love to work? / A: Yes, He is always at work.
>
> Q: Do the angels work? / A: Yes, they do just what God tells them to do.
>
> Q: What does God say about your work? / A: Those who do not work do not eat.
>
> Q: What makes you lazy? / A: My wicked heart.
>
> Q: How do you know your heart is wicked? / A: I feel it every day.
>
> Q: Who teaches you many evil things? / A: The devil, and I must not let him teach me.[148]

Catechisms taught a three-fifths theology of self-negation for Blacks while affirming Whites. Enslaving Whiteanity served as a proxy for the Master by teaching Africans had a Master in heaven who commanded them to obey a Master on earth. The educational strategy of enslaving White religion focused on the afterlife as a way to avoid ethics (e.g., the slavery-question). Empire was already "heaven" for White "gods." Plantation Christianity taught there'd be both a "Negro heaven and a White heaven" where Blacks would "work [enslaved] in heaven's kitchen."[149] Blacks doubted if "Whites could even go to heaven or if Whites might work as slaves for Africans" in heaven. Most agreed "Whites would be condemned to eternal fire."[150] If heaven were a place of justice, it could not contain the souls of White folks.[151] Black Christians took consolation that, on Judgment Day, "Christian" enslavers would burn in eternal hellfire.[152]

Since biblical theology did not support hatred, enslaving Whites formulated a three-fifths theology — devising a doctrine of multiple creations (polygenesis) stressing everyone did not descend from Eve and Adam.[153] What many reject as Christianity is actually the rejection of an imbalanced "Whiteyanity." Many Evangelicals live in an alternative reality: For example, a common claim made is that praying a prayer will magically ensure eternal security in heaven.

Certainly, portraying Jesus as White demands a stronger commitment to myth than reality which is telling about this toxic ideology. Some Whites have made Jesus White as a way to justify White supremacy — God in their own image. James Cone writes: "Thinking of Christ as non-Black" today "is as theologically impossible as thinking of him as non-Jewish in the first century. . . . If there's any contemporary meaning to the Anti-Christ, then the Euro-Church seems to be a manifestation of it."[154] The blonde-haired, blue-eyed Aryan Jesus was worshipped in Hitler's Germany. One pastor taught: "When people of European-descent can worship a Jesus who in his pictorial representation is Black, then and only then, will they have entered into a kind of therapy" to lessen their feelings of superiority against Black folks.[155]

When Jesus was asked who the most powerful people were, he responded that little children - the weakest, smallest, and most trusting people in any society - had the most authority. Power that is not shared is pure domination and abusive oppression. The opposite of faith includes the will to control others. Christian Nationalism today tries to control (to name just a few things) what we read, who we love, and when we can have children - our minds and our bodies. The path of Jesus is a love for truth that exposes ungodly power. Love always triumphs.

History shows that three hundred years after the life of Jesus the faith in his message that began by turning the world upside down was quickly domesticated by the very Empire that killed Jesus. Rejecting Jesus, a hybrid form of power-hungry nationalistic Euro-Christianity emerged during feudalism and came to imitate a "social structure where racialized-capitalism, Christianity, and the ubiquity of 'Whiteness' reign supreme as interlinked institutional discourses."[156] In Empire, people are commodified: *homo economicus*. In America's slaveocracy, Plantation Christianity began with the same Pilgrims who are honored at Thanksgiving. Puritans often "gifted" humans to their pastors.[157] The Puritans focused on the afterlife instead of ethics which made mute the "slavery-question." God-given power entitled "Christians" to enslave Africans. Calvinists taught God had cursed Blacks to be used for profit: It was "God's Will." Cotton Mather preached enslavement actually blessed Blacks because it allowed them to be "civilized" by godly White "Christians." Ironically, many Puritans later would become strident abolitionists.

Abolitionist William Wilberforce asked: "Is Christianity reduced to a mere creed? Does it consist only of a few speculative opinions and a few useless, unprofitable tenets?[158] Methodist-founder John Wesley forbade enslavers from receiving communion, but by 1840, American Methodists opted to see slavery as a "necessary evil." The Methodist circuit-preaching strategy began as a way to preach the gospel but was coopted as a way to support slavery. Among Evangelicals, Charles Finney championed abolition as did Mormonism's founder, Joseph Smith. When the "Great Disrupter," John Brown, raided Harpers Ferry, (West) Virginia, in 1859, Unitarians and Transcendentalists compared Brown's gallows to the salvific cross of Jesus.

A strident belief in Biblical literalism spread in the South as an in-arguable response to Northern abolitionist Christians who argued that enslavement was sinful. Plantation Christianity (now called Christian Na-tionalism), needing to justify owning humans, preached that the Bible — when read literally — accepted slavery.[159] Before World War II there were over 40,000 Southern Evangelical pastors who were part of what Woodrow Wilson called "a great KKK," an organization which made many financial contributions to White Baptist churches to cement support.[160] Cross-burn-ings were sermon, prayer, and hymn-filled services. Opposing Civil Rights, many White Baptists like Birmingham Police Chief (Theophilus Eugene) "Bull" Connor and the Methodist George Corley Wallace (and others) tied "Christianity" with White supremacy.[161]

D.L. Hugley said some Evangelicals love their White Jesus but hate everybody else. Recent forms of Plantation Christianity often confront the "sin" of a gay person, or trans-, and queer lives even though rarely mentioned in the Bible and not of the "seven-deadly-sins" (have you ever heard a ser-mon on gluttony.[162] During the Civil Rights Movement, the ethically-muted "gospel" preached by Billy Graham (and others) stressed an individualized faith where God was "in your heart" but not so much in your politics. While preaching with dogmatic assertiveness, they told about a personal Savior offering a personal mission for personal peace in a personal heaven. Their "Golden Rule" is that whoever has the gold makes the rules. Malcolm X said: "The Bible in the White man's hands, and his interpretation of it, have been the greatest ideological weapon for enslaving millions of non-White human beings."[163]

Religious zeal is a form of Whiteness-dislocation escapism. Plantation Christianity claims Jesus unites us all and, so, any Black-White distinction is divisive. Enslaving religion claims theirs is a non-ethnic, transcendent identity — a view which excuses them from confronting racist-oppression. God-zeal facilitates culture-erasure. White-erasure is weaponized indivisibleness. Because three-fifths theology supports oppression it has no desire to confront oppression. While Jesus lived in poverty, Christian nationalists valorize capitalism and the goal of living a comfortable life of godly wealth. In fact, Jesus started a revolution "led by, and among, the rejected."[164] He was born to an unwed mother and was raised among the oppressed. Howard Thurman taught Jesus was "disinherited from worldly influence but was rich in the things of God." A reporter asked Mother Theresa how she felt visiting a rich country like America, coming from a poor country like India. The saint replied that she had never been to a poorer country in her life than when she visited America.

Professor W. E. B. DuBois claimed the Black Church often aided oppression by "being caught up in religious and hysterical fervor."[165] In fact, the Black Church, among many things, is a "strategy to negotiate the brutality of systemic racism."[166] Negatively, queerphobia, homophobia, classist views, and other problems are still part of an often Eurocentric, often patriarchal, and often hierarchical Black Church. Far from being a monolith, the Black Church was born fighting White supremacy. Protests were often organized in Black Churches.[167] Even some Whites sensed the connection between Black faith and Black protest: At Selma's Edmund Pettus Bridge, Officer John Cloud shouted to protestors about to be beaten with nightsticks and rubber hoses laced with spikes to "Go home or go to your church! Is that clear?"[168] What wasn't clear to Officer Cloud was going to church for Black folks was the same as going to a bulwark for justice activism.

Jürgen Moltmann said Empire's most valid expression of Christianity were Black Churches where folks could be "loud and free and rattle the walls with song."[169] Churches were spaces to "deliberate, to think, to organize, to breathe."[170] They were refuges to feel supported, seen, and lifted up to find strength for another week. In one survey, while 49% of Whites told pollsters religion is "especially important to them," that number rose to 75% for Blacks.[171]

Orlando Patterson thought: "The tragic facts of slavery and Jim Crow show there are really two kinds of Christianity in America; one that has largely neglected the radical relational and spiritual message of Jesus preached by King and one that completely focuses on the personal meaning of Christ's death." Thirty-three long years of the life of Jesus are boiled down to only three memorialized days. Dr. King preached a faith "which takes the life and teachings of Jesus seriously as a way of life and not just as a way to avoid punishment and death."[172] White-centered ethno-evangelicalism teaches a religion *about* Jesus that is fixated on his death and not a religion *of* Jesus, which is based on his life and ethical teachings.

# Born In Violence

## THE MAAFA (1444–1865)

*I believe our slaves are the happiest three-millions of humans on whom the sun shines. Into their Eden is coming Satan in the guise of an abolitionist . . . The slave is certainly liable to be sold. But, perhaps, it may be questioned, whether this is a greater liability for the laborer who is dismissed by his employer without the certainty of being able to obtain employment or the means of sustenance elsewhere. The slave's duty is marked out with precision, and he has no choice but to follow it. He is thus saved the double difficulty of first having to determine the proper course for himself and then of summoning up the energy which will sustain him in pursuing it. . . . It is the duty of society to protect all its members.' . . . To protect the weak, we must first enslave them.*

**—George Fitzhugh, 1857.**

"Lew, first off, I just want to apologize for slavery." The Pastor was looking at me (Tait) in our first meeting and was weaponizing sorrow, four hundred years of pain, for his own tactical advantage. I wondered if he apologized to Japanese people for Hiroshima over a coffee or for Auschwitz with Jews before watching a ball-game. Whatever else — "slavery-regret" cannot become a tool to manipulate us. The "what" and "how" of slavery are ungraspable: "People were loaded onto ships and crammed together with sometimes less than eighteen inches between them. Here they would live for many weeks to several months in the bowels of a ship. They were deprived of any human comfort and shared in a collective misery. This disgusting place was where they slept, wept, ate, defecated, urinated, menstruated, vomited, gave birth, and died."[173] Slavery's audacity supports the claim: "The European receives pleasure from a feeling of control over other people."[174]

The word *Maafa* comes from Swahili meaning, "disaster or catastrophe – The Great Suffering of our people at the hands of Europeans."[175] The Maafa threw kingdoms into disarray. As many as thirteen million Africans came to Empire as prisoners-of-war with another thirteen million dying before leaving Mother Africa.[176] Captives came from West Africa, with the exception of about 15%–20%, of whom began in Eastern and Southern Africa.[177]

Enslavement is not where African America begins. Historians report explorers from Africa sailed to Turtle Island as early as the 13th century.[178] Almost two hundred years before Columbus — around 1311 — Africans came to the New World led by Mandinka King Abubakari II of Mali.[179] These explorers almost certainly encountered First Nations but there were no reports of any massacres. Archeologists have observed throughout Mexico traces of peaceful encounters with Africans. Waters claims that Incan, Aztec, and Mayan pyramids tell of African influence.[180]

Long shadows of the Maafa, the Middle Passage, and the African Holocaust, loom over Empire — boiling like seething rivers of molten-volcanic-lava capable of erupting any moment. Chattel slavery was an Empire innovation that made America the richest nation in history, with enslavers becoming the world's richest people. The foundation of Empire economy was torture and theft. Enslavement "was legal and sanctioned by the state and a web of enforcers . . . In American slavery the victims, not the enslavers were punished, subject to whatever atrocities the enslaver could devise as a lesson to others . . . for the first time in history one category of humanity was ruled-out of the human race and into a separate subgroup that was to remain enslaved for generations in perpetuity."[181]

Because the Africans who left with Europeans were never seen again, some wondered if "Christians" were cannibals. But "being eaten by White people was the least of their worries."[182] The Ibo assumed Whites were deformed evil-spirits since their traditional pictures of the devil represented him as White.[183] Some Whites have tried to soften slavery's horrors by claiming the enslaved "were well-fed and had decent lodgings."[184] In fact, as Huey Newton said: "Slavery is capitalism in the extreme."[185] The enslaved worked from "can't to can't" (before you could see anything when the sun came up to after sundown), stooping down, working like burden-animals before getting older, taking sick, and dying. Maybe they had one day a week to rest. Fredrick Douglass wrote: "I will, in the name of humanity, which is outraged, in the name of liberty, which is fettered, in the name of the Constitution and the Bible, which are disregarded and trampled upon, dare to denounce, with all of the emphasis that I can command, that everything that serves to perpetrate slavery in America promotes the greatest sin and shame of America!"[186]

James Baldwin argued some have written a "history" that's "nothing more than the Western interpretation of the life of the world."[187] The Maafa, along with the extermination of the First Nations, are the defining events of Empire. In 1776, "slavery was as customary as prisons are today."[188] At the time the Bill of Rights and Constitution were written, over 700,000 humans were enslaved.[189] Benjamin Rush said: "The war is over. But nothing but the first act of the great drama is closed. Let it not be said that the . . . strength of our young Nation perished of a heart blackened by atrocity and ossified by countless cruelties to the Indian and the African."[190]

For all Americans, "slavery is a sacred text."[191] Every year, churches such as Brooklyn's St. Paul's Baptist stage educational-dramas reenacting the *Maafa*. *Maafa*-services are springing-up to teach how past atrocities affect present realities. Today, dominators work to vampire-consume our souls. Elements of Empire's slaveocracy continue to try to imprison us in conformist cargo ships sailing in majorative Whiteness. Today, we're asked to dance to their discordant tunes and to enact the greedy plans of venture capitalists. Today, oppressors continue to chain those they oppress into impoverished neighborhoods, careers, schools, and jails.

Worldwide, the horrors of enslavement remain today: Over forty million people live in some form of forced-labor against their will: One in 200 people worldwide. "Distained work" is reserved for "distained people."[192] Of over ten million of these, 71% are women, and 25% are children, are slaves. Almost five million women (70% in Asia) are exploited in sex-slavery. Modern-enslavers "now earn up to thirty times more than their 18th-century counterparts. The one-off cost of a human in many places is $450. A forced-laborer generates about $8,000 in annual profit for their exploiter, while sex-traffickers earn about $36,000 per victim."[193] Owning-people occurs in at least seven African nations especially in the Sudan, Congo, Eritrea, Burundi, and Nigeria. Such tragedies show that "the Maafa continues to take its toll."[194]

## "DEVIL IN THE WHITE MAN - WHAT'S GOIN' ON?"

*Blacks can see clearly that America is a nation built on inhumanity. The signers of the Declaration of Independence put down their quills to go home and beat their slaves. Blacks have heard noble words, while the whip shredded the skins off their backs. It's no longer possible to hide the resistance-struggle that Blacks have constantly waged inside America.*

**—Julius Lester**

Christian Nationalists say America is a Christian nation. But if it were a Christian nation, no one would go to bed hungry, homeless, or uninsured, and every child would be safe to walk streets that were not awash in violence. Empire is "built on a foundation of profound inequality," where hypocrisy is the tax that "vice pays to virtue."[195] The "Declaration of Independence" proclaims freedom even as a third of its signers enslaved humans.[196] The 1776 *Encyclopedia Britannica* said a "Negro" was: "Filled with treachery, lying, cruelty, and impudence, intemperance, and a penchant for stealing, debauchery, and profanity . . . They are strangers to every sentiment of compassion."[197] Philosopher G. W. Hegel wrote: "The Negro exhibits the natural man in his completely wild, untamed state. We must lay aside all thought of reverence and morality - all we call feeling - if we would rightly comprehend him."[198]

Virginia began, not as a political organization, but as a business to cultivate tobacco, a labor-intense crop. Further South, the land was "suited for sugar-cane, rice, and cotton – crops for which the English had little experience but that Africans had already cultivated isn't Africa. Colonists soon realized without Africans (and their skills) their enterprises would fail."[199] When touring Thomas Jefferson's Monticello, I (van Gorder) saw a plaque reading "location of slave-quarters" and hearing tour-guides talking about "servants" as if they were area-teenagers needing extra spending-money. Both Washington and Jefferson became wealthy through slavery.[200]

Thomas Jefferson had five children with Sally Hemings.[201] The "Master of Monticello" called his enslaved "my family" even as he sold them. From 1784–1794 he trafficked at least eighty-five people: others were "gifted."[202] "Some ask, was Jefferson a good slave-master? That is an oxymoron: There are no good slave-masters."[203] When writing the Declaration of Independence, he possessed at least 150 humans. By 1822, he'd enslaved 267 people. In life, he freed only three prisoners and five more, all blood-relations, at death. In contrast, Washington freed all of his enslaved at his death.[204] One of Jefferson's ex-slaves, blacksmith Joe Fossett, spent his life vainly trying to buy-back his wife and four children sold by Jefferson.

Jefferson thought those who sustained his extravagant lifestyle, built his houses, cooked his meals, tilled and managed his fields, and obliged his sexual cravings were ugly and inferior.[205] Living under Jefferson's brutal dictatorship was simply about surviving.[206] He could barely stand to look at the "eternal monotony of their offensive features," suggesting "Blackness might come from the color of blood."[207] This "man of science" claimed enslaved Africans "secrete less by the kidneys and more by the glands of their skin which gives them a very strong and disagreeable odor . . . They are more ardent after their female, but love seems with them to be more an eager desire than a tender, delicate mixture of sentiment and sensation. Their griefs are transient."[208]

## "TROUBLE, O TROUBLE!"

*Slave-holders as men are proverbially brave, intellectual, and hospitable and whose women are unaffectedly chaste, devoted to the domestic life and happy in it. My decided opinion is that our system of slavery contributes largely to the development of these high and noble qualities.*

**—John Henry Hammond, 1845.**

In Pittsburgh's Lafayette Hall, a convention was held (1856), creating guidelines for a new political entity: The Republican Party.[209] They were led by abolitionists who preached "slavery was the buying and selling the image of God."[210] Some Black folks, hearing abolitionists' feverish justice language assumed that these people could not possibly be White or Christian.[211]

America's most notable abolitionist was Fredrick Douglass. Douglass was often introduced at meetings as "former-property" and often told gripping tales of torture to enthrall his White-majority audiences. Over time, however, Douglass found these sensational stories demeaning. Douglass, to echo what the New Testament says about John the Baptist, "was a voice and not an echo." He was unafraid to be unconventional, controversial, and confrontational. At the same time as Douglass, America's most famous White abolitionists were William Lloyd Garrison, Elijah Lovejoy, and "Potawatomi" John Brown. When John Brown was a child, he saw an enslaver beat a man with a shovel: This left an indelible mark on his heart. Brown raised his sons to share his abhorrence of slavery. They joined him in revolt at Harper's Ferry (West) Virginia that was finally crushed by the slave-owning commander Robert E. Lee (1859).

In 1860, Republican Abraham Lincoln was elected President. When re-elected in 1864 he picked Andrew Jackson, a Democrat, to be his Vice President. This attempt to forge a "unity- ticket" appealing to Southerners was easily the worst choice — other than going to see a play at Ford's Theatre — of his political life. While running for office (1858) Lincoln declared: "I am not, nor ever have been, in favor of bringing about in any way the social and political equality of the White and Black races. I am not nor ever have been in favor of making voters or jurors of Negroes, nor of qualifying them to hold office, nor to intermarry with White people . . . There is a physical difference between the White and the Black races which will forever forbid them living together on terms of social and political equality. And, inasmuch as they cannot so live, while they do remain together, there must be the position of superior to inferior. And I, as much as any other man, am in favor of having the superior position assigned to the White race."[212] Lincoln wrote (1863): "If I could save the Union without freeing any slave I would do it."[213] When questions arose about the future of freed slaves, Lincoln suggested that part of Louisiana be reserved for Blacks or to send ex-slaves to Haiti. One effort (1862), saw thirty ex-slaves sent to Haiti where all of them died within two years.[214] First Nations Americans also remember that Lincoln called for the federally-sanctioned execution of thirty-nine Santee Sioux in 1862. Lincoln was a complex politician who found himself, to use Shakespeare's phrase, "thrust into greatness." At his best, Lincoln wrote, "all legal distinctions between individuals of the same community, founded in any such circumstances on color, origin, and the like, are hostile to the genius of our institutions, and incompatible with the true history of American liberty."[215] Lincoln recognized: "If slavery isn't wrong then nothing is wrong."[216] Fredrick Douglass, who knew Lincoln, explained that, while the "early Lincoln" was "cold and indifferent" at the end, Lincoln became a "swift, zealous, radical, and determined" abolitionist.[217]

The Civil War was a bloody exorcism of slavery.[218] Freed Black folks who served in the Union Army faced particular brutality and, if captured, were almost always killed.[219] At war's end, almost 100,000 Black soldiers served in the military occupation of the South.[220]

## "EVERY DAY SEEM LIKE MURDER HERE"

*Sanctified by religion and legalized by the Supreme Court, "separate but equal" was enforced in the day by the agencies of the law and by the KKK under the cover of night.*

**—John Hope Franklin**

*Jim Crow* (a term based on a minstrel-song) was a time of endless lynchings and abuse in what William Pickens called the "American Congo."[221] Instead of using the term "Jim Crow" generated by Whites about theatrics mocking Black Americans, we'll refer to this era as "neo-slavery" or the *Era of Racial Terror*. Poet bell hooks calls this time "Apartheid America."

After the Civil War, Pennsylvanian politician Thaddeus Stevens proposed a plan to redistribute land to ex-slaves. Stevens plan (rescinded after four-months) gave Black folks "forty-acres and a mule." Normalcy never again was at the heart of Stevens views: "If it is just, it should not be denied. If it is necessary, it should be adopted. If it be a punishment to traitors, they deserve it."[222] This promising era called "Reconstruction" was a 10-year period that ended in 1876 when all Federal Troops left the South. This opened a flood-gate of terrorism: Groups such as the Ku Klux Klan (KKK),

White-League, and Night-Riders, without fearing punishment, terrorized Black lives. Terrorists castrated, mutilated, whipped, beat, and lynched folks. One "Christian gentleman" said that his proud KKK membership showed his godly allegiance to a "respectable organization of terrorists."[223] These White-power terrorist groups still exist today.

New laws were passed to ensure that Black folks remained poor. Voter fraud, bribery, and intimidation were enacted to limit Black power. Voter-suppression laws were so complex "one Black man with a doctorate failed to pass the literacy-test."[224] Blacks who were educated or successful were often targeted because they'd "stepped out of their place." If "Sambo" or "Mammy" were deferential, they'd be left alone: Their skin was Black-but-their-hearts-were- White.[225] If Whites thought Black neighbors had money, their homes would be raided. Ex-slave Ned Cobb said: "White folks hate to see N@#*s livin' like people."[226]

Lynchings were widespread across the Southland: On May 19, 1918, in Folsom, Georgia, "a pregnant Black woman named Mary Turner was hanged, covered with oil-and-gasoline, and burned. As she dangled from the rope, a man stepped forward with a pocket-knife and ripped open her abdomen in a crude caesarean operation. Out tumbled the prematurely born child. Two feeble cries it gave – and received for answer the heel of a stalwart man, as life was ground out of its tiny form."[227]

In Savannah, TN, 1911, Mr. Ben Pettigrew was in his wagon with his two daughters, taking his seed-cotton harvest to market. The KKK arrived and Mr. Pettigrew was shot dead. His two daughters were hung from trees. Typical of the Southland, those who did the lynching notified the next-of-kin (or an undertaker) to tell them when they could take-down the remains.[228] In Memphis, 1892, Mr. Thomas Moss, a mail-carrier, and two Black farmers, Mr. Calvin McDowell, and Mr. Henry Stewart, saved enough money to open the *People's Grocery Store* in the "Curve" — a Black neighborhood. All three were killed by the KKK when defending their property. Mr. Moss was a friend of the activist-journalist Ms. Ida B. Wells-Barnett.

Countless Black folks were forced into a "convict-leasing-system" where they were arrested for debt-peonage (or for no reason at all) and re-enslaved, once again, to work for free.[229] "If one died, a business-operator would call the State for a replacement. Life as a leased-convict was no better than life as a slave, and at times, worse. False criminal charges were often trumped-up as a means of legally securing large numbers of cheap human laborers."[230] In the South, the main enemy of justice was Southern justice. Chain-gangs thrived while, in Black areas, school-funding was sparse, health care was poor, and laws suffocated Black businesses. White supremacist zoning-laws decided where you could live, eat, work, swim, and everything else. The Supreme Court ruled segregation was legal if facilities were "separate but equal (1897)."

Neo-slavery was a way for defeated White Southerners to keep fighting the Civil War: This time they were winning. At this time, waves of European immigrants were sailing to America. While émigrés hoped for a better life, these hopes didn't usually line-up with being respectful towards Black folk. Immigrants were expected to side with other Whites against Blacks, and racist-oppression became a wedge-issue to unify immigrants into a shared complicity. In Empire, migrants learned how to perform Whiteness. There were no Whites in Europe. They were German, French, Italian, English, or something else, but they were not "White." In Empire, immigrants often seemed to become more bigoted after arriving here — seeking acceptance into a supremacist society where acting superior to Blacks was often the expected American way.

## RITUAL HUMAN SACRIFICE

*I was eight years old when I saw a photo of Emmett Till's body. The murder shocked me. I began thinking of myself as a Black person for the first time, not just a person. And I grew more distrustful and wary . . ., I could be hurt or even killed just for being Black.*

**—Kareem Abdul-Jabbar**

After the Civil War, over 5,000 Black men were victims of extra-legal slaughters — ritual human-sacrifices.[231] Over 90% of these 5,000 tortures and murders (1880–1960), happened in the "Bible Belt" of the Euro-Christian dominated Southland. Normalcy never again!

Mob violence ruled the Southland. When Black elected-officials tried to assume their positions, a mob of Whites killed 150 souls (Colfax, LA, 1873). The town erected a monument "to the memory of the heroes who fell in the Colfax Riot fighting for White supremacy."[232] Mr. Willie Holcombe chose to honor his father's request to earn an education which led to him being lynched: Mr. Holcombe thought he deserved respect and was taught otherwise by White supremacists.[233] Teenager Mr. Charles Jones, was lynched in Grovetown, GA for "stealing a pair of shoes and talking big." Mr. Henry Sykes was lynched in Okolona, MS for telephoning White girls and annoying them."[234] Mr. Henry Smith was tortured and lynched before 10,000 Texas "Christians" in Paris, TX (1893). Normalcy never again!

Some Euro-Southern "Christians" turned lynching into a highly-refined, practiced technical skill of racialized terrorism — their sport and their art.[235] The torture of Mr. Sam Hose (Newman, GA, 1899) included excursion-trains for 2,000 participants.[236] It was a public-ritual, a collective-experience, a carnival-like atmosphere, lasting for hours. Pieces of Mr. Hose were sold as souvenirs and some were displayed at an Atlanta grocery store. Postcards of Mr. Hose's body were sold across the South.[237] Public lynchings were scheduled in newspapers. Southern slaughters began and ended with prayer-benedictions.[238] Normalcy never again!

The "Red Summer" of 1919 saw race-riots break out in Texas, Georgia, South Carolina, Chicago, Washington, D.C., and over thirty other cities.[239] Violence was particularly devastating in Elaine, Arkansas, where Whites went on a five-day killing spree over a 200-mile radius.[240] When racial tensions erupted in Tulsa, Oklahoma (1921), the entire White citizenry was "deputized" to kill Blacks at-will and two hundred vigilantes roamed the streets killing. Over three hundred Blacks were killed and over 18,000 of their homes were burned to the ground.[241] Vigilantes surrounding Tulsa were joined by Oklahoma's National Guard, including machine-gun strafing-airplanes.[242] Normalcy never again!

White resentment was on full display in Wilmington, NC (1898) where another successful majority-Black community was burned to the ground. Decades of economic advances were erased in a few days. White-vigilantes roamed through Wilmington for four-days randomly "butchering people, taking them off streetcars, just killing them, that's all."[243] In Rosewood, FL the Black community was also torched (1923). Rumors flew of a Black mother and baby being thrown-off the Belle Isle Bridge in Detroit which led to a race-riot where at least twenty-five Black folks were killed and over seven hundred injured at *The Sojourner Truth Housing Project* (1943).

Nine Black free-loading teenagers (13–19) were kicked-off a freight-train (Scottsboro, AL, 1931). Also removed were White hobos and two prostitutes. One prostitute, Ruby Bates, accused all nine teens of trying to "chew-off her breasts." All were arrested for attempted-rape and taken to jail. Hundreds of White vigilantes stormed the jail to lynch them but were halted by police. Two- weeks later Alabama sentenced the "Scottsboro Nine" to the electric-chair.[244] Two Black teenagers, Mr. Richard Ponder and Mr. Ernest Hawkins, were arrested for attempted robbery (Leon Co., FL, 1937). The KKK went to the jail and abducted the teens who were taken to a swamp and riddled with bullets. A sign was left on their bodies: "Stay in Your Place."[245]

After World War II, some Mississippians organized a number of atrocities: Whites castrated, mutilated, and lynched two fourteen-year old boys for playing tag with a White girl. Whites "killed Reverend Isaac Simmons and cut off his tongue for refusing to sell his land. Whites whipped

Mr. Leon McTate to death for allegedly stealing a saddle. Whites beat Mr. Malcolm Wright to a bloody pulp because they didn't like the way he drove a wagon."[246] The KKK stopped delivery-driver Mr. Willie Edwards, Jr.; forcing him to jump to death in the Alabama River (1957). Mr. Mack Charles Parker, accused of raping a girl (who couldn't identify him in a lineup), was found dead in the Pearl River (1959).

Black soldiers were despised when wearing their uniforms.[247] Returning veterans were unable to get promised pay and disability-benefits. Some supremacist "Christians" responded: "You can die for us but you cannot vote with us."[248] Private James Neely was lynched in uniform asking for a soda (1898). After World War I, Mr. Charles Lewis was lynched in uniform (Hardin, KY). After World War II, veterans Mr. Joe Nathan Roberts and Mr. Isaiah Nixon were lynched (GA). Veterans Mr. Roger Malcolm and Mr. George Dorsey (and wives) were killed by a firing-squad (GA, 1946).[249] Black veterans returning from fighting Hitler watched train-transports of Nazi P.O.W.s placed in better class-cars than theirs.[250] Sometimes Nazi P.O.W.s and Southern "Christians" even sat together while Black soldiers "were relegated to the caboose."[251] Black soldiers, stationed in the Southland, reported wives and girlfriends were harassed or beaten.[252] One Black soldier stationed in Germany was taunted: "It's funny, you're here protecting us but no one's there to protect your people from the KKK and the Whites."[253] Normalcy never again!

Emmett Till, fourteen, was slaughtered on August 28, 1955, after whistling (a coping- device his mother taught him to deal with stammering) at a White store-clerk after getting candy. Mrs. Mamie Till Mosley tried to warn and prepare him, but said, "how do you give a crash-course in hatred to a boy who's known only love?"[254] At Master Emmett's funeral, his mother insisted "don't touch the face."[255] Mrs. Mamie Till Mosley wanted the world to see the truth of what Euro-Southern "Christians" had done. No one was jailed.[256] Normalcy never again!

Florida has electrocuted thirty-seven Black men for raping White women but has never electrocuted a White man for raping a Black woman. Mr. Abraham Beard (17) was electrocuted for supposedly raping a White (1954). Mr. Beard was convicted, in the same courtroom where Mrs. Betty Jean Owens failed to win justice against her guilty rapists. In Groveland FL (1949), Mr. Samuel Shepard, Mr. Walter Irvin, and Mr. Charles Greenlee were accused of raping a White. Declared guilty, the case was overturned (1951). While transferring Mr. Shepard and Mr. Irvin from prison, Sheriff Willis McCall took them out of his squad-car and told them to change his tire. He then shot both of them in the back and gleefully told his boss: "I got rid of them, boss: Killed them sons-of-bitches."[257] Mr. Shepard died but Mr. Walter Irvin miraculously survived.

## "HELP ME JESUS!"

*Is White America really sorry for her crimes against the Black people? Does White America have the capacity to repent- and to atone? . . . Indeed, how can White society atone for enslaving, for raping, for unmanning, for otherwise brutalizing millions of human beings for centuries? What atonement would the God of Justice demand for the robbery of the Black people's labor, their lives, their true identities, their culture, their history – and even their human dignity?*

### —Minister el—Hajj Malik el—Shabazz Malcolm X

Lynchings have continued: Eleven people named "Africa" (five children) in a Black countercultural organization called MOVE were killed while the West Philadelphia row-houses of 250 people were destroyed when Philadelphia police "pumped more than 7,000 rounds of ammunition" and dropped a bomb — a C-4 Satchel Bomb on the neighborhood. No charges were filed (1985). Normalcy never again!

Mr. Mulugeta Seraw was jumped by skinheads in Portland, OR (1988), returning from work. As they smashed-in his head with baseball bats, their girlfriends, watching from a car, cheered: "Kill him! Kill him!"[258] Four Los Angeles Police officers (1991) beat Mr. Rodney King.[259] This attack revealed "a plain type of evil, the type that cannot be disputed."[260] Riots, the language of the disregarded, broke out. When police responded, one officer, not re-alizing he was being recorded, exulted it was "monkey-slapping time."[261] Three weeks later, Miss Latasha Harlins (15), was shot dead by a grocer after stealing a $1.79 soda. The murderer was sentenced to 16-years, but the Judge revised his sentence to probation, community service. Normalcy never again!

On December 16, 1995, twenty-six-year-old ex-college cheerleader Mrs. Sonji Taylor was enjoying a Los Angeles sunny afternoon of Christmas shopping. While reacting to her crying baby in the parking-lot of the Pico Union Medical Center, police responded to a call that a Black mother was doing "odd things" to a baby. The police arrived and immediately shot Sonji eight times when she started reaching back to comfort her crying baby. Her last words: "Help me Jesus! Help me Jesus!" James Baldwin penned: "We all came here as candidates for the slaughter of the innocents."[262] Mr. James Byrd was dragged behind a pickup-truck by an eight-foot iron-chain by neighbors (Jasper, TX, 1998). Police claimed Haitian immigrant Mr.

Abner Louima punched an officer (1997). Mr. Louima was brought to the precinct where he had a toilet-plunger forced up his anus before an officer demanded Mr. Louima take it, covered in blood and feces, and put it in his mouth. Guinean immigrant Mr. Amadou Diallo was shot at forty-one times and died (1999). Police claimed Mr. Diallo reached for his wallet to show his I.D. and they thought it was a gun. Police admitted no wrongdoing; no officer was charged. On Christmas Eve (2002), twelve-year-old Master Michael Ellerbe was shot dead by police (Uniontown, PA). Unarmed, Mr. Sean Bell (23) was celebrating his bachelor's-party before his wedding when shot dead by fifty bullets (New York, 2006). In Jena, Louisiana, six high-school students were charged with "attempted murder" after beating a taunting classmate in the school-cafeteria (2006). Mr. Oscar Grant III was 22 when he was shot dead (Oakland, CA). Mumia Abu Jamal said: "Oscar Grant is you – and you are him — because you know in the pit of your stomach that it could've been you. You know this."[263] Normalcy never again!

February 26, 2012: Sanford, Florida: Young Trayvon Benjamin Martin was drinking ice- tea and carrying a bag of skittles for his little brother Fulton coming back from a convenience store.[264] He was followed and killed by George Zimmerman, "a would-be police officer, a vigilante . . . replicating the role of slave-patrols. Then as now the use of armed representatives of the state was complimented by the use of civilians to perform the violence of the state."[265] Seventeen-year-old Martin was lynched because he was wearing a hoodie and for being Black.

Ms. Kathryn Johnston (92) was shot dead in her home during a drug-raid at the wrong address (Atlanta, 2009). Miss Aiyana Mo'ne Stanley-Jones (7), sleeping on the couch, was shot dead by police while an A&E film-crew was filming an edition of a police reality-show (Detroit, 2010). Ms. Rekia Boyd was shot dead while in a park by an off-duty officer responding to a "noise complaint" (Chicago, 2012). Ms. Shelly Frey (27) was shot dead in a Walmart by a security-guard who accused her of shoplifting (Houston, 2012). Ms. Renisha McBride (19)unarmed and hurt after a car-accident knocked on the nearest door and was shot dead (Dearborn, MI, 2013). Mr. John Crawford (22) was shot dead when he picked up a toy-gun in the toy-section of Walmart (Beavercreek, OH, 2013). Mr. Freddy Gray was arrested for carrying an illegal knife (Baltimore, 2015). Mr. Gray was chained and put in a van on a deliberate "rough ride" with officers trying to hurt him. Mr. Gray died from injuries sustained to his neck and spine while being transported. Ms. Sandra Bland was pulled-over for failing to use a turn-signal after changing lanes when closely tailed by a police-vehicle she thought wanted to pass (Prairie View, TX, 2015). Her phone recorded the officer saying: "I'm going to light you up."[266] Ms. Bland died mysteriously, ruled a suicide, three-days later in police-custody. There was no reason at all for Ms. Bland being arrested. The officer was acquitted of any wrong-doing. Normalcy never again!

Traffic-stops are a chief "stop-and-poke/provoke" strategy to incite a response that will lead to incrimination. Public-school cafeteria-worker Mr. Philando Castile was shot seven times in thirty-eight seconds while his girlfriend and four-year old daughter sat in the car (St. Paul, MN, 2017). Mr. Castile had been stopped for a broken tail-light with the officer also claiming he fit the description of a known criminal: "Black." In the months previous, Mr. Castile had been pulled-over more than forty times for possible traffic violations. Days later, Afghan war-veteran Xavier Micah Johnson, murdered five Dallas policemen, claiming retaliation for Mr. Castile's murder.

When you go to Ferguson, Missouri, there's a makeshift monument to the victim of a state- sanctioned murder of an eighteen-year-old man. The message says in capital letters: "THEY CAN'T KILL US UNTIL THEY KILL US."[267] Mr. Michael Brown's hands were in the air, facing the police: "Hand's-Up-Don't-Shoot!" Mr. Brown was shot by police eight times and left on the street. Mr. Brown's body "was left to fester in the hot summer sun for and a half hours . . . keeping his parents away at gunpoint and with dogs."[268] Such disrespect underscores the idea some are beasts, "violently dangerous, as the dark embodiment of evil."[269]

Police responded to protestors with tanks and military weapons. Three organizers from Ferguson, Mr. DeAndre Joshua, Mr. Darren Seals, and Mr. Edward Crawford" were "found dead, shot in their cars."[270] When riots erupted, police blamed "outside agitators." Outside of what? And yet some Euro-Americans continue to say that they cannot comprehend why some Blacks don't trust police? Normalcy never again!

Dylann Roof went to a Bible-study at Emmanuel African Methodist Episcopal with a handgun (Columbia, SC) and killed nine folks in another saga of the "Black Parade."[271] After surrendering for arrest, police honored Roof's request to stop at Burger King for a free Whopper.

"Jim Crow is back."[272] Blacks are at least twenty-one times more likely to be killed by police than Whites (2012).[273] Often these murders are random: "Mike Brown was only walking down the street. Eric Garner was standing on the corner. Rekia Boyd was in a park with friends. Trayvon Martin was walking with Skittles and an Arizona Ice-Tea. Sean Bell was leaving a bachelor party. . . . Amadou Diallo was getting off work."[274]

Centuries of oppression taught Blacks "anger and violence were key ingredients necessary to ensure that their needs were met."[275] The Black Lives Matter (BLM) movement asked, in response to such lynchings: What kind of "fighters do we need to be."[276] BLM asks what is the generational-mission of this time and place: "How do we know what our mission is, what our role is, and what achieving that mission look like."[277] The old guard often made "too small demands."[278] Because these murders are, of themselves, what Professor Angela Davis calls "just the tip of the iceberg," joint-actions are requisite because it will be a "mistake to assume that these issues can be resolved on an individual level."[279]

## HUMAN GUINEA-PIGS

*The wrongs which we seek to condemn and punish have been so calculated, so malignant and so devastating that civilization cannot tolerate their being ignored because it cannot survive being repeated.*

**—Robert Jackson, U.S. Prosecutor, Nazi Doctors' Trials, (Nuremberg, 1946)**

Their names, voices, and stories are almost entirely erased to all but the Creator's storehouse of tears.[280] Of the many cruelties done by racist dominators against some Black folks in Empire, none may be more brutal than using unwilling subjects in non-therapeutic medical experimentation. It's no wonder *iatrophobia*," fear of doctors, is common among Black folks.

Statues have been raised in honor of Euro-Southern Christian J. Marion Sims, the "Father of Modern Gynecology," launched America's first women's hospital (NY). Like other Euro-Southern "doctors," Sims purchased at least seventeen women, and for years, conducted operations on their genitalia without anesthesia (AL, 1845-1865). Sims addicted women to morphine "in order to perform dozens of exquisitely painful, distressingly intimate vaginal surgeries."[281] One victim, Miss "Anarcha suffered under his knife thirty times" as Sims perfected a treatment for vaginal fistula.[282] Sims also experimented on a baby by cutting his scalp and boring holes in his skull.[283] Normalcy never again!

Thomas Hamilton (GA) tortured Black folks in search of a remedy for sun-stroke. One enslaved person was "poached to the point of fainting" while his skin was blistered and flayed. Hamilton, like Sims, Nathaniel Bozeman, and others "bought and raised healthy slaves for the express purpose of using them for experimentation."[284] T.S. Hopkins (GA) gave nitric-acid to five Black children with asthma. Francois Prevost practiced cesarean-sections on slaves. James Dugas perfected eye-surgeries on healthy slaves. Walter Jones (VA) poured boiling water on typhoid pneumonia patients and John Harden (GA) boasted that he had stripped blood vessels from the limbs of a healthy Black folks as well as from three hogs. Leeching and blood-letting were also "practiced" on healthy slaves in the Southland. Normalcy never again!

The primary source of income for most pre-Civil War Southern doctors was, basically, as "veterinarians" for enslavers. The focus was on the usefulness of the property. Enslaved people met doctors at slave-ships and on the auction block to see who was fit for exploitation.[285] Human traffickers made efforts during sales to hide deformities while the enslaved resorted to tricks to hinder their sale.[286] Physicians were often brought to enslaving labor-camps to punish sick enslaved seen to be avoiding work.[287] Enslaved people relied on African medical traditions such as the use of herbs, roots, and other natural remedies. Africans were the first to use citrus-juice for scurvy and inoculations for smallpox. For pain, Africans used kola-nuts, which eventually became Coca-Cola's main ingredient.[288]

At the time of the Civil War, enslaved people were worth the equivalent of four billion dollars and were the South's main economic wealth. When enslaved people were too old or sick to work, they were often given to physicians to settle debts and many were used in experiments. Dr. T. Stillman purchased fifty elders to study skin-diseases (SC, 1838). Southern medical schools offered students "abundant clinical opportunities" to work on the sick, dying, and on cadavers.[289] In "Virginia, limbs were removed solely to train medical students in amputation technique."[290] Normalcy never again!

Forced sterilizations were forced on over 30,000 Black prisoners and patients in mental hospitals in twenty-nine States.[291] According to the Southern Poverty Law Center at least half of the 100,000 to 150,000 people who were involuntarily sterilized using government funds" were Black Americans.[292] Later, birth-control options such as "The Pill, Norplant, and the Depo-Provera shot were evaluated in Mexico, Africa, Brazil, Puerto Rico, India," and Black America.

In one "scientific-experiment" conducted by the U.S. Public Health Service for over forty years, over four hundred Black men (201 of which were "control" patients) were misled and injected with various syphilis treatments (Tuskegee, AL, 1932–1972). Black nurse, Eunice Rivers, was used by study-administrators to recruit, reassure, and befriend Black victims. Rivers served as a trusted liaison and help participants feel they were not lab-animals. The only reason these horrors were stopped is that they were finally exposed. An out-of-court settlement (1974) compensated each victim with a paltry amount once legal fees were deducted. The cost of these experiments was the early deaths of unwitting subjects. Normalcy never again!

The Tuskegee Syphilis study was the longest and most famous — but not the worst. A trucker, Mr. Ebb Cade, was injured in an auto accident (NC, 1945) and found himself subjected to "fiendishly toxic radioactive" plutonium-239 injections.[293] In the 1970s, sixty-six Black children were placed in studies of the cardiotoxic "fenfluramine" and were given a $25 toy-store gift card while their parents received $100 each.[294] Dr. Harry Bailey did CIA-supported experiments on prisoners (through Louisiana State University) including testing the effects of LSD and other mind-control substances.[295] Near Miami, in a majority Black neighborhood called "Carver Village," the Fort Detrick Army Chemical Corps released boxes of mosquitos infected with Yellow Fever and other biological agents to trace their spread.[296] Normalcy never again!

## SHADOWS ON CAVE-WALLS

*Many Whites refuse to remember what Black folks cannot afford to forget. I've seen Whites stunned to the point of paralysis when they learn the truth about lynchings in this country—when they discover that such events were not just a couple of good ole boys with a truck and a rope hauling some Black guy out to a tree. They were never told the truth that lynchings were often community events, advertised in the papers as 'Negro-Barbecues' involving hundreds and even thousands of Whites who would join in the fun, eat chicken salad, and drink sweet tea.... Most Whites desire, or perhaps even require the propagation of lies when it comes to our history. Surely, we prefer lies to anything resembling, even remotely, the truth."*

**—Tim Wise, Blog, 3/18/2008**

Individual stories help us see a larger narrative which can help us create alternative narratives. All of us should remember to say their names and remember their specific stories to bring order out of chaos. Maybe "Littlefinger" (Game of Thrones) is right: "Chaos isn't a pit. It's a ladder."[297] We need to face hard facts so we can overcome the widest Grand Canyon in the world — the eighteen inches between our hearts and heads. When an Irish storyteller was asked why he repeatedly told the same story he said not everyone was listening closely the first time.

Things didn't happen by accident: A Black man was lynched every four days non-stop from 1889 until 1929.[298] While the seeds of racist-oppression may've been sown four hundred years ago, they're based on "perennial noxious weeds with deep roots."[299] Most know from the margins about George Washington Carver, but few know about Arctic explorer Matthew Henson, Garret A. Morgan, Norbert Rillieux, Granville T. Woods, Lewis H. Latimer, or characters like cowboy Bill Pickett, Seattle's Dr. Homer Harris, and many others. "The truth is if we don't author our own stories, there's someone else waiting to do it for us. And those people, waiting with their pens, often don't look like we do and don't have our best interests in mind."[300] It's a good thing that there are civil rights museums in many cities. It's a good thing that Birmingham, Atlanta, New Orleans, Jackson, and Baltimore's airports are named after Fred Shuttlesworth, Maynard Jackson, Louis Armstrong, Medgar Evers, and Thurgood Marshall. It's a good thing that there's a Negro League Baseball Museum in Kansas City and a Smithsonian Museum of African American History in Washington, D. C.

What does it say about the power of history that those Euro-Americans who openly confront parasitic White supremacy are also those most trusted as strategic-partners with Black folks? What does it say about the power of history that those Black folks who overlook the facts of the Maafa and neo-slavery are the most trusted accomplices of anti-Black White supremacy?

In the "Parable of the Cave," Plato describes a cavern where folks saw shadows on walls and thought they were real. When light flooded the walls, folks were slow to shift false views into an accurate view of reality. Carl Jung writes: "when our shadows are repressed for a long time, when we begin to emerge from the dark, they come out primitive as nonlogical entities."[301]

Any society is in a constant struggle between "memory against forgetting."[302] James Joyce lamented: "History is a nightmare from which I am trying to awake."[303] Positively, cherishing Africa led to the wisdom principles of *Ma'at* and the celebratory ideals of *Kwanzaa*: *Umoja* (unity), *Kujicahagulia* (self-determination), *Ujima* (collective work and responsibility), *Ujamaa* (cooperative economics), *Nia* (purpose), *Kuumba* (creativity), and *Imani* (faith).[304]

Educating these truths into life offers a constant reinforcement of the healing value of collective responsibility and shared vision. The principle of *Umoja*, for example, helps us understand our world. *Umoja* teaches we are part of a village greater than ourselves alone. We are part of each other's lives. We are not lost hobos, rootless aliens, and isolated strangers, but we are at home wherever we are and we belong to each other and to our Creator.

## RECY TAYLOR CONFRONTS HER VIOLATORS

*I've known rivers / I've known rivers ancient as the world and older than the flow of human blood in human veins. / My soul has grown deep like the rivers. / I bathed in the Euphrates when dawns were young. I built my hut near the Congo and it lulled me to sleep. / I looked upon the Nile and raised the pyramids above it. / I heard the singing of the Mississippi when Abe Lincoln went down to New Orleans, and I've seen its muddy bosom turn all golden in the sunset. / I've known rivers: Ancient dusky rivers. / My soul has grown deep like the rivers.*

**—Langston Hughes, *The Negro Speaks of Rivers***

In Atlanta, while Martin Luther King was still in high-school, in Abbeville, Alabama, twenty-four-year-old Mrs. Recy Taylor, a young mother and newlywed, was fighting for her life.

One night, walking home from revival at The Rock Hill Holiness Church, Mrs. Recy Taylor met six White "Christians" who stopped her on the road. Army Private Herbert Lovett pointed a shotgun at her and forced her into his green Chevy. Mrs. Recy Taylor was raped by six White men as she pleaded for her life — to return home to her nine-month-old daughter and husband.

Mrs. Recy Taylor sought help from the *National Association for the Advancement of Colored People* (NAACP), who sent investigator Ms. Rosa Parks to document the dreadfulness of September 3, 1944.[305] Mrs. Recy Taylor never got justice in the South but she opened a path for others to follow her. Her sharp testimony brough to light White-on-Black sexualized violence.

## HOW MUCH MORE OF THIS CAN WE TAKE?

*The Lord gave me the name "Sojourner" because I was to travel up and down the land showing people their sins and being a sign unto them. . . . You know children, I don't read small stuff as letters. I read men and nations.*

**—Sojourner Truth**

The *Maafa* was brutal for Black women and girls whose bodies were commodified as property. They had no protections over their own bodies because their "Blackness" separated them from the concept of "woman." Enslavement was enforced and reinforced through rape. In slave-castles, women resisting rape "were chained naked to a steel ball in the center of the courtyard and denied food and water as a warning to others."[306] On slave-ships, women and girls were raped at will. On auction-blocks, many women and girls were bought by White "Christians" for the purpose of sex-slavery or breeding.[307] They were often put on public-display with little or no clothes in order to show their "breeding potential."[308] For domestics and fieldworkers, every hour held the demonic possibility of being harassed, abused, or even worse by White devils.

And what of an enslaved mother trying to raise her enslaved daughter? Dr. Joy DeGruy writes that the mother knew a day would come when "these men or boys would use her fragile young body to satisfy their sexual cravings. That day might mark the initiation into manhood for the slave master's son, or perhaps the day she might be offered as an evening gift for White male visitors. The mother no doubt anguishes over this fact, but still, she hopes to lessen the tragic event by at least acquainting her innocent child with the particulars of being raped. She tries to help her little girl understand what will happen and why it is happening at all. She endeavors to explain how it will feel, how her vagina will tear, burn, and bleed. She attempts to tell her how best to prepare and survive the ordeal; tells her to lie still, not to resist, and to try to bear the pain. But there are limits to what she can tell her child to better prepare her. She cannot tell her how often they will come, how long it will last, or how many there will be. This mother cannot protect her. Nor can the father, who looks on powerless, defeated, and emasculated."[309]

Rape was a systematic weapon "to extinguish a slave woman's will to resist, and in the process, to demoralize their men."[310] Enslaving "Christians" commodified women's bodies in order to breed more slaves.[311] Enslaved women and girls were sometimes exchanged as gifts to other plantation slave labor-camps to sexually "initiate a son or younger nephew." Enslavers claimed such actions, what they called "night- time integration," protected White-female chastity by raping enslaved women as an "outlet for male frustrations."[312] Some White "Christians" raped Black women and girls even while claiming to be against "race-mixing," James Baldwin chided: "You're not worried about me marrying your daughter. Your worried about me marrying your wife's daughter. I've been marrying your daughter since the days of slavery."[313]

Ms. Ida B. Wells-Barnett, editor of the *Memphis Free Post*, carried a gun.[314] She was a scholar-activist who "wasn't about to die without a fight."[315] Akiba Solomon wondered how Ms. Ida B. made her "trauma inflammable," and how she "collected the evidence without becoming the evidence" and how she managed to avoid a non-violent death.[316] Although Ms. Ida B. lived a century ago, she knew what we know: "In America the principal conception of the black body is as chattel. This is the foundation on which all other racially stereotypical perceptions of the black body are grafted."[317]

Ms. Wells-Barnett., born into slavery (Holly Springs, MS), refused to be invisible and refused the invisibility of others. She refused to accept the unacceptable and refused to let anyone forget what no one should forget.

She refused to be silent in the face of caricatures of Black men as "a race of outlaws or monsters . . . to be feared and policed" and Black women and girls as always accessible for use by the whims of White "Christians."[318] Ms. Ida B. explained: "To conceive of the Black-body as chattel literally renders it a commodity to be bought and sold on the open-market, with all other commodities. The implications of this are vast, especially in relation to Whiteness as cherished property."[319] Whites, she explained, are not united as a group "by a shared ethnicity – they are unified by access to institutional power."[320]

Florida A&M (FAMU) criminology-student Miss Betty Jean Owens was returning from the "Orange and Green Ball" (1959) with her date when a blue Chevy blocked their car. Miss Owens was pulled from her car and thrown into a back-seat to be raped seven times by four Whites. The FAMU community rallied around their classmate as a "Black Everywoman." FAMU students shared how unsafe they felt: One said, "it felt like all of us had been raped." Banners at a FAMU solidarity-rally read: "It could've been your sister, wife, or mother," and "My God How Much More of this Can We Take?"[321] At the trial against the four rapists, KKK Attorney Harry Michaels sneered: "The crime here is insignificant." Another attorney shouted: "Are you going to believe this N@#*-wench over these four boys?"[322] Florida found them "guilty with a recommendation for mercy" — meaning they would avoid Florida's electric-chair.

Miss Annette Butler (16), a high-schooler, was sleeping beside her mother on Mother's Day when four White "Christian" Mississippians — claiming to be police — broke into her home and kidnapped her, taking Miss Butler to the Bogue Chitto Swamp where she was repeatedly raped. Miss Gertrude Perkins was raped at gunpoint by two White Alabama police. A Euro-Arkansan raped Miss Melba Patillo (12). Kidnapped, Miss Lila Belle Carter (16) was raped by a White insurance-salesman (Pine Island, SC, 1945). She was found dead, lying face down in a pool of mud. Mother Nannie Strayhorn accepted a ride home from two White police-officers who drove her into the woods and took turns raping her at gunpoint (Richmond, VA, 1946).[323] Miss Janie Mae Patterson, age eleven, accepted a ride home only to be driven to an abandoned mill and raped (Clio, AL, 1948). Mrs. Mamie Patterson, mother of six, was taken to the woods to be raped by two White farmers (Tuscumbia, AL).[324] When Miss Daisy Bates, a freedom-fighter was seven, she watched her mother being raped and murdered before her eyes: She never forgot.

Eleven-year-old Miss Endesha Ida Mae Holland was raped on her birthday (8/29/1955) when a White neighbor asked her to clean their house and promised her a "birthday bonus." A few years later, Miss Holland became a *Student Non-Violent Coordinating Committee* (SNCC) voting-rights activist. Speaking of her SNCC work, Miss Holland said: "Being treated with respect was something wholly new for me. Being around SNCC people, had turned my narrow space into a country bigger than I've ever imagined."[325]

Fifteen-year-old Miss Rosa Lee Coates was raped (Hattiesburg, MS, 7/13/1965). Her attacker was found guilty — but the all-White jury recommended mercy. Nonetheless, this guilty verdict for rape by a White "Christian" in Forrest County was the first ever. Jail guard Sergeant Jerry Helms tried to rape prisoner Ms. Joan Little (Washington, NC, 8/27/1974). Helms entered the cell with an icepick but she killed him in self-defense when he dropped the weapon. Dr. Angela Davis, and others, launched a nationwide effort to secure her freedom from criminal wrongdoing. The trauma Ms. Little experienced underscores that prisons are "designed to turn its residents into animals in a zoo – obedient to their keepers but dangerous to each other."[326] Rosa Parks, who had first fought for Mrs. Recy Taylor, organized a chapter of the *Joan Little Legal Defense Committee* (Detroit). At the trial, a woman met the brute power of a White jailor, and the putrid stench of his lust was no longer silent — emboldened to confront her rapist. When the jury unanimously acquitted Ms. Joan Little, she sighed with relief: "It feels good to be free."[327]

Thousands of other Black women, girls, and femmes have been traumatized by a long reign of White-on-Black sexual-terror that continued for centuries without fear of accountability — taught by hyper-sexual fathers to sons. Rape often motivated the Great Migration North. Leaving the Southland made pure sense since Blacks knew they had no legal justice if attacked.

Mrs. Mary Ruth Reed, a pregnant Black sharecropper, accused Lewis Medlin of attempting to rape her in front of her five children (5/5/1959). At the trial, the White defense attorney, faced the all-White jury, pointed to Lewis Medlin's wife, and said: "You see this pure White woman, this pure flower of life?" Then the White "Christian" lawyer pointed at Mrs. Reed and said: "Do you think he would've left this pure flower, God's greatest gift, for *that*?"[328] Mrs. Reed burst into tears when a not-guilty verdict was returned within only ten minutes.

White Ruby Floyd accused seven Black men of rape, and within a month, they were sentenced to death (Martinsville, VA, 1/8/1949). Mr. Mack Ingram was walking through a field when, seventy-five-feet away, Willa Jean Boswell saw Mack, screamed, and told her father Mr. Ingram had been "looking at her in a leering manner." (6/4/1951) Judge Ralph Vernon sentenced Mr. Ingram to two-years hard labor for what the Casswell County Court called "eye-rape."[329]

In June 2015, police in McKinney, Texas man-handled fifteen-year-old Black girl, Miss Dajeria Becton, at a children's swimming-party. Far more tragic, Tulsa, Oklahoma police-officer Daniel Holtzclaw was sent to prison for 263 years (2016) on 18 of 36 counts of rape and sexual violence against thirteen Black women while he was working on duty to protect the community.

## "A REALITY IN NEED OF FIXING"

*Old Satan am a liar and a conjurer too and if you don't watch out, he'll conjure you too!*

### —Spiritual

Dr. King, on December 5, 1955, preached to 5,000 folks at Montgomery's Holt Street Baptist. He said: "There comes a time when people get tired of being trampled over by the iron feet of oppression. There comes a time when people get tired of being plunged across the abyss of humiliation, where they experience the bleakness of a nagging despair. There comes a time when people get tired of being pushed out of the glittering sunlight of life's July and left standing amid the piercing chill of an alpine November."[330] Normalcy never again!

Dr. W.E.B. DuBois wrote Black Americans have a "double-consciousness." Black women and girls have a triple-consciousness and Muslim, gay, or trans-women have even further degrees of embodied nuance. What is certain is that Black women, girls, and femmes, are often unprotected victims of physical, sexual, and emotional abuse. For some, the home is a confining context of violence or threatened violence. Many married women are raped. Disrespect is normalized: In churches, some teach a 2,000-year-old Bronze Age Biblical message: "Women, submit to your husband as the weaker vessel."[331] In some businesses, women are paid and promoted at an inequitable rate. Gender stereotypes, which are both "prophecies and prisons," push our daughters toward jobs traditionally held by women.[332] While many men are becoming more sensitized to gender issues, women still must deal with men who "man-splain," sexualize, or marginalize them in other ways. Patronized mostly by men, pornography is a billion-dollar fantasy-promoting business. Women still have to deal with light-dark skin-tone issues (colorism) and have choices of make-up foundation become an issue because "people don't hear you at first – they see you."[333] Miss Saira, a nine-year-old, rejected by a boy because her skin was too dark, crying, took a rock and tried "to rub the brown off my skin."[334] Normalcy never again!

Women politicians — Black and White — deal with media-attention on their hair, clothes, weight, or even the tenor of voice. Straight-male counterparts rarely experience such scrutiny. Baptist Pastor Tony Perkins told Republican nominee Sarah Palin that, although Palin couldn't be a pastor, she could be America's Vice-President because she had her husband's "permission."

Is gender-bias stronger than race-bias? One thing is certain: Most Black women, girls, and femmes, face greater obstacles than most White women. In Mother Africa, women have also battled millennia of mistreatment. Positively, many African traditions honor women: Many creation-legends begin with the Creator first fashioning women. Social-values affirm a man cannot hold a position of honor if he doesn't respect women. Africa is resplendent with accounts of "Queen of Shebas" or "Queen Nzungas" who've led kingdoms with wisdom and strength.

Black women and girls often live in spaces that both "fetishizes and despises Black people."[335] Men brand Black women with sexualized, negative stereotypes "alternately idealizing and vilifying" but "rarely who they really are.[336] Women are sometimes seen as your "home-girl" who fixes you when broke, or as immoral "Jezebels" or subservient, self-sacrificing "Mammys."[337] Those involved in "tone-policing" see women as "ghetto" or having a bossy "attitude." But this is often an insistence on not being erased. Sexist tropes include "single-mother-welfare-queen" and "crack-hoe." Ms. Hortense Spillers laments: "Face it. I'm a marked woman, but not everyone knows my name. 'Peaches' and 'Brown Sugar,' 'Sapphire' and 'Earth Mother,' 'Aunty,' 'Granny,' 'God's Holy Fool,' a 'Miss Ebony First,' or 'Black Woman at the Podium': I describe a locus of confounded identities."[338] Sadly, single mothers are often "demonized" as deficient. Racialized caricatures of patriarchy render Black women, girls, and femmes a messy, uneven "reality in need of fixing."[339] Normalcy never again!

## "TIRED OF BEING TIRED"

*"Who would be free must themselves strike the blow.*

**—Frederick Douglass**

Black women, girls, and femmes, swim in a shark-infested "toxic sea of racism and sexism."[340] The Civil Rights Movement was a collective enterprise and the "foot-soldiers" for freedom were often Nubian queens. Women in D.C. (1934) "hung small pieces of rope from their necks to symbolize lynching victims" and also (1938) "carried empty coffins through the streets to evoke victims of police-violence."[341] During Montgomery's Bus Boycott, car-owning women — often Whites — helped folks get to work: Ms. A. W. West (80) drove her green Cadillac each morning offering rides to anyone. Boycotters faced Whites throwing trash and cups of urine.[342] Yet, hundreds of women kept moving forward for justice.

"Sheros" were fighting for substantive changes against an unending hamster-wheel of reactivity. Angel Kyodo Williams writes: "Black women have long been the canary in the coal- mine of the social structure of America, and as the canaries seek the air that is most clear because they know what it is to suffocate."[343] In the "1950s, some 90% of Black women were domestic workers."[344] Today, "25% of Black women are without health insurance and 65% of new AIDS diagnoses are among Black women and femmes. Black women are as likely to be evicted as Black men are to be imprisoned" (2016).[345] Positively, "Black women are the fastest growing group of entrepreneurs" in America in many creative, successful wealth-generating contexts.[346]

Ms. Fannie Lou Hamer, who grew up in the Mississippi Delta, fought for the social power of women. Her grandmother, Mrs. Liza Bramlett, had twenty-three children, twenty of which were the result of rape. Mrs. Hamer's mother also suffered a series of rapes. When Mrs. Hamer went to a hospital to have a small cyst removed, she was instead given a forced hysterectomy (1961). She said: "A Black woman's body was never hers alone . . . I went to the doctor who did that to me and ask him Why? Why had he done that to me? I would've loved to have children."[347] Mrs. Hamer was "tired of being tired." Many relish the spotlight but "dedication is not about the big splashy moments: it's about the quiet ripples of preparation and hard work before and after you jump in."[348] Mrs. Hamer worked at Pastor Medgar Evers' office above "Big John" Mora's Big Apple Inn.[349] She worked with SNCC where she was arrested (1963) and then the *Mississippi Democratic Freedom Party* when she was denied recognition at the Democratic Convention (1968). Asked why she was once beaten, Mrs. Hamer said: "I wouldn't say 'Yes, Sir.'"[350]

Mrs. Dorothy Height of the *National Council of Negro Women* (NCNW) and Mrs. Jeanne Noble (of *Delta Sigma Theta*) documented re-peated beatings and rape by activists arrested in the Southland. Ms. Bessie Turner, for example, was beaten in prison during the "Freedom Summer. (Clarksdale, MS, 1961)" Mrs. Marion King was beaten in prison when 7-months pregnant (Albany, GA, 1962). She gave birth to a stillborn baby. Ms. Amelia Boynton Robinson was beaten unconscious and left for dead, on Selma's Edmund Pettis Bridge. Normalcy never again!

## THREAT OF SALE

*It is not my anger that launches rockets, spends over $60,000 a second on missiles and other agents of war and death. Anger is loaded with information and energy . . . There is a "symphony of anger [against Whites]: I cannot hide my anger to spare your guilt, nor hurt feelings, or answering anger.*

**—Audrey Lorde**

During enslavement, "Ole Miss" was the "queen of White supremacy."[351] Most White plantation maidens rarely beat slaves. Instead, Ole Miss often used the threat of sale as an empowering affirmation of her superiority. Many White women forced Black women to nurse their children while neglecting their own. Many White women, whose greatest currency was "innocence," hated Black women and girls because White husbands raped them and then lynched Black men "on behalf of their infantilized "damsels in distress" needing "protection.

After the Civil War, White abolitionists Susan B. Anthony, and Elizabeth Cady Stanton — when launching a feminist movement on the sacred lands of the Iroquois Confederacy (Seneca Falls, NY) — refused to support Black men or women gaining the right to vote. White womanhood has often been "the vanguard of Whiteness;" with some women demanding membership privileges in the KKK.[352] Stanton, who insultingly referred to all African American men as "Sambo," wrote: "I would not trust a Black man with my rights; degraded, oppressed, himself, he would be more despotic than even our Saxon rulers are."[353]

Positively, there were White women allies, like Ms. Jesse Daniel Ames, in early 1930s Texas who formed the *Association of Southern Women for the Prevention of Lynching*. Mostly, however, a White-led feminist movement was "designed for the freedom of White women and not for the freedom of all women."[354] One Washington D.C. suffragist parade (1913) saw Black women consigned to a separate group at the far back instead of with their State delegations.

The Civil Rights Movement helped many White women gain greater empowerment in educational, medical, and legal fields.[355] White women can visit the intersections of racist oppression and sexism more as visitors than those with a permanent address. A statistical gap has grown between the advancement of Black women and White women. Black women, for example, make 58 cents for every dollar made by a White woman.[356] One percent of all CEOs are Black women while, in 2014, 60% of all Black women have loaned money to friends or family, and 73% of Black women worry about not having enough to pay their bills.[357] "The world doesn't stop for the tears of Black women."[358]

Frances Ellen Watkins Harper stated: "You White women speak of rights. I speak of wrongs . . . I do not believe that White women are dewdrops just exhaled from the skies."[359] Audrey Lorde states Black women use anger as a weapon against White "exclusion, unquestioned privilege, of racial distortions, of silence, of ill-use, stereotypes, defensiveness, misnaming, betrayal and co-option."[360] For Lorde, "a well-stocked arsenal of anger" is a response against those "who brought their anger into being."[361] Many Euro-Americans are "anger-inducers" and anger can serve as a "strengthening act of clarification." Lorde writes: "It is not the anger of Black women which is dripping down over this globe like a diseased liquid."[362]

Alicia Garza thought: "Historically speaking, there is little reason for Black women to have much faith that White women will fight for Black women."[363] Toni Morrison writes: "Black women look at White women and see the enemy, for they know that racism is not confined to White men and that there are more White women than men in the country." Some White women opt to preserve their own self- interests instead of promoting sisterhood against sexism. Sometimes, patriarchy happens in ways not perceived. Sometimes liberal Whites imagine themselves as actors in *Driving Miss Daisy* or *The Help* as heroes for their weak Black sisters. Sometimes, White feminism keeps Black women from controlling their own agendas. Unity, "in the midst of madness" is possible, but it's not the task of Black women to seek White validation.[364] Ms. Ruby Hamad writes: "White women can dry their tears and join us, or they can continue . . . on a path that leads not toward the light of liberation but only in the dead end of the colonial past."[365]

## LIKE A MIGHTY RIVER

Ms. Sojourner Truth (born Isabella Baumfree) asked a jeering crowd: "Ain't I a Woman? Look at me! Look at my arm! Ain't I a Woman? I can outwork, out eat, outlast any man! Ain't I a Woman!" (Akron, OH, 1851)[366]

A contemporary of Sojourner Truth was General Harriet Tubman (born Araminta Ross) who is renowned for saving so many escaping enslaved people. President Obama announced that General Tubman's visage would grace Empire's $20 bill but this plan was revoked by Trump.[367] General Tubman had planned to be at Harper's Ferry (West) Virginia in October 1859 but poor health (possibly a life-saving epileptic fit) made her unable to attend the rebellion.

Ms. Mary McLeod Bethune (1875–1955), businesswoman and advisor to presidents, founded Bethune-Cookman College (Daytona, FL). She was "made resilient by racism."[368] Ms. Bethune wrote in her "Last Will and Testament": "I leave you a thirst for education. Knowledge is the prime need of the hour . . . I leave you finally a responsibility to our young people."[369]

Black women should never have to feel like they need to be a "superwoman" or "wonder women." Black feminism has always led anti-blackness efforts to make a more inclusive world. Controlling self-destiny, rejecting fabrications about limitations, and self-skin comfort are why women are often leaders. Like the women and girls of Africa for centuries whispering at trees, our neighbors, sisters, wives, and mothers, are capable of whatever is in their hearts.[370]

Womanist theologians provide another fresh way of thinking about spirituality and liberation from a Black woman's perspective. It may be a moment-by-moment process to recapture a sense of freedom, but even with rough edges, the path is there to follow. Ancestors cut this path before we were born. The healing wisdom of Africa exposes false narratives, misrepresentations, misconceptions, and illusions that are not our inheritance. Warriors for Black human-rights include Anna Julia Cooper, Mary Church Terrell, Frances Harper, Charlotte Forten-Grimke, and, recently, *Black Lives Matter* founders Alicia Garza, Patrisse Khan-Cullors, and Opal Tometi. They follow in the tradition of Shaw University's Mother Ella Baker, Victoria Earle Matthews, Susan McKinney, and Josephine St. Pierre Ruffin who organized Black Women's clubs (in Brooklyn) in 1892. The *National Association of Colored Women* (NACW) was another group of feminist women fighting both sexism and racism.

The cost of racist-oppression has been high: Ms. Breonna Taylor, Ms. Sonji Taylor, Ms. Rekia Boyd, Ms. Alberta Spruill, Ms. Miriam Carey, and many others have been lynched by police violence. Dr. Angela Davis grew up in Birmingham and knew the families of those killed when their Sunday School class was blown up by terrorists. Professor Davis knew such a tragedy sprung from a systemic context, requiring aggressive mass-mobilization. She argued: "In a racist society it's not enough to be a non-racist, we must be anti-racist."[371] Privileged Whites need to be self- critical and recognize that passive avoidance works to protect racist-oppression. What many Whites need to do is to do the work of "unlearning [the religion of] Whiteness every day."[372]

Professor Davis claims the intersections of various injustices must be seen as separate pieces of a large whole. The globalizing forces of predatory, racialized-capitalism are about exploitation in every form. Capitalist racist oppression wages war on social solidarity and tries to make you think you belong nowhere when, in fact you belong everywhere. The promises of capitalism are declaratory and not real and actual. The anti-racist struggle, according to Professor Davis, is a global struggle. We cannot accept any divide-and-conquer strategy but need to see that systemic problems are global realities. Whites are not the majority — from a global perspective. All of us need to cultivate a fresh way of understanding what is actually happening in our world.

Black women voters are critical to elections as America's "most loyal voting bloc."[373] Politicians Val Demings, Keisha Lance Bottoms, Susan Rice, Stacey Abrams, Kamala Harris, Elaine Browne, Cynthia McKinney, Barbara Lee, Barbara Jordan, Shirley Chisholm, and Septima Clark —to name a few — have forged principled coalitions. Writer-scholars Maya Angelou, Alice Walker, Kelly Brown Douglas, Chanequa Walker-Barnes, Kimberle Crenshaw, Wilda Gafney, Michelle Alexander, Nikki Giovanni, Jacqueline Grant, Toni Cade Bambara, Gwendolyn Brooks, Angela Parker, and Asha Bandele — and others — give voice to those marginalized by hetero-patriarchy.

The term "Black is beautiful" has a centuries-long history.[374] In *On the Exhausting Notion of Guarding our Beauty*, Ayanna Byrd writes: "When Black women watched the 2018 film Black Panther and the bald, braided, kinky-haired brown bodies on the screen, we cheered the beauty and it had nothing to do with White people. The dazzle of Wakanda was all ours."[375] Thinking about his mother, Hanif Abdurraqib wrote: "Black women, sitting at the intersection of race and gender experience more than I do, more than their male counterparts. Tabbed as angry, and only angry. I think of my mother. How she always made sure to laugh louder than anyone in the room. How in every picture, she smiled with all of her teeth. How in markets by our house she'd call everyone by their first names . . . and ask about their families."[376] Thinking about their mothers, Patrice Khan-Cullors and Asha Bandele wrote: "Has my mother ever been allowed to lose herself in the laughter of her children, the silly baby games, the simple adolescent struggles – do your homework, do your chores? I do not remember ever going to a movie with my mother or window shopping. I do not remember us together as relaxed, as human 'beings.' We have always had to be humans 'doing.'"[377]

# Freedom Fighters

## DENMARK VESCEY AND NAT TURNER

*The genius of our Black foremothers and forefathers was to create powerful buffers to ward off the nihilistic threat, to equip Black folk with cultural armor to beat back the demons of hopelessness, meaninglessness, and loveless-ness.*

**—Cornel West**

Enslaved Africans did not accept bondage with docility. About three hundred major slave rebellions (the largest being the German Coast Uprising) were led by freedom fighters Denmark Vasey, Martin Delaney, Nat Turner, Cinque Joseph, Gabriel Prosser, Charles Deslandes, Deacon Samuel Sharpe (who led the West Indian "Baptist War"), Gaspar Yagna, the unnamed leaders of the Stono (1739) and New York City Uprisings (1741), and many others.

Gabriel Prosser, an enslaved blacksmith, mobilized an army who could "slay White people like sheep" and "fight White people for freedom."[378] He planned to capture some unguarded rifles and kidnap Virginia's Governor James Monroe (1800) but was betrayed by two slaves.[379] Gabriel avoided capture for almost a month until he was betrayed and then executed in Richmond.

In 1811, over five hundred Black freedom-fighters captured a few plantations near New Orleans. When they moved toward the city, they met the U.S. military: "In the brutal aftermath, militia members chopped-off the leader's hands and burned him alive. They then executed and beheaded over a hundred slaves, put their heads on spikes and lined them along the river."[380]

In 1818, freedman Denmark Vesey ("Telemaque"), and member of the Emmanuel A.M.E in Charleston, SC launched a revolt inspired by the Haitian revolution. In fact, Vesey planned for four years before setting the date for revolution as July 14, 1822. Slave Peter Prioleau exposed his plans. In gratitude for this betrayal the State of North Carolina freed Prioleau and awarded him seven enslaved human beings. Vesey was hanged with thirty-five comrades. A man of faith and a multilingual education, Vesey knew true success in life was measured in terms of freedom.

Nat Turner was a "seer and holy man" who spoke in poetic language about the visions which inspired his actions.[381] His revolt, led by seventy former-slaves, killed at least 57 enslavers across a twenty-mile path of destruction (Southampton Co., VA, 1831). Turner was caught and hanged but his bold uprising left a lasting impression on the South. Nat Turner lived his truth.

## "THE GREAT ACCOMMODATOR"

*No people have ever risen out of the shadows and into the sunlight without fierce opposition. We have been no exception to the rule . . . but we shall win in the end because we have God and justice and fair play on our side.*

### —Booker T. Washington

Booker Taliaferro Washington believed in Empire although Empire never believed in him. He embodied Shirley Chisolm's view: "I don't measure America by its achievements but by its potential."[382] Booker T., born in slavery, became the first President of the Tuskegee Institute which was founded to equip Black folks with marketable skills. Because Booker T. was focused on economic empowerment, he sometimes allied himself with White supremacists.[383] His belief was there was "little race prejudice in the American dollar."[384] Once, Alabama's Governor W.C. Oates told Tuskegee's graduates: "I want to give you N@#* a few words of plain-talk and advice: This is a White man's country, as far as the South is concerned, and we are going to make you keep your place. Understand that. I have nothing more to say to you."[385]

Booker T. traversed Empire lecturing and fund-raising. When Theodore Roosevelt invited Booker T. as the first Black man to dine at the White House, Euro-Southerners spat: "Now that Roosevelt has eaten with that N@#* Washington, we'll have to kill a thousand N@#* to get them back to their place." Another Southern "Christian" said: "The White House was so saturated with the odor of N@#* that the rats have taken refuge in the stable."[386]

Today, however, one speech is remembered, a message, he gave at the Atlanta Exposition (1895): Booker T. told Whites to disregard Black agitation for equality and focus on enlisting Black usefulness in the Empire economy. Because it's impossible to imagine the unending pressures Booker T. felt in neo-slavery Alabama, the flippant label "Uncle-Tom" is unfair.[387] Bottom line: Booker T. got things done. He was a pragmatic accommodationist encircled by White supremacist terrorists stealthily lurking to grind him into fine powder at any unguarded instant.[388]

## LIVING ABOVE THE VEIL

*I sit with Shakespeare and he winces not. Across the color-line I move arm in arm with Balzac and Dumas. . . . So wed with Truth, I dwell above the veil. Is this the life you grudge us, O knightly America? Is this the life you long to change into the dull red hideousness of Georgia?. . . Actively we've woven ourselves into the very warp and woof of this nation – we've fought their battles and have shared their sorrow. We've mingled our blood with theirs and generation after generation we've pleaded with a headstrong, careless people not to despise justice, mercy, and truth, lest the nation be smitten with a curse. Our song and our toil and our cheer and warning have been given to this nation in blood-brotherhood.*

### —Dr. William Edward Burghardt DuBois

William Edward Burghardt DuBois, a warrior against racist-oppression, was the first Black man to earn a Harvard doctorate.[389] In another era, DuBois might've lived a quiet life.

Professor DuBois was a questioner: "How does integrity face oppression? What shall honesty do in the face of deception?"[390] Some labelled him a "Marxist" — others a Pan-African Nationalist.[391] He became a strident voice for justice and helped found the NAACP. As a child of African and Dutch French Huguenot parents, Marcus Garvey mocked the Professor with the derogatory term "mulatto"[392] The Professor, however, thought Black Americans could embrace both their African and American heritages and that Black pride needn't equate with an "individuality entombed in Blackness."[393] Ironically, Dr. DuBois' Pan-African ideas evolved over time and came to partially parallel Garvey's ideas. The Professor came to believe that only socialism, and not racialized-capitalism, could break cycles of exploitation at the greedy heart of Empire. For the Professor, a realistic Pan-Africanism meant the integration of Diasporic Africans.[394] Dr. DuBois called for a "race-conscious movement without being racialist."[395]

Comparisons between Booker T. Washington with Dr. DuBois can play into a "divide-and- conquer" strategy. These two men lived in different areas, with distinct social-networks and opportunities. Both worked to empower Black lives. Both thought Black power demanded bicultural fluency. But, unlike Booker T., the Professor warned Black Americans that White supremacy would "bleach" their souls.[396] Much is made of tensions between the Professor and Washington's "Tuskegee Project" where Booker T. tried to bridge social-alienation gaps through vocational-training. DuBois said education fostered rational skills and mental development.[397] Wisdom-education – the arts and humanities – empowered the dominated to defeat a "tangle of thought and afterthought" rooted in the memory of slavery's "death ships;" embodying both external and internal inferiority.[398] DuBois hoped to "dwell above the veil" of racist-oppression but wasn't naïve about his enemies. He held to "a hope not hopeless but unhopeful."[399] On his ninety-fifth birthday (in Ghana) Dr. DuBois said Whites saw him as "nothing but a N@#*."[400]

## FIGHTING IGNORANCE

*Talk! Talk! Talk will not free the slaves. What is needed is action! Action!*

**—John Brown**

Carter G. Woodson, a major catalyst behind Black History Month, was born the son of former slaves (1875). He earned a Harvard doctorate in history before launching an academic society and journal promoting Black history. Dr. Woodson was a man of "Black prophetic fire."[401] He taught we must comprehend the past to understand the future. In the 1930s, Dr. Woodson accurately predicted "the maltreatment of Negroes will be nationalized."[402]

The English word "education" comes from the Latin, *educare*, to "bring forth" (Igbo – *mmutu*, Swahili – *elimu*). A dog can be trained, but a dog cannot be educated. Before his death (1950), Dr. Woodson wrote sixteen books including *The Mis-Education of the Negro* — an Afrocentric classic. Miseducation is the "cultivation of an alien identity."[403] It's the process of negating our own genius. Dr. Woodson noted the mere impartation of knowledge was not education: Education was "what we agree that the young should carry in their minds" instead of a tool for state-sponsored propaganda.[404] Dr. Woodson taught when an oppressor can control your thinking they don't have to worry about your actions: "You don't have to tell him to stand here or go yonder. He will find his proper place and will stay in it."[405] Transformative education keeps us from being controlled by other folks and their toxic influences. Knowledge of ourselves protects us from being destroyed by racist-oppressors or by becoming oppressors ourselves.[406]

Dr. Woodson warned Empire education was designed to "handicap a student by teaching him that his black face is a curse and that his struggle to change his condition is hopeless. It is the worst sort of lynching."[407] Dr. Woodson declared: "I am ready to act, if I can find brave men to help me."[408] To be a "Woodsonian" is to be one who "encourages and inspires African Americans to do things such as support and start Black businesses, admire the varied greatness of Africa's past, and not blindly imitate others in religion, education" or in any other area of life.[409]

## "NO USE LYING ABOUT IT!"

*"Those who profess to favor freedom and yet deprecate agitation, are people who want crops without plowing up the ground." / "If there is no struggle there is no progress."*

### —Frederick Douglass

Marcus Aurelius Mosiah Garvey was born in Jamaica (1887). From 1919 until 1940, he preached to two million followers a message of self-respect, self-empowerment, and support for Africans throughout the Diaspora. Prophet Garvey strongly confronted controlling structures by training folks to be powerful with pragmatic, and confident agency in every sphere of life.

FBI Director J. Edgar Hoover said that Garvey was "one of the most powerful personalities I've ever seen on a platform."[410] Garvey gave folks a "backbone where before they only had a wishbone."[411] Garvey taught pride in Africa and rejected worshipping a White God. He noted Pontius Pilate was White and Simon of Cyrene (who shared Christ's cross), was Black.[412] Garvey said we shouldn't be serfs or dogs envying the soul-killing leprosy of Whiteness. Garvey expected no alliances with Whites who "had the power to oppress" and would always do so.[413]

Garvey made many enemies. He attacked the NAACP as an "enemy of the race. . . . Between the KKK and the NAACP, give me the Klan for their honesty of purpose toward the Negro. They're better friends to my race for telling us what we are and what they mean; thereby giving us a chance to stir for ourselves, than all the hypocrites put together with their false gods and religions, notwithstanding. . . . potentially, every White man is a Klansman, as far as the Negro in competition with Whites socially, economically, and politically is concerned. There's no use lying about it."[414] He believed: "There's a need for a pure Negro race. . . . slavery brought on us the curse of many colors within the Negro race. Mulattos are evil and in the future the Negro race should not be stigmatized by bastardy."[415] This is a major blind-spot because love — not hate — leads us to see that "the interracial body is disruptive because of what it indicates as well as the ways in which such bodies must perform through these realties."[416] Problematic terms like "mixed, and biracial, are remixed versions of terms like mulatto, quadroon, and octoroon."[417]

Marcus Garvey was accused of many things but, finally the FBI entrapped him in a mail- fraud scheme connected to his Black Star Steamship Company (1926).[418] Empire deported Garvey to Jamaica where he remained. Detractors accused Garvey of being an egotistical "virtuoso." Even though Garvey's "Back to Africa Movement" seems regressive, it exposed that any future for African Americans in Empire must combat the crippling effects of leeching White supremacy. He emphasized self-reliance and diasporic nationalism.[419] Garvey sought to develop independent Black institutions (IBI's) fostering Black flourishing.[420] Most significantly, Prophet Garvey was a forerunner to Malcolm X in that his remedies combined spiritual and psychological emancipation. *Garvey Lives!* Barry Beckham's play (1972) relates: "I've been sleeping all my life. And now Mr. Garvey done woke me up, I'm goin' stay woke."[421]

## "EQUALLY GOOD TO LIVE OR DIE"

*Only thing we did wrong – stayed in the wilderness a day to long. You know the one thing we did right was the day we began to fight. Keep your eyes on the prize! Hold on! // I love everybody! I love Hoss Manucy (KKK, St. Augustine FL) when he'd just beat us up! I love everybody // You know I wouldn't want to be Governor Wallace and I'll tell you the reason why, I'm afraid my Lord might call me and I'd not be ready to die.*

**—Civil Rights Freedom Songs**

Master Fuzzy Simpson (8) and Master Hanover Thompson (10) were boys playing an innocent "kissing-game" with White seven-year-old, Sissy Sutton (Monroe, NC, 1958). When Sissy told Daddy about her game, police arrested the boys for attempted rape. The eight and ten-year-old were beaten bloody and, a week later, were found guilty of "molestation" in a juvenile-court and sentenced for "indeterminate terms" in reform-school. Robert F. Williams, NAACP activist, organized the *Committee to Combat Racial Injustice* (CCRI) to work for the release — which they eventually gained. Even President Dwight D. Eisenhower called on North Carolina's governor to free the boys back to their mothers who had not seen them for four months.

Thousands of activists and martyrs led the Civil Rights Movement. Rev. George Lee was gunned down while helping register voters (1955). Rev. Medgar Evers, Mr. James Cheney, and Euro-American Civil Rights workers Mr. Michael Schwarmer, and Mr. Andrew Goodman were murdered. Other martyrs from voter registration drives include Mr. Lamar Smith (1955), Mr. Vernon Dahmer (1966), and Euro-American Episcopalian seminarian Jonathan Myrick Daniels (1965). Third-grader Miss Linda Brown was stopped while enrolling in a Topeka elementary-school. Miss Brenda Travis, age sixteen, was arrested for sitting at a lunch-counter. Ms. Diane Nash was arrested for "contributing to the delinquency of minors" in a lunch sit in. Fiery mottos at boycotts included: "Don't buy where you can't work! Don't buy where you can't eat!"

On December 5, 1955, a forty-two-year-old seamstress, Ms. Rosa Mc-Cauley Parks changed the world by getting on a bus (Montgomery, AL). She was tired of going to the back-of-the-bus to accommodate White terror. Her refusal to accept a second-class designation set-in-motion a tsunami. A boycott was launched as others followed her example: "The moment you set an example, the spell of the status-quo is broken, and others will follow."[422] Nine-months before Ms. Parks, 15-year-old Miss Claudette Colvin (and Miss Mary Louise Smith) had been arrested for the same crime, but her case was "de-prioritized" because she was an unwed, pregnant teen.

Imprisoned, Rosa Parks became "Inmate #7053." Racist-oppressors singled Ms. Parks out for focused punishment and her life was often threatened. But she never fought alone: Black folks united together in every way imaginable. One group of women, led by legendary cook, Georgia Gilmore, even funneled money into the boycott-movement's coffers by selling baked goods to unwitting Whites who had no idea they were actually supporting a revolution.[423]

Ms. Parks didn't "emerge out of thin air." Folks embraced the work in the trenches to bring change because "there comes a time when it is equally good to live or die."[424] NAACP lawyer Thurgood Marshall began to publicly foreground specific injustices in order to expose White supremacist laws. Power comes through unity, change comes through organization, and justice comes through determination. Freedom-fighters should be "fierce believers in possibility, rigorous cultivators of presence, effective wielders of power and ardent lovers of people."[425]

## "DID YOU KNOW MALCOLM?"

*I loved having my own garden-plot and took care of it well. I loved specially to grow peas. I was proud when we had them on our table. I'd pull out the weeds when their first little blades came up . . . And sometimes when I had everything straight and clean for my things to grow, I'd lay down on my back between the rows and gaze up in the blue sky at the clouds moving and think all kinds of things.*

### —Minister el–Hajj Malik el–Shabazz Malcolm X

Minister Malcolm X was a gardener, who nurtured visions and brought strength out of hard work and love. Brother Malcolm lent defiant voice to the endless anguish of the oppressed. He was a "pulsating cultural archetype. He lives in the unconscious of every Black American."[426]

Born Malcolm Little in Omaha, he became Malcolm X, who became el-Hajj Malik el- Shabazz Malcolm X. His mother, Louise, was from Grenada and his father, Earl, was a celebrant of Garvey's gospel lynched by the KKK. Afterwards, Mama Louise Little was committed to an insane-asylum and young Malcolm was sent to a juvenile-detention home. His childhood knew the "humiliations of poverty" that "would haunt him for the rest of his life."[427] After being imprisoned, he converted to the *Nation of Islam* (NOI). When he joined, the NOI had fewer than a thousand members. When Minister Malcolm left the NOI it had over 40,000 members.[428]

Minister Malcolm experienced many lifetimes in his thirty-nine years. His life is a fluid metaphor of what it means to be an African in America. Minister Malcolm even had a university named in his honor (*Malcolm X Liberation University*, MXLU, 1969–1973). He transformed broken shards of pain into a magnetic mosaic through discipline and relentless education. Throughout his pilgrim-life, he valorized the positive, nurturing, healing wisdom of Mother Africa. Minister Malcolm fought against actions with words and against words with actions.

Minister Malcolm was an inspiring soul "who did not stop seeking answers."[429] His creative pragmatism led him to conclude the best solution for his beloved community was not in moving to Africa. Instead, he taught we could take an inward *hajj* back to the Homeland of souls. Minister Malcolm realized, after visiting Ghana, that Africans everywhere were interdependent and responsible for each other's constant encouragement and ongoing empowerment.

Minister Malcolm is known for preaching all Whites were "devils."[430] How could racist perpetrators of the African Holocaust be called anything else? When once asked directly "Do you hate the White man?" He answered:

"We don't even think about him. How can anybody ask us do we hate the man who kidnapped us 400 years ago, brought us here and stripped us of our history, stripped us of our culture, stripped us of our language, stripped us of everything that you could use today to prove that you were ever part of the human family."[431] It wasn't honest to be nice. What Whites needed to hear was the truth: "Stop sweet-talking them. Tell them how you really feel. Tell them what kind of hell you've been catching."[432] After converting to Orthodox Islam, Minister Malcolm thought everyone, made in God's image, need not be consigned to a constructed identity. Race-traitors, seeking to be divested of being White, are welcome to share at our sacred table.

Minister Malcolm, like Gandhi and Thoreau, didn't reject Christ but rejected slave-promoting Whiteyanity. The inclusive justice-message of Islam won his heart. Minister Malcolm called himself a "Black Nationalist freedom fighter."[433] He "articulated Black rage in a manner unprecedented in American history.... [he] highlighted the chronic refusal of most Americans to acknowledge the sheer absurdity that confronts humans of African descent" in America - the incessant assaults on Black intelligence, agency, beauty, character, and possibility.[434]

## INMATE #7089

*Being Black in America means trying to smile when you want to cry. It means trying to hold on to physical life amid psychological death. It means the pain of watching your children grow up with clouds of inferiority in their mental skies. It means having your legs cut-off and then being condemned for being a disabled person . . . It means the ache and anguish of living in so many situations where hopes unborn have died.*

### —Rev. Dr. Martin Luther King, Jr.

In 1959, Dr. King visited India, where he was introduced as an "untouchable" and an "outcaste." He was shocked but responded: "Yes, I am an untouchable, and every Black person in the United States of America is an untouchable."[435] Dr. King's lived a Black Social Christianity that rejected the toxic superficialities of Empire — a business-venture based on an exploitation model. His prophetic criticisms were counter-resistance to the recurring forces of hatred.

Michael Luther King (his name was later changed) was born in January 1929.[436] He excelled in school and skipped the ninth and twelfth-grades. Dr. King followed his father and grandfather into ministry. While studying sociology at Morehouse, his mentor was Rev. Dr. Benjamin Elijah Mayes.

Warrior-scholar King studied theology at Crozier Theological Seminary (Chester, PA) and philosophies of personalism at Boston University. He was impacted by Thoreau and Gandhi's non-violent actions which met injustices with moral authority. Dr. King agreed with Walter Rauschenbusch that true Christianity was always a prophetic force for justice. His path emphasized a unity between inner, soul-change and transformative, steady social change.

Family nurtured Dr. King: "When all else fails, you need to be able to go home again and have people call your name in a way that is familiar only to them."[437] He was a proud Atlantan and never missed a chance to dine at his "second home," Paschal's on Hunter Street.[438] Whenever troubles mounted — he went home — Ebenezer Baptist Church. There, congregants "knew Martin before he knew himself and they knew him better than he knew himself."[439]

Dr. King's preaching was prophetic and he is "the most celebrated orator in the American tradition. He's our Churchill. Why? Because he was able to convince White people, in the middle of Jim Crow apartheid segregation, that there was "racism" going on and it was bad! It took a world-class Cicero or a Churchill in the middle of apartheid to show that. That's not [only] about Black speech; that's about White listening. White listening that tunes out and turns down the volume when certain truths start coming."[440]

Defenders of a static status quo offer us a sanitized version of St. Martin of the Poor that limits Dr. King as an inert hero preaching tolerant restraint; not a prophet inciting rebellion. Empire dominators honor Dr. King because he's dead. They hope we forget Dr. King denounced the Vietnam War, Empire imperialism, and exploitative racialized capitalism. At his funeral, a Bible verse was read: "Let us kill the dreamer and see what becomes of his dream?"[441] Today, this question is a taunt against those who've turned his call for justice into an antiseptic ideal. Today, we need to hear Dr. King's view that "it is necessary to realize that we have moved from the era of Civil Rights to the era of Human Rights."[442] Today, there are "more than nine hundred streets named after Dr. King in forty States" but this practice deflects attention away from the fact these streets are often contexts of poverty.[443] Remember Dr. King's warning: "The whirlwinds of revolt will continue to shake the foundations of our nation until the bright day of justice emerges"[444] He has to be "dis-remembered" from inaccurate misrepresentations.[445] He was hated by the ruling elite for saying the truth that "the bombs in Vietnam explode at home" because money was wasted in a war instead of rebuilding America.[446] MLKs life was a synergy of the pastoral, pragmatic, and idealistic. A quiet introvert with a heart for the world, he wrote six books and won the Nobel Peace Prize (1964).[447] When Dr. King went to Oslo to accept the award, he invited twenty-six guests, "the largest entourage in Nobel history."[448] He had a big heart! Reverend King was taken suddenly from his wife and beautiful children one chilly April evening in Memphis, 1968. He was there fighting for poor garbage-workers. James Baldwin said the Civil Rights fights "clarified once and forever and in the sight of the world the real intention of our co- citizens towards us. When Martin's head was blown off, we learned something."[449] Immediately after his murder, riots broke out in 125 communities. History will record him as America's finest soul. Arrested during the Montgomery Bus Boycott "for driving 30 miles-per-hour in a 25 miles- per-hour zone, he was placed in a police car and taken to the city jail" where the State of Alabama designated the future Nobel Peace Prize Laureate as "Inmate #7089."[450] Today, "his message is neither understood nor seen as relevant to a new age of conservative ascendancy."[451] Few appreciate Dr. King's views about cancerous, racialized-capitalism's prison-inducing chains. He fiercely loved justice more than self-security. Dr. King claimed Black folks are the "conscience of America. We are its troubled soul. We will continue."[452]

## MARTIN AND MALCOLM TOGETHER

*The White man's Christian religion further deceived and brainwashed this 'Negro' to always turn the other cheek, grin, scrape, bow, be humble, to sing and to pray, and take whatever was dished out by the devil White man. He was told to look for his pie in the sky and for his heaven in the hereafter while, right here on the earth, the slave-master White man enjoyed his heaven.*

**—Minister el–Hajj Malik el–Shabazz Malcolm X**

They met only once — and then by accident — in a hallway for a few minutes. As they were going separate ways, someone suggested a photo. Not long after, Malcolm was assassinated at Harlem's Audubon Ballroom late on a Sunday afternoon.[453] Both men were lynched at age 39. Both embodied values of "justice, love, and hope."[454] Time links Malcolm and Martin together.

Today, Malcolm's pragmatic nation-building instincts combine with Martin's pragmatic call for intercultural respect. Attempts to divide Martin's call for "redemptive suffering" from Malcolm's call for "reciprocal bleeding" fail to see the concord between both realities. Both loved community. While some need a little more "Malcolm" in non-fawning rhetoric and a little more "Martin" in tireless activism, these warriors show us the same path. A "Malcolm-Martin" balance combines the *yin* of hopeful idealism with the *yang* of angry passion. Walking a tightrope, we'll keep our balance best with both sober realism and determined effort. The alternative to a "Martin- Malcolm" prophetic-contextualization approach — to use a term from Kosuke Koyama — is an era of increasingly hateful polarization and intercultural violence.

By returning to the hallway of that singular photograph, we see Malcolm and Martin as partners in a way circumstances prevented in life. Their unified heartbeats throb in strong rhythm with Middle Passage ancestors — still beating bloodied knuckles against slave-ship walls. Martin calls, and Malcolm responds, "Amen." Malcolm calls and Martin responds "Preach!" They are watching us, arms wrapped around each other's broad shoulders, seeing us with fierce love.

## CHANGING SAMENESS "THIS IS OUR COUNTRY!"

*"You know, you don't want to live with them either." (1973) // "I've always had a great relationship with the Blacks."*

**—Donald J. Trump (2011).**

James Baldwin wrote, in "the sunlight prison of an American dream," Whites are "in the grip of a weird nostalgia."[455] White students at the University of Chicago's 1903 commencement ceremony heard Presidential candidate John Temple Graves call for Blacks to be relocated to the Philippines. Graves proclaimed: "This is *our* Country. We made it. We molded it. We control it and we always will. We have done remarkable things. We have important things to do. The Negro is an accident – an unwilling, a blameless but an unwholesome, unwelcome, helpless, unassimilable element in our civilization."[456]

Under enslavement, Blacks risked being sold or lynched at any instant. Founders of this slaveocracy designed a system designed to exclude Black people, women, and First Nations from power.[457] We weren't on the radar. The Electoral College, for example — a relic of slavery — was designed to preserve White supremacy. It has always been undemocratic and needs to quickly go the way of Betamax and the sundial.

Today, we don't have the luxury to have short-term strategies. If you're planning to stay inside this system you should understand the way power and resources are distributed. Inside a slaveocracy, Black progress will be won, step-by-step, in a protracted struggle for justice. It takes both protestors on the outside, and pragmatists on the inside, to generate power and unlock the resources of Empire. Our context demands long-term planning centered on specific objectives, acted on with agreed-upon (de-centralized) strategies, and then, moved forward with unity and discipline. A long-range plan looks past just simply burning down the Big House.

In Empire, "politics is the place where power operates."[458] This is why voter-suppression (which should be called voter-theft) is a tool to keep control in a "pseudo-democracy."[459] In 1896 Mississippi, there were over 130,000 Black voters, but by 1904, that number was reduced to 1,300.[460] Suppression comes in many Janus-faces: Southern postal-workers sometimes simply didn't deliver voter-registration cards. Votes aren't counted or machines "malfunction." Voter-theft has included many variations on poll-taxes and literacy-tests. Some voted easily like "Uncle" Ike Pringle, praised by Whites (Lincoln, MS) as a "totally unreconstructed, a true Negro of the Old South who always sided with White folks."[461] Sometimes voter-thieves asked impossible questions: "How old was Christ when he was born?" One applicant was handed a Chinese script and asked if he knew what it meant: "Yeah, I know what it means: It means that N@#* ain't gonna vote in Mississippi again this year."[462]

We must never forget the organizers and protestors who died for our right to vote. Churches for decades have organized "souls-to-the-polls" efforts. White supremacist terrorists murdered Rev. George Lee for registering voters (1955). Mr. Lamar Smith (60) was also killed while helping folks register (1955).

Many folks feel "captured" by both parties, not happy with either option. In terms of party-affiliation, Minister Malcolm said: "I'm not a Democrat. I'm not a Republican. I don't even consider myself just an American."[463] Today, Black abolitionists like Malcolm Kenyatta, Aryanna Presley, Jamal Bowman, and Chevron James are working inside the system to change it. Yet, the majority of Black folks don't vote because they feel that they don't have much to vote for. Some feel "the biggest lie in American politics" is the idea that "if we just vote everything will be okay."[464] This is self-imposed voter-suppression: stealing your own vote.

To be clear: Voting is a weapon, a right, an obligation, and a responsibility for every citizen. Voting is political currency — wasted if unused. To not vote is a self-erasure of your own role in civic society. It's understandable — just misguided and shortsighted — why some folks feel they're "too good" to vote. Mr. Colin Kaepernick explained what many feel who don't vote: "You know, I think it would be hypocritical of me to vote. I said from the beginning. . . . I was against the system of oppression. I'm not going to show support for that system. The oppressor isn't going to allow you to vote your way out of your oppression."[465] This quote is an example of agreeing and disagreeing with a view at the same time. Voting's not a panacea to solve every problem any more than flu-medicine "solves" the flu. It might not help — but it might — and not taking it might kill you.

Jean-Paul Sartre authored an essay entitled *Elections: A Trap for Fools* (1973). Henry David Thoreau claimed voting was a waste of time because the system was rigged.[466] Both criticized voting as "the least you can do." Okay. So, do it! High-minded outrage may be great in theory but it has real-world results that hurt folks in real-world ways. In 2016, for example, 42% of America's 200 million eligible registered voters didn't vote.[467] While most Americans don't live in "battle-ground" States, every voter has civic and local ("down-ballot") election results, such as choices about who is District Attorney, Judge, tax-assessor, or Police-Chief, that directly affect our lives.

Systemic problems — in a context rooted in exploitation — will not only be resolved through elections. Yet, the fact so many folks don't want you to vote should tell you how meaningful it actually is. Not voting is a self-inflicted wound. A vote won't solve all your problems, but it's a starting point. Think of it as brushing your teeth or using a handkerchief. Voting is only one weapon in our arsenal of action. Dr. Angela Davis is correct that grass-roots activism is "the most important ingredient of building radical movements."[468] In 2016, "only a few dozen out of the more than 2,300 elected prosecutors nationwide were Black folks. The overwhelming percentage of the elected-officials responsible for many consequential decisions in the criminal-justice system" are White.[469] Voting is part — however small — for justice-building. It is an exercise in agency: Erase and silence your own voice at your own peril.

## "THE WHOLE COUNTRY'S SOUTHERN!"

*The problem of the twenty-first century is the problem of civilizing White people.*

**—Nikki Giovanni**

In 1968, Robert F. Kennedy predicted, "in forty years a Negro can achieve the same position my brother had."[470] President Lyndon Baines Johnson (LBJ) could've enacted the Civil Rights Act in 1964 but waited until after the election because he feared losing Southern votes. In the Southland, it's always been true "the lowest White man counted more than the highest Black man."[471] LBJ's main opponent was Dixiecrat George Wallace of Alabama.[472] LBJ won easily but Wallace noticed the strongest supporters of his race-baiting message, were mostly Northerners. He exulted: "They all hate Black people. That's it! . . . The whole United States is Southern!"[473]

Wallace was right: In 1968, Richard Milhous Nixon won with Wallace's Law-and-Order "Southern Strategy" which was filled with code-words like crime, busing, welfare, and quotas. Wallace, a White supremacist, won the ear of Whites by whispering race-baiting dog-whistles. Nixon parroted this tactic and brought Wallace's thinly-veiled White supremacy into mainstream politics. Nixon cultivated class-resentments against "elitist-leftists" who look down their noses at industrious, gun-owning, devout, god-fearing, ordinary Americans. Nixon's Chief of Staff, H.R. Haldeman said: "You have to face the fact that the whole problem is really *the Blacks*. The key is to devise a system that recognizes this while not appearing to."[474]

Extremist conservative social-Darwinism — framed as culture-wars — came with Barry Goldwater and devotee Ronald Reagan. Goldwater warned of the evils of civil-rights for Blacks: "We're being asked to destroy the rights of some under the false banner of promoting the civil- rights of others."[475] Extremist conservatives endorsed a strategy towards Black empowerment of "benign neglect" that milked White-backlash.[476] Goldwater, Wallace, Nixon, Reagan, two Bushes, and Trump have continued playing the old game of "solving" racism by declaring it solved. Politicians sell a Golden-Corral buffet of code-words against Black empowerment while supporting systemic White-affirmative action.

The grand-fatherly, Ronald Wilson Reagan — elected President in 1980 — tried to deliver a "death-sentence" against Black empowerment.[477] The ever-upbeat Reagan began a "new era where thinly-veiled contempt for racial minorities . . . unleashed a racist backlash."[478] Reagan invoked the deferential "pure and true Americans" who knew to "stay in their place." If politics and patriotism are the last bastions for scoundrels, this B-movie actor-turned-politician took "patriotic-racism" to new levels. Reagan fused a "possessive investment in Whiteness with other psychic and material investments-especially in masculinity, patriarchy, and heterosexuality."[479]

When Reagan was California's Governor, the Black Panthers briefly occupied the Statehouse. This led Californian legislators to enact the nation's strictest gun laws very quickly. Speaking of United Nations delegates from Africa, Reagan said: "To see those, those monkeys from those African countries – damn them, they're still uncomfortable wearing shoes."[480] Reagan's (who had only one Black cabinet member in his two-terms) "virtue-loving" Education Secretary, William Bennett, said: "I do know it's true that if you wanted to reduce crime, you could – if that were your sole purpose – you could abort every Black baby in this country, and your crime-rate would go down. That would be an impossible, ridiculous, and morally reprehensible thing to do, but your crime-rate would go down."[481] White identity-politics is effective in unifying White America against a common-foe. Lee Atwater

(1981) defined the Republican's "Southern strategy": "You start out in 1954 by saying, 'N@#*, n@*#, n@#*.' By 1968, you can't say 'n@#*' – that hurts you: Backfires. So, you say stuff like forced busing, state's rights, and all that stuff. You're getting so abstract now [that] you're talking about cutting taxes, and all these things you're talking about are totally economic things and a byproduct of them is [that] Blacks get hurt worse than Whites. . . . I'm saying that if it is getting that abstract, and coded, that we are doing away with the racial problem one way or the other. You follow me – because obviously sitting around saying, 'We want to cut this,' is much more abstract than even the busing thing, and a hell of a lot more abstract than 'N@#*, n@#*.'"[482] Dog-whistle racist oppressors euphemistically "talks about race without ever explicitly mentioning it."[483]

Implementing the politics of disposability, Reagan criminalized mental-illness sending thousands of mentally-ill folks to homelessness or prisons. Reagan savaged social-welfare programs and re-distributed wealth through tax-cuts and business de-regulations so complete that, when he left office, the top 1% of all Americans had more wealth than the bottom 90% combined.[484] James Baldwin said of Reagan, "What I found unspeakable about the man was his contempt, his brutal contempt, for the poor."[485] Under Reagan, long-term unemployment rose only 2% among Whites but rose 72% among Blacks.[486] He attacked Affirmative Action as a "leaking poison in the American soul. . . . America must once again try living with inequality as life is lived."[487] Reagan grimly promised to "send the welfare bums back to work."[488]

Reagan launched a "War on Drugs" while creating a permanent underclass, which actually increased both drug use and America's prison-population. It was a gold-rush boom-time for prison-builders. Sentencing often disproportionately criminalized Black criminals in comparison to White criminals.[489] For most extremist conservatives, even the Christian idea of loving everyone doesn't seem to apply to criminals. Reagan lavished vast sums of welfare on expanding government to build prisons. This "system was better designed to create crime and a perpetual class of people labelled criminals, rather than to eliminate crime or reduce the number of criminals."[490] It was a failure for justice but a booming success for a new kind of business.

Reagan's ahistorical preaching of "reverse-racism" claimed most Euro-Americans were victimized by Affirmative Action. For Reagan, individual rights were the goal of Civil Rights. Reagan saw Affirmative Action as a liberal bribe he refused to pay — in exchange for Black cooperation. Reagan re-framed debates on "racism" by claiming America was a "color-blind" meritocracy. The cheery Irishman led relentless attacks on Black America while not seeming to be a mean-spirited racist. Reagan made the birthday of his version of a domesticated Martin Luther King, Jr. a national-holiday to show injustices against Blacks were ancient history. He claimed ending Affirmative Action was "very consistent with what Dr. King had in mind."[491]

## KINDER, GENTLER RACIST OPPRESSION

*By age thirteen, I had intuitively developed the cardinal guidepost for emotional health: the "Never-wanna-be" rule. Never want to be with the people who do not want to be with you.*

**—Randall Robinson**

In 1988, George H. W. Bush ran attack-ads against Michael Dukakis featuring Willie Horton, a Black criminal in Dukakis' home-state of Massachusetts who, on furlough, raped a White woman and then stabbed her boyfriend. Down 17% in the polls right before the election, Bush claimed: "If I can make Willie Horton a household name, we will win the election."[492]

Steven Shull summarized the Reagan-Bush Era: "By playing on the fear and frustration of lower-class Whites, both Reagan and Bush left a substantial civil rights legacy, but it was not a kinder and gentler one."[493] Bush more than doubled the billions of dollars invested in the "War on Drugs" claiming what was needed was "more prisons, more jails, more courts, and more prosecutors."[494] George W. Bush, like his father a decade earlier, was careful to avoid offending White Southerner conservatives. When Hurricane Katrina slammed New Orleans, Bush waited four days before responding to those unable to flee the storm (2005).[495] After Katrina, slanted news reports seemed to say that "Blacks looted stores" while "Whites found bread."[496] Bush's glacial response sent to some the message that "the value of life is persistently specified along racial lines."[497] Rush Limbaugh and Tucker Carlson said victims were responsible for their plight because they didn't own cars. Barbara Bush observed, since many victims were poor, the "loss of their homes and relocation to other cities actually worked out well for them."[498] One official said: "We finally cleaned up public-housing in New Orleans. We couldn't do it, but God did."[499]

Goldwater, Nixon, Wallace, Reagan, the Bushes, and Trump sought to represent a status quo that equated the "American Way" with majority White ways. Their narrative of ethno-tribalism communicated to supporters a view that welfare keeps lazy, poor non-White people eating Cheetos, smoking weed, and watching reality-TV. A majority of non-Whites are reliant on aid that conservatives are forced to pay. In contrast, the true, industrious Americans (who happen to be White) break their backs at work to support the ungrateful indolence of the stupid poor.

## THE SAX OFFENDER

*Racism is so universal in this country, so widespread and so deep-seated that it's invisible because it is so normal. . . . The difference between de-jure and de-facto segregation is the difference between open and forthright bigotry and the shame-faced kind that works through unwritten agreements between real estate dealers, school officials, and local politicians.*

**—Shirley Anita Chisolm**

Even though William Jefferson Clinton (1992–2000) was the first Euro-American inducted into the Arkansas Black Hall of Fame as an honorary member there's not much honorable (other than playing the saxophone on Arsenio Hall for four minutes in 1992) about his intercultural policies. He gave tepid support for Affirmative Action while calling for "fairness." Basically, Clinton blamed the problems of Black lives on Black lives: We are our own worst problem. Clinton's party-platform (1992) was the first in five decades to entirely avoid mentioning racist-oppression.[500] Clinton preached the high-sounding language of "color-blindness." Candidate Clinton (1992) was determined not to be outflanked on the Right so he returned to Arkansas to oversee the execution of Mr. Ricky Ray Rector, a mentally incapacitated Black man. He also staged a political-stunt by attacking rapper Sister Souljah."[501] As President, Clinton slashed funds for government-housing, which led to scores of evictions that disproportionately affected Black women by a wide margin. Clinton infamously signed into law a crime-bill that changed America. When Clinton left office there were 800,000 Black men in prison and 600,000 Black men in college.[502] This was more folks in prison than had been in slavery in 1850. Clinton was able to smoothly offer Black voters' style over substance because voters saw him as the "lesser-of-two-evils." Michael Eric Dyson observed: "Clinton is just the sort of political figure that Malcolm often warned us against."

Clinton went to the Memphis church where Dr. King gave his final sermon and said, if Dr. King were alive, he'd say: "I didn't fight for the right of Black people to murder other Black people with reckless abandonment."[503] Both Bill and Hillary Clinton also spoke about 'Super-predators,' with the "savage behavior of lawless vandals who do not share our values."[504] Hillary Clinton, when running against Obama, assured that she'd never have had Rev. Jeremiah Wright as her pastor because she represented "working-class,

you know, White, Americans."[505] She tried to link Obama to Minister Louis
Farrakhan and, in 2006, leaked a picture of Obama in Somali dress "a thinly-
veiled attempt to evoke fears about so-called Muslim terrorists."[506] She went
to a church near Ferguson during the height of BLM-protests to assure "all
lives matter."[507] For both Clintons, all too often, fiery or fine words joined
with slow-molasses inertia.


## "KENYAN ANTI-COLONIAL BEHAVIOR"

*An intelligent thief does not steal in his own quarter of the town. // The Devil does
not destroy his own house.*

### —Egyptian (Kemet) Proverbs

It was the best of times and the worst of times: When Barack Hussein Obama
was elected, and when I (Tait) first heard his middle name, I thought, didn't
we just kill a 'Hussein'?

Michelle — a great-great-granddaughter of slaves, held the Abraham
Lincoln Bible while Barack pledged the oath-of-office. In Abbeville, AL,
Mrs. Recy Taylor, 89, watched this moment — with tears in her eyes —
from her home. John Lewis and C. J. Vivian stood behind Obama on the
Presidential dais. Forty million African Americans felt in that moment a
breath of fresh air.

Four years earlier, at the Democratic convention, a skinny Illinois
Senator named Obama strode to a microphone and gave one of the most
moving speeches in America's political history. Four years before that,
Obama wasn't allowed admission into the 2000 Democratic convention.
The son of a Kenyan economist and Kansas school-teacher, he was born in
Hawaii. After law school he became a community-organizer with churches
in Chicago while being mentored by the Reverend Jeremiah A. Wright, Jr. of
Trinity United Church of Christ. Obama seemed to relish the unique calling
of a community-organizer, a task "simultaneously selfless and selfish."[508]

When teaching a course, *Racism and Law* at the University of Chicago,
he compiled a textbook featuring Frederick Douglass, Dr. W. E. B. DuBois,
Dr. King, and Minister Malcolm X. The spry teacher also assigned his law
students a catalogue of neo-slavery's slaughtered victims.

Obama broke the mold of what was possible in Empire politics: As
David Axelrod joked before the 2008 election: "How can we lose with a
Black candidate named Barack Hussein Obama?" On Obama's first day as
President one elder observed that, before him, the only Black who could

spend any extended period of time inside the Oval Office would've been a janitor.

Some Whites claimed President Obama's success was proof "racism" was eliminated. Tim Wise responded: "Not only does Obama's success not signify the death of White racism as a personal or institutional phenom-enon; if anything, it may well signal the emergence of an altogether new kind of racism. Consider this, for lack of a better term, Racism 2.0."[509]

Obama was accused of being Muslim, Kenyan, socialist, and a friend of terrorists. One survey (2008) showed a majority of Whites felt British leader Tony Blair was more "American" than Obama. The President was too White for some and too Black for others.[510] Rod Blagojevich said: "I'm blacker than Barack Obama. I shined shoes. I grew up in a five-room apart-ment. My father had a little laundromat in a Black community not far from where we lived."[511] Harry Reid said the President was a "light skinned Af-rican American with no Negro dialect unless he wanted to have one." Bill Clinton told Ted Kennedy: "a few years ago, this guy would've been getting us coffee."[512] J. Gresham Barrett tweeted, "I just heard Obama was going to impose a 40% tax on aspirin because it's white and it works."[513] Missourian Rusty Deposes joked that an escaped gorilla from a zoo was "just one of Michelle's ancestors."[514] Mike Huckabee inferred Obama was raised in Ke-nya and embraced Mau-Mau revolutionaries (was this a hot-button issue?). Newt Gingrich thought Obama exhibited "Kenyan anticolonial behavior."[515] Steven Forbes claimed Obama was "anti-American."[516] Over 50% of Whites thought it possible Obama was a Muslim.[517] Houston's First Baptist Pastor Gregg Matte prayed: "Today, Hollywood is our pastor, technology is our Bible, charisma is our value, and Barack Hussein Obama is our President."[518]

The New Yorker ran a satirical cover where the President wore Mus-lim garb while the First Lady was portrayed as a Black Panther beside a fireplace with a burning flag. "At least 50 new Right-wing militia groups" were formed in 2008-2009.[519] Protestors rendered Obama as Hitler, an ape, the "Joker," and a "be-feathered African witchdoctor."[520] One poster said, "Obama's Plan: White Slavery."[521] For Whites, Obama did not "think or look like them."[522]

Obama often chose the policy path of consensus-avoidance about deeply systemic realities. Little changed: "there was a Black man in the White House and nearly a million Black men and women in the Big House."[523] On the other hand, Obama brought to the office a knowing smile, apt-word, stylish gesture, or a graceful touch. When we heard Obama begin a speech in Jamaica shouting, "Wha Gwan Jamaica!" or when he dropped the micro-phone at his last correspondents-dinner, we knew such a time might never quickly return.[524] At least, Barack Obama was a good man — a politician who never sought to be a political "messiah."

## WALLMERICA

*"There's no question that Charlottesville wouldn't have occurred without Trump. It really was because of his campaign and this new potential for a nationalist candidate who was resonating with the public in a very intense way. The alt-right found something in Trump. He changed the paradigm and made this kind of public presence of the alt-right possible."*

**—Richard B. Spencer, American neo—Nazi leader**

The same folks who thought Barack Obama was a Muslim Kenyan thought Donald J. Trump (DT) was a Christian. Extremist conservatives sought a "political savior" and turned to a serial-groper, wall-builder who critics called Donald-the-Menace, Agent Orange, the Great-White-Dope, Darth Tax-Evader, Adolf-Twitter, the White Kanye, Trumpty-Dumpty, the Lyin' King, Benedict Donald, and Groper-in-Chief. He talked about "American carnage" — fueling the backlash of White supremacist hatreds.[525] Tiffany Cross writes: "If you take all of Trump's actions and rhetoric together, the pattern is clear: He is, by definition, a White supremacist."[526] Non-Whites watched as many Whites closed "ranks around their Whiteness."[527]

Trump, a misogynistic "self-confessed p@#*- grabber" was elected in a nation where many White men have long had "the right to sexual access to all women."[528] Trump promoted himself in a strategy to "deliberately seek to occupy every ounce of our attention. . . . Trump aims to distract us from distraction by distraction."[529] Trump announced oddly: "I love the poorly-educated."[530] The failed casino-manager, failed mail-order meat-seller, failed university-starter, and consummate day-trader turned to politics by challenging Obama's "Certificate of Live Birth" even though a newspaper reported his birth (1961). This ploy was in his long history of answering odd questions that no one had ever even thought to ask.

Truth-decay was in full-force in the Trump Era, culminating in a failed government coup. Kelly Ann Conway spoke of "alternative-facts" while Rudy Giuliani said, "truth isn't the truth."[531] Trump rallied to save Confederate monuments and names of Confederate Generals on military bases.[532] Of course, it's no coincidence most Empire statues — from the European features of the Statue of Liberty to Mount Rushmore, to the men on our currency — embody the ethno-cult of Whiteness.[533] As the man on the $20,

Andrew Jackson said: "It is vain to deny that the Blacks are an inferior race, very inferior to the European variety."[534]

Ironically, Trump — may have done "more to advance racial understanding than the election of Barack Obama. . . . Trump's clear anti-otherness makes it impossible for Whites to deny the existence of racism in America."[535] Nigerians certainly have a clear view of Trump's views when he said they would "never go back to their huts" after visiting America, called African nations "sh@#*-hole countries," and said Empire "should have more people from places like Norway."[536] James Baldwin observed: "Most of the White people I've ever known impressed me as being in the grip of a weird nostalgia, dreaming of a vanished state of security and order."[537]

Trump returned to the Presidency in 2025 after defeating a Black woman, Kamala Harris. In contrast, Trump lost the 2020 election to Joe Biden who once famously "complimented" Obama by saying that he was "the first mainstream African American who is articulate and bright and clean and a nice-looking guy."[538]

To quote Fredrick Douglass, most Whites live in a world of fiction: "Self-deception is a chronic disease of the American mind and character. Americans are masters of the art of substituting a pleasant falsehood for an ugly and disagreeable truth and of clinging to a fascinating delusion while rejecting a palpable reality."[539] Although "democracy dies in darkness it can also die in Whiteness."[540]

# The Weight of White

## A TALE OF TWO CITIES

*They lived on the surface of their days; their smiles were surface smiles, and their tears were surface tears. How far apart in culture we stood! All my life I had done nothing but feel and cultivate my feelings; all their lives they had done nothing but strive for petty goals, the trivial material prizes of American life. We share a common language, but my language was a different language from theirs. It was in the psychological distance that separated the races that the deepest meaning of the problem of the Negro lay for me. For these poor, ignorant White girls to understand my life would have meant nothing short of a vast revolution in theirs.*

**—Richard Wright, *American Hunger*, 12–13.**

"There are days when the places we're from turn into every other place in America."[541] I'm (CVG) from Pittsburgh — a working town and "capitalism's first-city."[542] It's steep valleys, and high hills hug rivers crossed by more bridges than any city but Venice. My mother was an immigrant, whose father – fleeing pre-war Nazi Germany, settled beside the Monongahela. Dad's family were farmers near the Ohio River. But my experience of home was vastly different from the experiences of Black Pittsburghers such as twenty-four-year-old Romir Talley, killed by Wilkinsburg Police (12/21/2019).

Pittsburghers are proud of Andy Warhol, Jonas Salk, Rachel Carson, Gene Kelly, Art Rooney, Honus Wagner, Mario Lemieux, Arnold Palmer, and, most of all, Mr. Rogers.[543] Pittsburgh's always had a thriving Melenated community led by nationalist Dr. Martin R. Delaney, journalist Robert Vann, painter Henry O. Tanner, librarian Virginia Florence, politician K. Leroy Irvis, writer August Wilson, musicians Billy Eckstein, George Benson, Billy Strayhorn, Wiz Khalifa, Jasiri X, Olympians, and hall-of-famers Cool Papa Bell and Josh Gibson.[544] The first Black American appointed to the United Nations was Pittsburgher Edith Samson (1950).

When the city began, forty-two descendants of Africa were present when the French Fort Duquesne became the British Fort Pitt under Colonel George Washington (1758).[545] In 1787, African American Benjamin Richards was an original signer of Pittsburgh's incorporation petition. The last enslavement-sale was in 1786, even though Pennsylvania's "Abolition Act" became law in 1780. At that time, when Blacks and Whites fell in love, they were criminals: If a Black married a White, they'd be enslaved while a White-faced indenture for seven years.[546] In the 1790 census, there were 880 slaves in the area and by 1830, twenty-seven people remained enslaved.[547]

In 1936, the White Crusaders of the KKK wanted to "put the Mason-Dixon line north of Pittsburgh."[548] Pittsburgh is only fifty miles from the Mason-Dixon line, and before the Civil War, it was a central station on the Underground Railway.[549] Many runaways made it their home while others (especially after the Fugitive Slave Act) continued on to Canada.[550] At least 40,000 escaped freedom-seekers moved through Western Pennsylvania enroute to freedom in Canada.[551]

During the Civil War, over 2,000 Black Americans called Pittsburgh home. The most notable was Dr. Martin Robinson Delaney.[552] There was nothing passive about Delaney who said (1865): "We barely acknowledge Whites as equals – perhaps not in every respect."[553] Frederick Douglass introduced Dr. Delaney as a man of "most defiant Blackness" saying: "I thank God for making me a man simply, but Dr. Delaney always thanks God for making him a Black man. This man completely identifies himself with a people and a time at once wonderful and perilous."[554]

By 1900, there were over 20,000 Black Pittsburghers, but, because of the Great Migration (1916–1945), that number soared to over 100,000 by 1960.[555] Pittsburgh's steel-mills once quaked the earth — dwarfing humans with giant magnets, trawling cranes, steam shovels, and other mammoth machines that must've seemed strange to Southern farmers. The mills were dirty and deafening — a harsh rumble that never ended in twelve-hour workdays. In the summer, Blacks were often assigned blast-furnace jobs carrying scraps of hot-metal or slag-molten-leftovers. Workers fought noxious fumes, thick dust, and heat while stoking coal into boilers — jobs no one else wanted. Others worked in pick-and-shovel gangs lifting logs or steel beams.

Blacks were paid less than Whites and were mostly excluded from unions until the 1930s.[556] In one effort to "keep Blacks in their place," one mill recruited Southerners as foremen over crews of Black laborers. Workers fought for fair wages, equal promotion, and safer conditions. One mill boss lamented at their unity: "The Negro refuses to be yelled at."[557]

Black Pittsburghers had trouble finding work outside steel-mills: Whites at restaurants or shoppers at some stores refused to be served by Blacks. Women had an even harder time: Over 90% (1910–1930) of Black Pittsburgh women were domestic workers.[558] Pittsburgh steel tycoons some-times recruited Black Americans as strike-breakers during times of labor unrest.[559] Recruits, sometimes transported in sealed-cars, found themselves locked into mills surrounded by displaced strikers. One recruit explained: "All we knew, we was getting a job. I wanted to work. I didn't know what the strike was all about."[560] After the strikes, fuming racist pressures often exploded.

A pillar of Black Pittsburgh was Robert Lee Vann who launched *The Pittsburgh Courier* (1910).[561] In its time (similar to Jasiri X today), Vann shaped a world where Black folks, without apology, defined themselves.[562] The *Courier*, America's largest Black-owned newspaper, was distributed nationwide while also reporting daily-life in the "Hill District" ("Little Haydi"), Beltzhoover on the bluffs of the Mon, and Homewood-Brushton. Special attention highlighted the Burg's key role as a music-rich "Northern Pole" of American Jazz.[563]

The *Courier* described strains between newly-arrived Southerners and OP's ("Original Pittsburghers") who forbade children fraternizing with newcomers. OP fraternal societies often excluded newcomers.[564] OP's were often Presbyterians or Episcopalians while Southerners were often Baptists or Pentecostals. Bethel AME was the first Black church in Pittsburgh begun in 1808.[565] By the 1920s, Pittsburgh's Melenated community had thriving barbershops, pool-halls, boardinghouses, dance-halls, brothels, taverns, shops, laundries, and diners like the Crawford Grill.[566] Playwright August Wilson spent hours at the B & M Restaurant eating fluffy biscuits, grits, and hotcakes and hearing the frustrations of neighbors that went into his plays.[567] Of Pittsburgh's demoralizing plight one visitor lamented: "A month in Pittsburgh would justify anyone committing suicide."[568] Even then, every resident was true to their love for the 'Burg.

A huge funding source in Black Pittsburgh was loans provided by those who ran the "numbers game" (the "policy"): "Pennies, nickels, and dimes slowly converted into millions of dollars, where were used by men of influence to uplift Black business ventures."[569] Pittsburgh's leading Black millionaire was "Mr. Big," ("The Caliph of Little Harlem" and the "Jesus of Negro Sport") Gus Greenlee, who poured money into his greatest love – the Crawfords baseball team – which became a leading star of Negro League Baseball (NLB). Along with the Homestead Grays, the Crawfords made the 'Burg the center of Black baseball. Unlike some cities, both teams were Black-owned and managed. The quality of competition was fierce: Seven of eleven NLB players in Baseball's Hall of Fame played for these two teams, including Satchel Paige. The greatest of all, Josh Gibson, was considered even a greater hitter than Babe Ruth.[570]

Because Pittsburgh is a drinking town with a sports problem, my core experience with "Blackness" when growing up was through our local "religion" — sports. The NFL's first Black quarterback was New Kensington's Willie Thrower and the first Black NBA player was Chuck Cooper of Westinghouse for the Boston Celtics. Willie "Pops" Stargell led the first team in MLB history to host an all-Black squad during a game.[571] Mr. Stargell was also known for his active local involvement in confronting sickle-cell anemia — a disease he personally experienced.

When segregation ended, something was lost as well as won. Schools, for example, had their own spirit reflecting values at the heart of the culture. Sports, entertainment, and business contexts expressed distinctive merits such as mutual affirmation. After integration, many Black businesses were closed. Pittsburgher August Wilson wrote of the era of segregation: "If you're all together standing outside the doors of White American society and you cannot participate in this society, then there's a certain strengthening in who you are as a people."[572]

## JOURNEY TOWARDS SATORI

*To be woke is to see and say what has gone unseen, unspoken.*

**—Tomi Adeyemi**

Buddhism is a liberation spirituality. It begins with a story about protective parents fearing a worrisome prediction: Before Buddha was born, his father received a prophecy his son would either be a rich ruler or a poor teacher. The king, deciding to protect his son from poverty, shielded his son with a life of privilege. I grew up in Bethel Park, a homogenous, secure-urbia. Like Buddha's world, it was an island of ignorance upheld by privilege. Like Buddha, my tidiness was pierced by the intrusion of aliens. Mom said — when learning colors — I saw a Black man and shouted: "Look! A green person!" My Grandpa was racist and I first remember hearing about "Blacks" from Grandpa when he complained *they* had moved into *his* neighborhood and were driving down property-values (Boynton Beach, FL). This mystified me: Who were these commanding people who could change everything so radically just by showing up? What was their Black magical power?

Bethel Park began as a coal-mining town called "Coverdale," where miners spent their days underground getting black lung disease for little pay. Black miners faced unrelenting racism. Some mines, especially in West Virginia, were called "Ku Klux mines" for refusing to hire Blacks.[573] Even today, Coverdale is Bethel Park's only majority Melenated neighborhood. In Bethel Park there were three Black families (we knew) — the Richardsons, the Hutchinsons, and the Taylors. Positively, Dad decided a family-vacation should include stops in Montgomery and Birmingham to "see what was going on" and "to see what it was like to be a minority." (1968) This kind of "drive-by education" is typical for some liberal Euro-Americans. Maybe it does more harm than good if it underscores the idea others need White benevolent care. Christ United Methodist taught me that the White Jesus loved "Red or Yellow, Black, or White." But, curiously, I never saw any "Red, or Yellow, or Black" recipients of God's love at that church. Gaps between lofty ideals and unforgiving realities began to take root in my segregated world.

White liberalism visited my horizon again when I landed a job with Mr. Elton Hickman, a landscape-architect who hired Black kids as a way to empower them and educate us. I don't doubt the earnestness of this Latin teacher in the inner-city Pittsburgh School District. When the boss was gone, however, those in his grand-experiment whined about how *they* didn't work as hard as *we* did. No doubt, being beaten-up a few times by Mr. Sam Richardson helped support my emerging stereotypes. At sixteen, I got my driver's-license and was told not to drive through Homewood-Brushton at night and use "common sense" in Edgewood-Swissvale: It was "iffy."

At eighteen, I was off to college: Six-Flags-Over-Jesus-Oral-Roberts-University where it seemed every Black brother or sister either played basketball or a trumpet. At least, that's what I assumed. All of us were "united" in Jesus but didn't date, eat, or study together. I never considered dating a "sister" until marrying one decades later! Social times with a "brother" were like "exotic-adventures" at Epcot-Center; learning we both liked football (but not hockey)!

After college, I avoided Blackness for another decade while serving Jesus in Asia as an Evangelical missionary (the ultimate White-flight). Whenever a Chinese student asked me about the KKK or "racism", I'd explain about uneducated red-neck racists but how I wasn't one because I cried when I heard the MLK "I Have a Dream" speech. But their questions planted doubts in my soul: I knew that, although I spoke authoritatively, I had no idea about what I was talking about. When speaking about Black America, I might as well have been talking about the Planet Neptune. Maybe this sensitized me when moving back to Empire to rescue my life from myself. When I got home, all I could see — which I'd never seen before — was how segregated my church (and everything else) was. A Messiah College student named Sheena Styles, challenged my views. I knew I didn't know a lot and what I did know — probably wasn't accurate. My address-book was all-black on the cover but all-White on the insides.

Then I went to Harambee Church in Harrisburg and met Dr. Lewis T. Tait, Jr. At Harambee, it wasn't uncommon for visiting Whiteys like me to "come and experience Black Christianity." But I stayed because Harambee was a world I didn't know existed. All of a sudden, "racism" was everywhere and I wasn't off the hook! I heard dramas beyond my imagination and realized how sheltered my world was. The simplest way my Evangelical-self knows how to say it was I was converted and born-again. Ever since, I'm a "recovering racist."

When I talk about this to other Euro-Americans, some assume I'm hinting they're racists. We're never the problem — only the solution. But most of us are as blind as bats in a blizzard. When you realize most of your education, especially in history classes, was propagandistic it takes time to process. We must admit: "Our education has filled us with strong prejudices."[574] My isolation growing up wasn't intentional: Was it? Our ignorance wasn't avoidable: Was it? Meanwhile, the lady at Burger King — I never could pronounce her name — seemed so nice. The lady at the cafeteria — never got her name — seemed so nice. The guys who picked up our trash — we gave a tip at Christmas — were also probably nice ex-cons. Better to avoid grim issues: Move on! *Kumbayah!* Dr. King was great! Slavery was bad! Glad it's over!

## PATRICK VAN GORDER: UNPACKING THE CONFUSED RELIGION OF WHITENESS

*You must be the solution to the problem that you face.*

**—Mahatma Gandhi**

My parents were missionaries, and my earliest memories are of being different. Called by a Pentecostal God, my folks took me to bring the Gospel of Jesus to China. I was raised in one of the stoutest traditions of White saviorhood — a White light in a mission-field of black hair.

I found a group of friends — the children of other expats enrolled in a local "International Academy" — that were almost all White. Our in-and out-lines weren't explicitly racial: for parents it was neatly labeled boxes of "saved" and "unsaved," but for me, it was English and non-English: kids with whom I could communicate. Here, my story mirrors the archetypical White

American story: De-facto segregation without the harsh moral baggage of explicit segregation.

After God said we were done in China, our family roamed the earth for a few years, so I had no chance to put down roots. Then, when I was 12, we moved to the rural wonderland of Boiling Springs, Pennsylvania, where the high-school was small and lily-White. To their credit, my parents wanted to expose us to some diversity. That's how I came to spend long Sundays at Dr. Tait's Harambee Church, forty minutes from home, in one of Harrisburg's Blackest neighborhoods.

We were welcomed earnestly and without any agenda by Dr. Tait and the Harambee family. I don't remember ever being singled-out or admonished for my Whiteness. But I had a front-row seat to watch my Dad wrestle with the weight of his burdensome guilt: A White, male, straight, Christian, German, etc. Grateful as I'm now for this formative perspective, back then it was a mixed blessing. I was a hormonal teenager trying to understand my place in an America that'd never really been home and I felt far from the vested privilege for which my father now wept.

Of all the memories that stick from Harambee, the *Maafa* is the most poignant. Every year the church would stage a dramatic retelling of the transatlantic slave trade — the Middle Passage. Members of all ages would play the roles of kidnapped Africans sold into slavery and their sufferings through the Middle Passage before lives as slaves. As two of the few White folks in our church, you can imagine the roles Dad and I played — and our resulting grim emotions.

In one scene, I played a young enslaver who hatefully whipped a swaying, moaning line of half-naked men, women, and children. I verbally and physically assaulted ("N-word" and all) an older man trying to shield a girl from my whip. In front of the church, I thrashed the shirtless, sweat-drenched Deacon Kler Jones — one of the kindest men I knew — as he moaned in pain.

I'm very appreciative to the Harambee family for their kindness and generosity of spirit. Those Sundays were central to my understanding of race and Christianity. But as a fourteen-year-old, I remember complex feelings about my Dad's tear-filled journey of contrition. Why did he feel guilt for actions of distant, unknown ancestors, but not his own actions? It was certainly easier for me to make the story about Dad than about the racist-oppression Dr. Tait fought.

I spent high-school in a drug and alcohol-fueled haze, trying-on identities like costumes. After a summer of landscaping with a work-crew of "salt-of-the-earth blue collar White men," I put on a new costume of cowboy boots, old pickup-truck, country-music, bourbon-whiskey, the whole nine-yards. Casual racist oppression, sexism, xenophobia, and homophobia were sometimes part of the mix. Moving to more diverse (than Boiling Springs — the bar is low) Pittsburgh for college should have disinfected me, but at first, my "country-boy" identity came to the fore as I sought to find my place as an insecure nineteen-year-old in a new city.

Unknowingly, I convinced myself my costume as a "simple man" with local dreams was truer than the performative wokeness and missionary-external focus of my parents who preached about a shared humanity. At Pitt, I sometimes wore a Confederate-flag bandana from a promotional box of *Rebel Yell Whiskey*. I'd keep it in my back-pocket, to dab sweat, opposite my "Skoal ring." Today, seeing that flag fills me with disgust. Back then, it was another part of the costume. One day I was driving down Forbes Avenue (near Pitt) when I approached a protest march. As I passed, I waved the rebel bandana from my pickup-truck. In the years since, I've often wondered why I didn't connect that action to the lessons of the *Maafa* and the empathy I've always felt at my core. I guess I saw the protesters as condemning my fictionalized White-Americanness. I projected my own identity-insecurities on the marchers: I was being *attacked.*

Complicity is violence and my denial of being a racist — and at the same time — promoting anti-racism demonstrates White privilege. I'm not the lies I tell about myself. I can never be impartial. The distance between me now — in the crowd crying out for Pittsburgh's own Antwon Rose, or for Ahmaud Arberry, and Breonna Taylor — or the "me" back in the pickup waving a rebel bandana is close. The man in the MAGA hat could've been me: That scares me.

I have a lifetime of work finding a path forward. But the arc of my own grappling with racist oppression has taught me that being a strategic partner is not to be saved-by-Jesus-no-matter-how-I-act Whiteyanity way. Nor is partnership simply a journey of self-discovery. That's as self- centered as the "saved" view is passive. To be a strategic-partner is to take responsibility for where we're going. It's to act, not to be.

## LEARNING FROM THE GERMANS

*No White person, even when he wants to, can understand what it means to be Black living in America today, any more than a combatant can understand what it means to be a non-combatant.*

**—Margaret Halsey, 1946**

The Germans enjoy constructing elaborate words. One is *Vergangenheitsau-farbeitung* which means "working-off the past" and coming-to-terms with horrific dimensions of history: It's a distressing — but necessary — process if you're a German or a German-American.

After Hitler, if you're German, you have to face resurgent intolerance in order to ensure such atrocities never happen again. After the War, Germany banned all Nazi symbols or flags. German school children are required to visit concentration camps. Symbols matter: In Germany, you even need to be careful what kind of moustache you wear, how you part your hair, or how you raise your arm in greeting. When neo-Nazis stage protests, since they cannot fly Nazi flags, they fly Confederate Rebel flags.[575] Germans get it.

Amazingly, in Germany when Hitler sought election some Jewish citizens voted for him in hopes a "gesture of loyalty would bind the system to them. That was a vain hope."[576] Oppression needs "otherness." In 1936, the Germans launched a set of anti-Jewish, anti-otherness laws called the "Nuremberg Codes" which was based on a two-year study of Southern Jim Crow laws. One Nazi explained their inspiration: "For us Germans, it was especially important to know how one of the biggest countries in the world with Nordic stock already has race-legislation which is quite comparable to that of the German Reich."[577] The Nazis were impressed by the lynching custom which served as a ritual torture-humiliation. Hitler marveled enviously how America's Southern "Christians" could enact all these horrendous racist atrocities with a self-righteous "knack for maintaining an air of robust innocence in the wake of mass-death."[578]

Jews didn't have to return from Death-Camps to see statues of Josef Mengele in their towns. How would Whites feel if they were enslaved for four hundred years and then had to live in places where others erected statues honoring enslavers. When America held anti-Nazi Nuremberg Trials, a key goal was educating all Germans about past unspeakable atrocities.

Susan Neiman writes: "Nazis are not just a German problem. You may prefer to call them demonstrators, White supremacists, but that's a distinction without a difference. The deliberate use of Nazi symbols – swastikas, torches, and slogans ("Blood and Soul;" "You will not Replace Us,") – leaves no room for doubt."[579] Hitler hated Blacks and forcibly sterilized German Blacks. The final defeat of Nazism was a victory for all Germans and the defeat of White supremacy will be a victory for all Euro-Americans. The end of Nazism tied to Germany — and the end of White supremacy tied to America — is what liberation looks like. Ironically, there are more Holocaust museums in America than in Germany, Israel, and Poland combined, but only a few dedicated to teaching about slavery.[580] Most Germans are dealing with the past while most Americans are not.

In 1946, after the Nazi demise, the Nobel Prize for Literature was awarded to the German writer, Hermann Hesse who used his acceptance speech to share an alternative story of another Germany — the peasants of the past. Hesse hoped the world would see that "German" was distinct from "Nazi." This is how a broken people heal. Hesse asked the world to remember a Germany of fine workmanship and simple pleasures. For Hesse, Germans going forward from Hitler needed to disavow arrogant superiority. The goal going forward from this lesson would be living from the best — and acknowledging the worst — in each of our own historic and multivalent cultures.

I (CVG) am a proud German and Dutch-American. Gratitude for being German, however, happens in light of the fact that 11 million people were killed by Nazis in the last war. Whatever is affirmative must also acknowledge truths that are evil and ugly. This is what Albert Einstein meant when saying his activism for civil rights came because he was a German.[581] The resources of heritage are both a blessing and a curse, and it's within my agency to renounce the curses of the past while also embracing past blessings. The poison of atrocity isn't all it means to be German — there's also Goethe, Mozart, sweet, fine Mosel wine, and tangy peach-schnapps.

I'm a culturally-embodied person, a first-generation Euro-American. I cherish a culture of Kattie Kollwitz, Ernst Barlach, Bach, Bayern-Munich football, wurst-with-mustard (eating some now!), and potato-pancakes. I'm also benefitted in cultural sensitivities because other Whites tried to kill Grandpa during World War I when he fought for the Kaiser and in World War II when they tried to kill him at his steel-mill. I benefit as an outsider-insider because my Mom was pushed off the path every day in Pittsburgh en route to school because she was seen as a "kraut" and "Nazi."

James Baldwin wrote something new in the world is "desperately trying to be born – but the old ghosts have the baby by the throat."[582] Today, "virtually all Germans acknowledge the ugliness of their past and the culpability of perfectly nice, respectful people."[583] Germany paid reparations to Jews because they knew that an aching past must be met with an exorcism.[584] Reparations embodied the claim that Germans wanted to resolve the irresolvable. Reparations must come before reconciliation. While resentment nails people to their past — telling the truth brings soul-healing. Germans, delighted with that which is good within their culture, know it is dishonest to acknowledge only the good without also admitting past evils. In fact, the vitality of modern Germany is rooted in a confession of deep legacies of brokenness. As Rabbi Nachum articulates, "There is nothing more whole than a broken heart."[585]

## MYSTERIES TO EACH OTHER

*White privilege is like an invisible weightless knapsack of special provisions, assurances, tools, maps, guides, code-books, passports, visas, clothes, compass, emergency gear, and blank checks.*

**—Peggy Macintosh**

Dr. King once preached a sermon about Washington Irving's drama "The Legend of Rip van Winkle." In this tale, Rip Van falls asleep and doesn't wake-up for twenty years. While asleep, a revolution takes place and wall-portraits shift from England's King George to George Washington. Dr. King's point was we shouldn't slumber through a revolution with a "Rip-van-Winkle Syndrome": Falling asleep and unaware while history is being made all around us.

In America today, many are insensible. There are about 45 million African Americans held in curious regard by 235 million Euro-Americans. We tell different versions of a shared history. Ralph Ellison pronounced Blacks as "Gulliver's" with bodies pinned down for the bemusement of the tiny White Lilliputians. Of course, stereotypes go both ways: One Jim Crow song laments: "White-man in a starched shirt, setting in the shade – laziest man God ever made. Bee flies high. Bees makes honey. Black folks makes cotton, White folks gets money."[586]

Dr. King is a national hero now because he's dead. Will Rogers said if an American wants to be a hero (e.g., Lincoln or Kennedy), they have to find the right time to die. Michael Jordan or Jackson are heroes because they're relationally "dead" — far-away, exceptional, remote. Black "ambassadors" can rent space in our brains because they don't rent property on our streets. Some Whites embrace Black athletes or entertainers because they're not in their "neighborhoods, schools, and private lives."[587]

We tell distinct stories about "Whiteness" or "Blackness." My mother (CVG) never knew she was White until she came to America. My wife Vivian and her family in West Africa never knew they were "Black" until they came to America: Before that, they were just human.

Parasitic White supremacy constantly reinvents itself because "the anti-Black idea is so contagious that it now affects, in varying degrees, almost every person in this society."[588] Racist- oppression exists for one reason: It works. It doesn't need to be rational because it is always systemic before it's personal. Many Whites often talk about "racism" from two starting points — either "things are better than they were" or "get over it."[589] Empire has morphed into a society of racist-oppression without observable racists. Why? Our biases are deeply embedded. The concept of "color-blindness doesn't make sense because you can't tell me that you don't see my Blackness when you have to see my Blackness to even make that statement."[590] Some make odd "compliments" to me (Tait) like: "I didn't notice you were black." Really? What do you think of me as? Such a comment would sound ridiculous if someone said they didn't "notice" you were fat, ugly, rich, short, or a woman. Racist-oppression functions without the need for racial animus because the same Whites who preach intentional color-blindness (erasure) will, at work, for example, hire Whites before non-Whites and then claim choices were based on factors such as experience."[591]

To those who consider themselves beyond the designations of race, the idea of a "racist" is something quite specific.[592] For them, "racism" is a problem for those spending too much time in the sun getting drunk at NASCAR tracks waving confederate flags. They enter "good-behavior liberal heaven" by name-dropping a recent book or Spike Lee movie: Performative virtue-signaling.

We are mysteries to each other.[593] While still embracing Dr. DuBois' concept of "double-consciousness," we must accept we're all stuck in one place together. Mother Sojourner Truth thanked the Creator every day that she hadn't been created White. Mother Truth never had to admit that it was her people who built an exploitation-mechanism business-country on the twin foundations of genocide and slavery.[594]

## "WOULD YOU LIKE TO BE WHITE, BROTHER?"

*He has understood the system so well because he felt it first as his own contradiction.*

**—Jean Paul Sartre in Albert Memmi's,**
***The Colonizer and the Colonized***

America is a "country built on individualism and selfishness."[595] Extreme conservatives celebrate the "rugged individual" who fights and wins alone. Ironically, this emphatic stress on individualism is used to promote an anti-individualistic, conformist message. American individualism fixates on competition and is "the epitome of selfishness."[596] It fosters "pathological loneliness."[597] Empire's founding laws claimed to protect individual rights at the same time that most laws relating to First Nations and Black people were group-categorizing initiatives.

Extreme conservatives are those who think "hierarchy or inequality are the result of a natural social-order in which competition is not only inevitable but desirable."[598] They want government to stay out of social problems with the noticeable exception of a woman's abortion rights.[599]

Today, the mantra of "individualism is everything" spreads like poison-ivy across extreme conservativism. This view reached a nadir when William Bradford Reynolds avowed: "We're all- each of us - a minority in this country: a minority of one."[600] In this logic, if you're sinking on the Titanic, you've no one to blame but yourself for buying a ticket. The Right White supports political policies to keep Black folks "in their place" and out of "our place."

How do extreme conservatives reconcile a fight against every dollar for so-called entitlement programs for others while enjoying a host of entitlement programs for themselves? Taxpayers have bailed-out farmers, bankers, manufacturers, the airline-industry, and others. Military and space programs receive ample funds, while schools and infrastructure are underfunded. Empire foreign policy is basically one vast global welfare-program with massive amounts of aid sent to places like Israel (we are writing in 2025) and Egypt.

Extreme conservatives preach individualism while following a civic-religion complete with ancestor worship-shrines in Washington D.C. At the same time, they claim they're under assault. In Knoxville, TN, a 123-foot-long billboard declares "anti-Racism is a code word for anti-White."[601] Some even claim they're victims of "racism." At Temple University (1988), Michael Spletzer organized a *White* Student Union to protect Euro-Americans from injustice. Mostly, however, extremist conservatives simply "solve racism" by ignoring it. James Baldwin lamented: "It comes as a great shock to discover the country which is your birthplace – to which you owe your life and identity – has not in its whole system of reality evolved any place for you."[602]

## A HAPHAZARD KINDNESS

*America is false to the past, false to the present, and solemnly binds herself to be false to the future.*

### —Frederick Douglass

Liberals love to fix things: Watch out if you're in their way. They will try to fix you. Entitled liberals, like extreme conservatives, wallow in "White privilege." The problem is that advantage is least apparent to those who enjoy it. There is nothing some extremists do that is "qualified, limited, discredited, or acclaimed" simply because of their reliance on racist categories.[603] Escaping discomfort is a refined art of the privileged. The shameless with benefit assume the gains they enjoy have been earned from their own merits. White privilege refuses to acknowledge how much their successes spring from "stolen goods." In reality, the primary function of White privilege is to maintain the sanctity and order of White privilege.

Dr. King wrote in *"Letter from Birmingham Jail"* that the biggest enemy of justice was not the KKK, but "the White Liberal who is more devoted to order than to justice and who prefers tranquility to equality . . . [while they say] I agree with you in the goal that you seek but I cannot agree with your methods of direct action" because they wanted to make changes on their own timetable.[604] King chided liberals for retreating from fighting systemic, racist-oppression — preferring, instead, to focus on symbolic changes. White performers, costumed with a liberal- savior-complex, have empowered the slow-rise of resentful White-adjacent Black conservatism. In Miguel Cervantes' *The Man of LaMancha*, Don Quixote attacks windmills while fantasizing he is fighting giants. Quixote joins courage with misguided fantasy. Entitled liberalism is often performative: They focus on their own agendas while thinking they're investing in Black power. Who are Whites to help Blacks (at least, not without asking for help)? Many well-meaning social initiatives are top-down, with little regard for local input. Is it any wonder some liberal initiatives, tossed like bones to a yard-dog, are rejected as paternalistic?

Privileged liberals crave a "wokeness-medal" — praise for admitting the obvious while all extremists cannot imagine any problem their solutions can't fix. Some liberals want to be your friend in weird ways while, on the other hand, some conservatives invite you to be just like them. Van Jones states "It's hard for Whites to hear the pain of the subjugated people in this country . . . to realize that we are living in an Apartheid-society where you can literally spend your whole life thinking you live in the 'Bay Area' when you don't live in the Bay Area, you actually live in your racialized-bandstand just like everybody else. So, we live together in these bubbles that touch, and we call that diversity, but we don't know each other."[605]

Some privileged liberals assume they know what it is to "be Black" and that they know "both worlds." They lead organizations "helping" Blacks while relating to other Whites as "experts on us."[606] It is an "imposter syndrome" where, if you listen to some folks talk about you then you might begin second-guessing yourself if you're not careful.[607] Of course, the ultimate expression of appropriation happens when folks like Rachael Dolezal and Jane Kraus pass themselves off as "Black." Misplaced empathy happens when "woke-folk "center themselves in someone else's story."[608] Some liberals crave to have their consciousness eased and may gain prestige or economic benefit from being "experts" in a context where other Whites are more ignorant. Such posers are easily exposed: As anyone in a circus knows — if you spend enough time backstage watching the magicians rehearse — it becomes hard to be impressed by the magic-act. There's too much "sleight of hand" to see anything but "theatre" over substance.[609]

Most privileged liberals are only temporary "visitors" into Black injustice realities. Breathtaking cowardice blossoms at the first sign of inconvenience if courage is rooted in self-affirming self-interest. In contrast to extreme conservative Jesus-adventurer-explorers who go on "missions" into urban Blackness with Chevy Suburban's filled with canned-goods from their White Jesus, privileged liberals parachute into these same urban leper-colonies to pick up trash or give political advice before escaping from their discomfort back into their brand-new electric Volvos; back into their cozy, safe suburbs before night-fall.[610]

Privileged liberals "use" justice-issues to carve out a space for themselves. Tiffany Cross writes: "Many White people including the recently 'woke' bunch, have existed in a bubble that gave little credence to my lived experience in this country."[611] For many, "Blacks are a series of statistics framed in exotic categories that "work like cages, trapping us in images and assumptions."[612]

Some privileged liberals have a "father-knows-best" paternalism, an "elitism of getting it right" with flourishes of compassionate rhetoric often nullified by timidity once elections are won: Dealing with racist-oppression is a sideshow.[613] Of paternalism, Malcolm X said: "I don't want anybody working with me because they are doing something for me."[614] For Whites, Abdurraqib observes: "It must be something to be able to decide what volume, tone, and tenor you will allow Black people to enter your life, for praise or for scolding."[615]

## MAYFLOWER POWER

*If we tell ourselves that the only problem is hate, we avoid facing the reality that it is mostly nice, non-hating White people who perpetrate racial inequality.*

**—Ellis Cose**

In May 2020, Chris Cooper was out birdwatching in Central Park (Manhattan) as he did many clement mornings. A woman approached the birding-area with her un-leashed dog. Cooper told the lady to obey the law and leash her dog. What followed was the woman calling 9-1-1 (where she used the term "Black-man" three times) to report she was being threatened. It all came so easily, so naturally. She intended her use of the term "Black-man" like Nazis did to "yellow-star" Jews, forcing them into cattle-cars of compliance. Later, when the video went viral, the lady apologized to Cooper— assuring everyone she wasn't racist and had a liberal soul that loved Obama — or platitudes to that effect. She was contrite once exposed: A polite racist.

"Polite-White-finishing-schools" keep privileged liberals from saying blatantly inappropriate remarks. From that foundation, good grooming makes this ugly issue a topic to be politely avoided. For the policing-polite, racist-oppression is a peripheral artifact of someone else's distant past. For Black folks, dealing with the amused contempt of polite-Whites it is an everyday occurrence. At a CVS one morning, I (CVG) kindly offered $10 to a Black woman in the parking-lot whom I assumed was homeless until she said "no" and hopped into her BMW. But condescending politeness is not a small issue because fear and ignorance can quickly shift into cruelty and recklessness. Polite-Whites are afraid of impolite Black men based on unquestioned fears resident within crippling Whiteness-psyches. It's ironic that — after 400 years of Whites initiating constant violence against Blacks — polite-Whites fear "Black power." And it starts young: One survey showed White kids, as early as six-years old, most often telling psychologists "they did not want to be Black and liked least people from Africa."[616] Recent surveys reveal most respondents guessed most welfare-recipients were Black while, in actual fact, two-thirds of those below the poverty-line are White. One study of 1,200 respondents, including 150 Black folks, showed that over half of those polled thought, "Blacks were less intelligent than Whites while 40% said they were equally intelligent and only 6% said they were more intelligent than Whites. Also, 60% of those surveyed rated Blacks as lazier than Whites."[617]

## STRATEGIC INTERCULTURAL PARTNERSHIPS

*I was, for all practical purposes, a "made-in-America" person. Yet, the making itself had not convinced me that I was truly part of the process that governed the society. Black and White, two colors, two origins, two destinies; that is what intervened in the midst of reflections on place for a young African in the South of Georgia.*

### —Professor Molefi Kete Asante

In ancient Greece, there was a myth about King Sisyphus cursed by fate in a challenging way. Each day, Sisyphus spent all day rolling a heavy boulder to the top of a mountain which demanded all his energies. When the boulder reaches the summit, and the task is complete, the gods (and gravity) force the boulder to roll back where it started in the morning. Time to start all over again: A futile task. That's exactly how some folks feel confronting injustice and trying to flourish in Empire. How can we co-exist? Thinking in terms of "co-existence" is a more honest goal for America's future. Mutual coexistence will happen slowly since leeching White supremacy is so widespread. A Chinese proverb states: "One who hurries cannot walk with dignity." Equality is proven in power-dynamics: Who's in control and making decisions? Anglo-conformity leads to blaming victims for their own social marginalization. Those defending the status quo often don't look beyond their own self-interests. Because they benefit from a system they designed, their intercultural goals are more about cooperation than justice.

While folks talk about being allies, they also often want to be the decision-makers and maintain control. What is a true ally? Speaking of his White mother Clay Cane wrote: "Allyship is jargon my mother never learned, but in many ways, it describes her to a T. She wasn't a savior or some great White hope but operated from a space of compassion."[618] An ally isn't a "fixer" who offers their solutions to your problems. Strategic partnerships for justice are directly tied to shared power-dynamics. A strategic-partner isn't a tourist. Public White-grief over Black-death is often a theatre of point-scoring self-justification. One legacy of the civil rights era was that, once the "party" was over, most "allies" returned to their regularly scheduled programs . The World Council of Churches organized a grassroots effort for churches to advocate for the Civil Rights Act of 1965. As soon as laws were passed, however, those "allies" vanished. Why? Black activists saw passing laws as a *first* step while many Whites saw these laws as the end-point.

Building any kind of justice-movement demands building both long-term and short-term partnerships. Do African Americans look for allies or strategic-partners (accomplices)? The problem with the idea of being an "ally" is it suggests we'll always share the same mission and focus. In one sense, all of us do share a deep humanity. In terms of justice-fights, however, Whites who are strategic-partners cannot be "allies" in the sense that they're socially located in a position of privilege and power. White strategic-partners, however, can work to make theoretical Black empowerment become actual Black power. In this, Whites have to clean up their own side of the street: White strategic-partners, whatever else they do, should work to confront White myths. One major demolition project that merits dismantling is the myth of monocultural "patriotism." When Whites talk about the Constitution, they sometimes forget when it was written, Black folks were in iron-chains in cotton-fields: It wasn't written with Black folks in mind.

Another myth is the troublemaker narrative: If Whites design a system for the benefit of Whites and that system fails then who is to blame? Another myth is the "melting-pot pretense: Let's admit the "melting-pot" has always been a forge to foster Anglo-conformity.

Abolitionist William Lloyd Garrison had many flaws, but he spent his life in the mission of shattering "the conspiracy of silence" about racist-oppression. From morning to night, Garrison preached one message: "Slavery was a crime, a damning crime."[619] Accomplices such as Garrison, Levin Coffin, Elijah Lovejoy, Thaddeus Stevens, Charles Sumner, Silas Soule, John Brown, Harriet Beecher Stowe — and others worked for justice alongside Black Americans. They used their privilege for others. During the Civil Rights era, some Euro-Americans — like Unitarian Pastor James Reeb and Rev. Bruce Klunder in Cleveland — died for justice.[620] Yet, even these martyrs were beneficiaries of a system which allowed them to choose levels of involvement. Today, the "dismantle collective" is helping folks to stop "talking about being allies" and actually engaging in performative alliances.

## PLANET OF THE WHITES

*You want to integrate me into your anonymity because it is my right you think to be like you. I want your right to be like yourself.*

**—Gerald W. Barrax, *Black Narcissus***

Finally, let's talk about the "reconciliation-myth." What some Euro-Americans mean by "reconciliation" often looks like lobotomization. George Yancey writes: "the way we define a social problem will affect the way we conceive of its solution."[621] "Reconciliation" is a lofty term that doesn't apply to most Black justice demands. What does "reconciliation" mean? The "re-prefix" means to go back to something already existing. To what point in our relationship are "re-concilers" asking us to revisit? The best answer might be the early 15th-century; before White supremacist-motivated pillage-conquest emerges as the dominant characteristic of African-European relations. Black America doesn't need either retaliation or "symbolic reconciliation." Theatric pantomimes never equate with substantive justice. Reconciliation is often the "default-button" that some Whites — especially religious ones — push in order to avoid doing the challenging work of facing systemic racist oppression and the recognition that we've never shared a mutual, equitable relationship. "Reconciliation" has often been about placating White-guilt and keeping Blacks in steaming "cotton fields" of designated, controlled assimilation.

Another odd term is "integration" which looks a lot like conformity. One dictionary definition of the verb to "integrate" is to "make complete by adding parts into the unified whole."[622] This kind of integration has never happened in Empire where rivers, roads, and railroad tracks have always been red-lines of segregation. Striving for "integration" when rooted in a "White-is-right" mentality is a really toxic demand for conformity to a dominating culture.

Yet another strange term is "multiculturalism."[623] Previously, it had been called "diversity" or "pluralism", and, at its best, multiculturalism is a corrective to melting-pot notions of a monocultural America. Euro-American conjurers of multicultural programs can feel good about offering lip-service to dreams of equality while offering a pleasant "add-on" to the dominating culture. "Usually when folks speak of multiculturalism, what they really mean is 'Yes, let's all get together, but on White terms.'"[624] If you doubt that, just ask the average White in "multicultural" America to name ten Black men who aren't athletes or entertainers. Folks singing "Lift Every Voice" is not as sonorous as equitable hiring-practices. Genuine recognition is about more than sharing ethnic-foods or ethnic-dances. Diversity agendas may warm hearts but can often be smokescreens for inertia. Professor Angela Davis warns many multicultural initiatives are celebrations of "difference that don't make a difference."[625] No doubt, multiculturalism springs from sincere intentions, but the opposite of good is not evil, but good intentions. Any effort that avoids facing structural inequalities is tangential.

## "DISNEYFIED" OPTIMISM

*There was not, no matter where one turned, any acceptable image of oneself, no proof of one's existence. One had the choice, either of "acting just like a Nigger" or of not acting just like a "Nigger"- and only those who have tried it know how impossible it is to tell the difference.*

**—James Baldwin**

Many American-dreamers describe Empire as a "can-do" country and tell stories of pioneers, immigrants, and astronauts who faced every challenge and solved every problem. A few things are left out: slavery and genocide. Actually, most White immigrants came to Empire because they were poor, uneducated, hungry, or on the wrong side of the law or social-status.

Issues become "Disneyfied." Utopian optimism may help folks feel better but they don't touch Empire's deeply-rooted justice problems. "Optimism" can become a cover for inertia. Our response has to be creative, assertive, and focused: Turtle Islanders practiced shape-shifting and slave-folk shamans could fly. We need to lead a long-term resistance rooted in tangible hopes.

Black optimism can be naïve insanity and liberal optimism can be a stalling-tactic to keep unpleasant issues "off the radar-screen." Who knows if folks would've noticed Mr. George Floyd, Mr. Philando Castille, Ms. Breonna Taylor, Ms. Sandra Bland, and Mr. Ahmaud Arbery if they weren't caught on video or if Covid-19 hadn't delayed their NBA basketball season?

Unless you're a Jewish-American, Mormon, or a Democrat in Texas, others probably never ask a White person to represent everyone else who's in your tribe, yet "being Black is a 24-hour a day, lifetime job!"[626] Reverse-racism? Now that's funny! Have you been teaching your boys since age-seven how to deal with angry Black police-officers? George Wallace once insulted Blacks by saying they probably didn't even know where Alabama was and they probably didn't know where America was. Oh yeah, Black folks certainly know Wallabama. In fact, we love an Alabama first in the nation with HBCU's and not your dismal swampiness. We love Alabama but we "don't love the State of Alabama."[627] Wallace's accusation of obliviousness can be thrown back at some Whites: Some have a better grasp of Burmese ethnomusicology or Latvian ringtone-options than they do about their own embodied White supremacist privilege.

There are ways to choose enchantment instead of illusion. The word "enchantment" comes from the French, "chanter," to chant or to sing. Declarations can be rhapsodic or prophetic. There are also many role-models available to help us envision the practical work needed to fight racist- oppression. Branch Rickey, far from being a revolutionary, simply used his power to dismantle privilege when signing Jackie Robinson to a baseball-contract. Rickey's primary motive was to win baseball games but making that the simple priority was a healthy step in the right direction. Abolitionist William Wilberforce fought racist-oppression by organizing a boycott of slave-grown sugar supported by 300,000 English people.[628] Maybe you can't do everything — but you can do something. Do something! Do what you can where you are with what you have.

## "REFUSE TO BE WHITE"

*'When I use a word,' Humpty Dumpty said in a rather scornful tone, 'it means just what I choose it to mean. Neither more nor less!' 'The question is' said Alice, 'whether you can make words mean so many different things.' 'The question is,' said Humpty Dumpty, 'who is to be Master. That is all.'*

**—Lewis Carroll,** *Alice in Wonderland*

When skillful chefs want to kill a frog, they drop it into cold-water and gradually turn-up the heat so the frog doesn't notice it is slowly being boiled-alive. Addressing injustice with symbolism may fool a few folks who aren't paying attention but they'll soon find themselves being boiled-alive. Every American of any and every ethnicity is somehow "trapped by race."[629]

Can Euro-Americans become "abolitionists" against their own crippling Whiteness? Ignatiev and Garvey in *Race Traitor* write: "The White-race is a historically constructed social-formation – historically constructed because it is a product of some people's responses to historical circumstances; a social-formation because it is a fact of society corresponding to no classification recognized by natural sciences."[630] Euro-Americans who reject incapacitating "Whiteness" and fight-White are "race-traitors" who, as James Baldwin says, refuse to be White. Whites created an exclusivist-club designed for Whites by denigrating others: "People were not favored socially because they were White; rather they were defined as White because they were favored. . . . as the White race exists; all movements against racism are doomed to fail."[631]

How do Whites become "race-traitors"? "Debilitating Whiteness robs Euro-Americans of their ability to actually be their full person in their fullest humanity . . . it's a creation that we all need to resist."[632] Angel Kyodo Williams says: "One of the most powerful things White folks can do is just call themselves 'White.' Of course, it's not the whole of who you are . . . but living and choosing to live in that discomfort of what gets foisted upon you when you wear that label is stepping into a place of your own . . . being on your own frontlines and not trying to be on folks of colors' frontlines. Being on your own frontline is where the work is juiciest and that's where it begins."[633] Ask yourself (if you are White) what was your last racist thought or action? Ask your White friends when the last time they were racists. Think hard!

## A MALCOLM X LAPTOP-STICKER SOLVES ALL!

*"You will never see hippies get more upset than on an Ultimate Frisbee Field. It can be jarring to see people who look like they should be playing acoustic guitars yelling at each other about whether or not Blake stepped out of bounds."*

**—Christian Lander (New York Times, 11/16/10, C6)**

Many Euro-Americans are complicitous in empowering racist-oppression because "the anti-Black idea is so contagious that it now affects, in varying degrees, almost every person in this society."[634] When I talk (CVG) about working to become a "recovering racist," students look at me as if I'd just confessed being Alabama's Grand-Dragon-Wizard of the KKK. In my own life, I'm trying to, as Glaude says, "kill-the-idea-of-White-people" because that's the best way for our society to escape this present morass: Anti-Whiteness is the best way — and maybe the only way.[635] 'Whiteness Studies' — as a new academic discipline — has a history of trying to explain the obvious to the oblivious. It should be obvious that anti-racist progress should be authenticated by African Americans instead of Euro-Americans. Frederick Joseph claims: "The actual problem with White people is that many just don't have any sense of accountability when it comes to people of color. Accountability not only for the things White people do that often make interacting with them the most frustrating and tumultuous part of our days. But also, accountability for the historic and current inequities and disparities plaguing Black people."[636]

In many contexts, Blacks have to "tiptoe around the feelings of White people" — often hyper-sensitive.[637] Their comfort is their privilege and protestations about being uncomfortable are forms of control that support White advantage. Cornel West is optimistic that Euro-Americans are gaining "an escalating type of consciousness."[638] Let's hope so: We need solutions. The reason there's so much awkward stress between Black and White Americans is that there's so much reason to be awkward and stressed. Some White Americans relate to Blacks the way a customer relates to a salesperson — with fake eagerness with fake friends in unnatural dialogue.

Well-meaning liberals often resort to virtue-signaling affirmations such as saying, "the X," or el-Hajj Malik el-Shabazz Malcolm X" instead of just "Malcolm X." Paul Ricoeur thought symbols are often more meaningful than beliefs because we are more emotional than rational. The tons of symbolic gestures and token affirmations could fill to the brim all the vacant spaces in the Mojave Desert. Just as the football-star in *Jerry Maguire* said: "Show me the money!"

"Hope deferred makes the heart sick": In 1963, eight White pastors cautioned Dr. King to slow-down. They loved his views but thought his tactics were too pushy. The problems of Empire aren't personal. The slave-trade wasn't personal, neo-slavery wasn't personal, racist-oppression is not personal. It is empowered and embodied by systems. In 2020, Dennis Chauvin put his knee on Mr. George Floyd's neck for eight minutes, forty-six seconds. Chauvin embodies an Empire working systematically with lethal effect. Euro-Americans must realize that as long as they have their knee on a Black man's neck, they can't go anywhere themselves. It's one thing to protest or click on Amazon to buy a BLM and Malcolm X sticker for your laptop — it's another to act.

## CIRCUS LIVING

*By going and coming a bird needs to rest.*

**—Ashanti Proverb**

An African (Ibo) proverb states: "Perhaps you do not understand me because you do not love me. Perhaps you do not love me because you do not understand me." Malcolm X said the one who controls the definitions controls the argument. After the Civil War, because the abolition of slavery ended White control over Black bodies in one way, minstrel-shows became a new form to put Blacks "in their place." "Darkies" became the focus of ridicule in public performed by Whites paid to play silly, black-faced caricatures. *Uncle Tom's Cabin* was Empire's first classic, the first epic-movie was *Birth of a Nation,* the first block-buster novel was *Gone with the Wind*, the first talkie was *The Jazz Singer*, and the most popular radio-show was *Amos n 'Andy*.[639] Minstrelizing Black folks reframed frustrated White insecurity with dissonant theatrics. Minstrelsy was a White shuck-and-jive emotive-release filled with insecure disdain for Blacks.

## "WE TREAT OUR NEGROES JUST FINE"

*The one who is guilty is usually the one who talks the most.*

**—Ashanti Proverb**

A modern form of the Empire minstrel-show has been the sports-world. Positively, through sports, some wealth has returned to Black America. Educationally, sports became the primary way HWCUs (Historic White Colleges and Universities) were desegregated — becoming wealthy in the process. Positively, a few folks found money-making careers and some have used their platforms to promote justice. Negatively, Black athletes have fought against being "owned" — forced to participate in their own muting mistrelization. Whites have often demanded Black athletes check their "Blackness" at the door — and quietly "stay in their place."

Historically, there's a complex relationship between Empire-sports and blaxploitation. Before the Civil War, bare-knuckled-heavyweight Tom

Molyneux earned his freedom through fighting. Today, sports is a huge in-dustry — the nation's tenth largest — generating over 220 billion dollars a year.[640] There's something "safe" about seeing folks perform in a sporting event.

The Harlem Globetrotters (HG) brought sports-minstrelsy to the fore-ground.[641] From the outset, owner Abe Saperstein had the Globies employ "Step'in-Fetchit routines." Amazingly, Abe paid his Globetrotter players less than half of what he paid their White faux-opponents. "Sap" once threat-ened to fire an entire HG team when they threatened to strike for better treatment. "Sap" also initially threatened any NBA team considering hiring his HG "property." Not-so honest Abe "made as much, if not more, money out of Black sport during the first half of the 20th century as anybody in America."[642] Fortunately, in 1993, Mannie Jackson purchased the team and this trail-blazing, barnstorming gem became the first Black-owned sports franchise.

In 2020, 81% of the players in the NBA, 70% of the players in the NFL, 8% of MLB were Black Americans while less than 2% of NHL hockey-players identified as "non-White."[643] Owners in plush-seats watch Black gladiators attack each other in symbolic deaths. Athletes are commodities — bought, sold, and traded. Careers are interchangeable and disposable.

Sports promise "a level playing field but the Faustian-bargain of ath-letics is that huge amounts of money can be earned quickly while, at the same time, bodies and freedoms are destroyed."[644] Black athletes are often forced to conform to White social expectations. In 1949, for example, Jackie Robinson was (basically) obligated by his boss to appear before a Senate committee to criticize the great entertainer Paul Robeson.[645] Robinson was a pioneer who "knew his place." The Boston Red Sox's first Black American, Earl Wilson, was chosen because, as his scouting-report said, "He is a "well-mannered colored boy, not too Black, pleasant to talk to."[646] Alternatively, some use sports as a platform to assert Black empowerment: At the 1968 Olympics, John Carlos and Tommie Smith raised fists in protest during the National Anthem.[647]

Boxing "is never a sport-of-choice" and boxers have often been poor-folk fighting to entertain rich-folk. America's first boxers were slaves: Planta-tion owners enjoyed "putting together the strongest slaves and having them fight it out while wearing iron collars."[648] Cassius Clay (Muhammad Ali) won Olympic Gold in 1960.[649] "The Greatest" said he was the best because: "I'm so fast, I can turn-off the bedroom lights and get into bed before it gets dark."[650] After converting to Islam, Muhammad Ali changed his focus: "I re-ally don't care about boxing. Boxing is a stepping-stone just to introduce me to the audience."[651] Ali used his social influence to refuse to fight in Vietnam saying that no one there "had ever called him a N@#*."[652]

When Paul Robeson was criticized for being ungrateful for what he'd been "given" he replied: "Nothing is ever given to us . . . human dignity cannot be measured in dollars and cents."[653] The vast entertainment context includes movies, television, radio, music industries, social media, gaming, publishing — to name a few — where Black creativity has been monetized, represented, and misrepresented in countless ways. The Harlem Renaissance, featuring Claude McKay, James Weldon Johnson, Langston Hughes, and others was a rebellion; a "revolt against myths" (that Whites invented) while countering with the authority of beauty.

Emma Goldman said about social change-agency: "If I can't dance, I don't want to be part of your revolution."[654] Akiba Solomon said: "I believe God used Nina Simone to open up the possibility that we might be haughty and angry rather than supplicant in the face of racism."[655] It was said that Miles Davis — part of "an aesthetic community of resistance," always played with his back to the audience because of his attention to artistic excellence.[656] For the greatest, for Farke Touré, Marley, Prince, Stevie, Marvin, Mariah, Ray, James, Aretha, Jimi, Louis, Billie, Train, Ella, Miles, Duke, Dizzy, Beyonce, Alicia, Lauryn, Diana, Michael, Muddy, Whitney, Chaka, Thelonious, B.B., Roberta, Patti, Barry, Smokey, Al, Lionel, Luther, Tina, Gladys, Otis, Fats, Fela, Etta, George, Gil, Isaac, Bird, Cook, Biggie, Rhianna, and Pac it was never about only recording supreme music, it was also about getting freer and singing their own strong truth.

In contrast to transformative artists, minstrelsy happens when someone performs only for money or fame. Minstrelsy happens when suffering is re-packaged for sale. Hanif Abdurraqib talks about one rapper who got rich selling "Black-joy" to White audiences: "The natural reaction to Black people being murdered on camera is the notion that living Black joy becomes a commodity – something that everyone feels like they should be able to consume as a type of relief point."[657] Abdurraqib also talks about Black sadness: "At some point a person figured out that the performance of sadness was a currency . . . If I can convince you that I am falling apart, in need of love, perhaps I can draw you close enough to tell you what I really need."[658]

Renowned entertainers like Denzel Washington, Cicely Tyson, Aretha Franklin, Hattie McDaniel, Samuel L. Jackson, Sidney Portier, Harry Belafonte, Halle Berry, Paul Robeson, Morgan Freedman, Viola Davis, Dorothy Dandridge, James Jones, Oprah Winfrey, Chadwick Boseman, and countless others are part of the "furniture" of American social-consciousness but have not always been free to openly express their "Blackness." Only recently, artists have enjoyed greater control over their own work. More changes are needed: It's relatively easy to remove sitcom-episodes featuring Black-face (or other efforts), but far more vital is shifting the economic levers of decision-making from exclusive White-control.[659] Normalcy never again!

## STRONG FAMILIES UNDER ATTACK

*Sticks in a bundle are unbreakable.*

### —Bondei (Kenyan) Proverb

Sometimes family-issues feel like a path littered with shards of glass. The "jarring madness" of jumbled family-issues are a key reason a *Sankofa* message must be amplified.[660]

Orlando Patterson observes: "African Americans are the most un-partnered and isolated group of people in America and quite possibly the world."[661] Kendi claims, "nearly one-fourth of Black families were headed by women, twice the rate for White families."[662] There are many types of healthy families and loving our kids is probably the most vital mission in our lives. Activist Rickell Howard Smith writes: "Now I know that parenting my children is the most revolutionary thing that I can do in this world. Parenthood transformed me from a lawyer to a freedom fighter for Black children."[663] "Home is where the heart begins."[664] Yet, "only 34% of Black men and 26% of Black women disagreed with the statement that there's often distrust between Black men and women."[665] Tensions abound: For example, to limit youth-alienation, divorced couples must set-aside animosities for the long-term interests of our kids. The healing *Sankofa* wisdom-vision of Africa is our way forward as Melenated communities become stronger. One of the greatest enemies against strong Black families and healthy communities are the policing (and prison) systems of Empire. For millennia, the concept of policing was confined to the military. In the last two centuries, policing philosophies have changed dramatically. Some argue that, in Empire, "slave patrols were the first instantiation of the modern police-force whose primary purpose has never been to 'protect and serve' the broader public but to protect the interests and property of the powerful."[666] Not long ago, however, Black Americans were strengthened by community-policing which focused on working with local neighbors in relational ways.[667] What is even more vital is the reinvestment of funds from policing towards meeting the pressing needs of Melenated communities with sufficient funds and targeted resources that will improve lives.

America is the world's largest jailer with about one-quarter of the entire world's prison population.[668] This system has waged war on Black families: The more police, the more folks are policed and become victims of police-violence. There are over 2.5 million folks in Empire prisons, and "there are more people with mental-health disorders in prison than in all" of America's psychiatric-wards combined (2015).[669] Prisons are money-making businesses that provide well-paying jobs for those who build and service the prisons and those who work there — guards, and a few nurses and counselors. Prisoners in forty-nine states are even billed for their prison-time: "In Florida they can charge you $50-a-day, payable upon your release."[670]

The profitability of punishment means many prisons are private-companies trading on the New York Stock Exchange. The most profitable sector of the prison-industrial complex are immigration detention facilities. "America's sprawling slave-labor system" is part of a vicious cycle that ties punishment with profit, criminals mean more "cargo" for the prisons, which means more profit for investors.[671] The more tightly cargo-prison ships are packed, the greater the profits for stockholders. The 13th Amendment abolished slavery "except as a punishment for crime."[672] Empire judges are the only people on the earth who can legally throw folks into slavery for crimes of poverty. What is needed are solutions generated by local communities. President Obama explained: "If lawful work were available for young men now in the drug-trade, then crime in many communities would drop; that, as a consequence more employers would locate businesses in these neighborhoods and a self-sustaining economy would take root."[673]

Whites sell more drugs than Blacks and yet Blacks are far more likely to be arrested.[674] More than 55% of all prisoners are of Black and Spanish-speaking backgrounds while their percentage of population is about 35%. Policing is more aggressive against drug-sales, prostitution, and other crimes of poverty. Enforcement is stricter in Melenated communities and more "tolerated" in others. Stop-and-frisk policies, while declining, often profile non-Whites.[675]

Mr. George Junius Stinney, fifteen, was sent to South Carolina's electric-chair, June 16, 1944, to become the youngest person ever executed in the Empire. At 5'1" and ninety pounds, "adjustments had to be made in order to secure his body to the electric chair."[676] In 2014 — a little late — his verdict was reversed and Mr. Stinney was ruled innocent of killing two White girls. Today, adult sentencing for minors is on the rise. Youth often enter truancy, discipline-punishment settings only to be offered "rescue" by joining the military or blue-collar labor.

"Prisons are racism incarnate."[677] Youth are "socialized in prisons and, like homing pigeons, [are] being conditioned to return."[678] Each young man imprisoned results in "reducing the pool of Black marriageable males."[679] Prison populations also have a high number of violent White supremacists, and there've been myriad racialized riots, and the majority of prison-guards are not Black. On the inside, "racism is the best tool of the prison officials to control volatile prison populations. The warden and his guards intentionally kept up their racial hostilities."[680]

Such human rights violations could not "happen in a society of merciful people guided by justice and integrity."[681] Countless innocent people are arrested simply because they "fit the description": Black. This isn't new: In the South, it was common for "White criminals to blacken their faces" and then, commit a crime and, then hope to "throw suspicion on a Black person."[682] The common racist notion of "Black-on-Black" crime makes corporate-White crime invisible. All crime, including the larger realm of White-on-White murders, happening at five-times the rate of Black-on-Black murders, is usually about internal communal violence.[683]

In the courts, the "innocent-accused" face a conundrum when there's a better chance avoiding harsh sentencing by accepting a plea-deal than fighting for truth. Judges can sway juries with variant jury-instructions. The quality of legal-services, the extent of legal-fees, and bond- payment potential are all factors that can translate into a difference of years in prison-sentencing. Judges empathetic towards those standing in front of them will naturally be more lenient. Black judges and White allies/strategic-partners can have a measurable effect on sentencing realities.

Policing is sometimes "White-rage, under the guise of law enforcement."[684] The widely espoused "few-bad-apples" narrative blurs the fact that the tree itself is rotten to the core. The "racism of the police is not the product of vitriol; it flows from their role as armed agents of the State. The police function to enforce the role of the politically powerful and the economic elite"[685] While legislation, training, and new policies are needed, that's not all that's needed. "We can have new legislation. We can put cameras-on-cops but it's going to be heart-to-heart that we expose these wounds" in the long-term as our society transitions into sanity.[686]

Empire policing is the most militarized police-force in the world — laden with excessive fire-power. Speaking of the police one young protestor asked: "Why do they hate Black people?" What most folks forget about racism is that it's often a social-bond "that occurs among people as a means of mattering and belonging. It is a currency that arises" in times of social change.[687]

A *Sankofa* vision teaches no one can manipulate your mind unless you allow yourself to be controlled. The brilliant writer Lerone Bennett warns:

"From birth to death, the Negro is handled, distorted, and violated by the symbols and tentacles of white power; tentacles that worm their way into his neurons and invade the gray cells of his cortex. . . . The Negro must not only don a mask; he becomes, in many instances, the mask he dons."[688]

## TRAIL-TO-JAIL

*Education? How much faith in education can be clung to by people whose minds have been raped? For three centuries Blacks have been told by Whites that they were intellectually inferior - and generations of Blacks have believed it and acted accordingly.*

**—Carl T. Rowan**

In Chicago's public-schools, Ms. Marva Collins' spent her career sharing "head-bread" to students hungry to learn. She rejected negative views of her students and thought education gave kids "a fighting chance at agency."[689] Ms. Marva Collins opposed student "aim-nesia;" the loss of hope. She tried to instill a "Black-bone" in her beloved students.[690] In a society where kids are seen as "cogs in a great machine," Ms. Marva Collins taught that no one is expendable.[691]

James Baldwin claims "the paradox of education" is that it should help students become conscious enough "to examine the society in which they are being educated."[692] In America's Eurocentric-education, however, schools are often spaces where children are trained "to serve another person's dreams, ensure another person's wealth, produce another person's vision."[693]

Educational opportunities are not equal: Michelle Obama's guidance-counselor told her she wasn't "Princeton material." White standards of 'normal' sent Miss Tiana Parker, age seven, home-from-school in Tulsa for her dreadlocks and forced Miss Vanessa van Dyke, age twelve, home-from-school in Orlando for hers.[694] School dress-codes and demands for conformity in minor issues are ways to reinforce control. Education should foster transformation zones; not conformity zones: This is a huge, unresolved issue in school detention-discipline strategies.

Integration (if it doesn't erase) can be a positive force if it promotes human truths and values instead of only Eurocentric truths and values. In many schools, honors-courses serve as a filter where Black youth perform to show mastery in normative White speech-patterns and attitudes. One's success relates to what clothes children wear in relation to White discomfort. In Oklahoma, one politician drafted a bill banning wearing a hoodie in public.[695] Integration, when weaponized, upholds the status quo with the option to "integrate or be marginalized."

Space-racism refers to places of controlling oppression: "Non-White students fill most of the seats in today's public-school classrooms but are taught by teachers who are 80% White" who, however unconsciously, may often have lower expectations for non-White students.[696] In Black-majority spaces, Dr. Angela Davis notes schools often "use the same technologies of detection as jails and they sometimes use law-enforcement officials. In Empire, some elementary-schools are actually "patrolled by armed-officers with metal-detectors and searchlights."[697] When I was in school (Tait) we had "truant-officers" to get kids into school and now they have police-officers to get kids into prison. In Texas, 83% of those charged for "failure to attend school" and fined over $16 million were non-White.[698] Suspensions, not part of any initiative-taking learning agenda, are inequitable: In Wisconsin, 21% of Black schoolgirls (compared to 2% of Whites) are suspended at least once.[699]

Black high-school students have the nation's highest dropout-rate. In New York City, Blacks graduate at 28%.[700] Only 12% of Black male fourth-graders are proficient in reading compared with 38% of White boys of that age.[701] Public schools are more segregated now than in 1970.[702] At college, low high-school graduation rates result in Black students making up 12% of all undergraduates and about 7% of all graduates. Biases become a factor in why there are more Black women doctorates (or academicians) than men.

Patterson notes "African Americans are the only ethnic group in the country where women outperform men in hard sciences including computer sciences, math, and physics."[703] In 2025, 55% of professors are White men, 30% White women, and 4% are Black (men and women). What about doctoral candidates? Only 5.4% of all doctorates were awarded to Black students. Black students earned 1.2% of all physics degrees, 0.9% of math and statistics doctorates, 1% of computer-science doctorates, 2% of chemistry doctorates, and 1.7% of engineering doctorates. In the areas of plant-genetics, wildlife-biology, medical-physics, atmospheric-physics, physical-oceanography, plasma-physics, geometry, logic, number-theory, robotics, structural-engineering, English as a second language, Italian, Middle/Near East history, classics, music, and music performance, not one doctorate was awarded to a Black person in America in 2017.[704]

Legacy college-admissions are a form of White Affirmative Action, while improvements need to be made in recruitment strategies. Some colleges have initiated initiative-taking mentoring and generous funding for scholarships. Calvin College (MI) brings high-school students of color to the campus for pre-college courses. When students arrive, these colleges should not be racially-charged environments. Yet, problems often arise when Black students, expressing themselves are mistakenly accused of racializing the situation or accused of separatism: "Many Whites seem captivated by an optical illusion . . . They see the Blacks separating themselves; they rarely see that the Whites have separated themselves as well."[705] White students sometimes view Black student-unions as forms of racial exclusion and not as supportive campus enclaves to preserve self-dignity.

"Power prefers to operate in obscurity."[706] Even as HBCUs are under siege, HWCUs must address their own sordid histories during the *Maafa* and neo-slavery.[707] For example, the University of Alabama (along with most Southern schools) owned slaves that built their campuses and worked as staff. Most Southern HWCU universities founded to support the inter-sections of slaveocracy and Christianity (such as Baylor) during the Civil War turned campuses into training- grounds for the godly Confederacy. In recent years, some of these defensive fortresses of status quo (such as Alabama and Baylor) have slowly recognized (but without financial repara-tions) historic abuses. Positively, Georgetown University, slave-owners until the 1840s, and nine (of twelve) colleges at Yale University named in honor of slave-masters have erased these names.[708] Brown University was founded by a donation of $160,000, from slave-trade profits. Brown became the first Ivy League institution to hire a Black president, Ruth J. Simmons.

The Juneteenth-legacy of Texas-racist oppression speaks of last-ditch efforts to delay justice long after it was dethroned. I (CVG) work at Baylor University, named after a devout Baptist slave-master and righteous slave-killing judge: Let that sink in for a minute. Shortly after the 2008 election, students burned an Obama-sign and hung a noose from a tree: National news. Afterwards, Baylor issued a press-release saying that Euro-American students had actually put-up a poorly-designed rope-swing that only "coin-cidently" coincided with the sign-burning. Black students were the ones to blame: They "over-reacted" and "jumped" to the wrong conclusions.[709]

Sometimes, Black students are asked to "educate" White students about "what it means to be Black."[710] Sometimes kids are judged, not on their merits, but as the "Black student" as if they represented 44 million people. When it comes to teaching history, Black experiences are often bracketed into an ocean of suffering. It's good African American History and Literature classes have been added but many remain "segregated" from the larger curriculum.[711]

Many spiritualities teach a Creator spoke worlds into being with words. There's a saying "talk is cheap" but what's really cheap is only cheap talk. When the "normal" is White then it's easy for non-White kids to feel inferior. Fortunately, the war on Ebonics has eased as educators accept that letting kids express themselves on their own terms isn't promoting poor grammar, it's promoting free-expression. Today, Ebonics is widely accepted among early-education reading-specialists as a "systematic, regular, and complex structure ... [with] a vocabulary or lexicon, a phonology or sound-system, and a grammar."[712]

## RED-LINING APARTHEID

*Housing residential segregation has proved to be the most resistant to change of all social realms. Perhaps this is because, in general, most racial change has been artificial.*

**—Thomas Pettygrove**

Neighborhood gentrifications raises the value of folks' homes so high they can no longer afford to live in their own homes. Just as the government organized First Nations onto reservations where they could be controlled, so also Black Americans have been pushed into urban ghetto-reservations. Minister Malcolm X said: "We live in the poorest houses and pay the highest rents, eat the poorest food, and wear the poorest clothing at the highest prices."[713]

In South Africa, a land-grab system of "apartheid" (rhymes with "hate") was as legal as it was evil. In Empire, segregation happens in spite of laws. The spatial isolation of Black America is by design. Transportation networks maintain segregation: See where they operate. Segregation is valued by supremacists because it reinforces "heinous stereotypes about African Americans."[714] Stereotypes "reduce complex human beings into cardboard cut-out" representations.[715] These stereotypes "are seared into the mental frying-pan" of Empire's "citizenry, swallowed whole," as it "eventually goes to the "social gut of America."[716] When they are advanced they "dissolve any requirement to take certain people seriously or empathize with them."[717] Normalcy never again!

Segregating spaces keeps Blacks invisible unless Whites — to quote songwriter Bob Cole — take "A Trip to Coontown" (1897).[718] Small kids learn that only kids who look like them will attend their birthday-parties or Sunday-school classes. Social segregation segregates information about possible jobs. Workplace segregation isn't a failure but a planned outcome: "They've succeeded in providing jobs to middle-class Whites, kept Blacks at outcaste, subsistence level, and out of the skilled-labor market with its high-paying jobs, allowed Blacks to remain a vast source of cheap labor and a readily available political scapegoat."[719]

For decades, the number of Black residents in many localities has been controlled through zoning-laws. For example, in 1916, Dallas approved an ordinance which designated blocks on which Blacks could live. In 1927, "Texas took the experiment with racially restrictive zoning-laws a step further than other States" by openly segregating Blacks and Whites by zoning-laws.[720] When some Blacks tried to circumvent laws, they were prohibited from entering homes that they'd built and paid for. In Grosse Point, MI (1946), Blacks, Asians, and Mexicans were forbidden to buy land through a checklist enacted to catch those who were "swarthy in appearance" or who had "characteristics" that were not "typically American."[721]

After World War II, when highways, airports, and stadiums were built — calling for massive "eminent-domain" seizures — many projects destroyed established Black communities. At the same time, even though the G.I. Bill was intended for all veterans — because it was managed through State authorizing-agencies, there were huge discrepancies in its administration. In Mississippi, for example, only two of the 3,229 home-loans were given to Black people.[722] Later, the "Fair Housing Act" attempted to dismantle the architecture of "red-lining" but deep legacies of past discriminations still remain. In 2009, former President Bush bought a house in Dallas that historically had a restrictive-covenant of Black exclusion. Public-housing projects are another way that spaces are designated as Black-only. One Judge, exposing measures to maintain segregation, claimed: "The primary purpose of the Dallas public housing project was to prevent Blacks from moving into the White areas of the city."[723]

"White flight" led to dramatic urban changes. Almost 400,000 Whites moved out of Los Angeles in the 1990s.[724] One issue that has emerged is Melenated communities without grocery-stores and other amenities.[725] At the same time, in 2024, more Blacks live in American suburbs (39%) than in cities (36%).[726] "Gentrification" (displacement) results in Melenated communities being transformed overnight. When an urban-core is hollowed-out, a "donut-effect" occurs where slum-lords become wealthy. In the 1990s, Washington, D.C., cleared out the city's southwest-quadrant, dislocating over 20,000 residents: turning homes into upscale-housing for the rich. Do politicians benefit from ghettos? Incompetent politicians seek proximity with Black voters at election-time in photo-ops but later vanish, "never committed to empower us."[727]

## BLACK FACES, WHITE SPACES

*"Come celebrate with me that every day something has tried to kill me and has failed."*

**—Lucille Clifton**

In Empire, it's easy to buy "unleaded-gas but you can't buy unleaded-water for our children."[728] Flint, Michigan is a city where one-in-six homes has been abandoned and over 40% live below the poverty-line.[729] Flint galvanized a nation that learned an entire Melenated community was drinking lead-poisoned water. In fact, there were about "4,000 U.S. areas – mostly poor and non-White – [that] have higher lead-poisoning rates than Flint."[730] This is a tragic cycle because, "higher childhood blood lead-levels are associated with higher adult arrest-rates for violent crime" and other societal and health-related problems.[731]

Majority-Black communities (such as Orlando and Jacksonville) have also "been victims of sustained toxic-chemical dumping and childhood rates of asthma among young Blacks" has reached "epidemic levels."[732] Air-pollution problems also promote asthma. Also, hazardous landfills (or toxic waste-dumps) are often opened near majority-Black areas. Instead of "ethnic-cleansing" this is "ethnic-churning" because some folks move out while others remain stuck when toxic-sites are opened. In 1988, Emelle, Alabama received 47,000 tons of toxic contaminated-soil from Geneva Industries of Houston. Additionally, these areas are not always serviced with adequate storm-protection systems against natural disasters. This creates nightmares whenever toxic-dumps are "scattered" by catastrophes, spreading lethal toxicity.

What about the "Great Outdoors"? Is there a "psychological-divorce" between some Blacks and America's wilderness areas? Rural settings were often the spaces where rapes and other terrors transpired. Some White-majority spaces were designated "sundown-towns" which meant Blacks had to "know their place." Restrictions often excluded wilderness-areas where Whites freely wandered without fear.[733] One way to cope with wilderness-stress is to replace geographies of fear with safe-spaces of protection. This leads to reinforcing behaviors where folks tell each other where they "belong" (where they're safe). Habits become encoded in family-lore and it can become an instinctive survival-strategy for folks to look for others that look like them to feel safe. Sometimes, wilderness-spaces were places of refuge from slave-catchers but often they were traumatic spaces. To many Black faces, too many White-majority spaces are not safe spaces. In the Black story of Empire South, a sense of belonging didn't usually correspond with wilderness spaces. Billie Holliday (and others) spoke of trees as symbols of violence. One Black Floridian sighed: "We've had so many atrocious things happen to us in the woods" that wilderness areas are "fear-places" of "isolation and helplessness."[734] One Texan was blunt: "There's a lot of trees in those woods and rope is cheap."[735] The spatial fears behind the idea of "Driving-While-Black" are not that different from fears about "Camping-While-Black."

Environmental-justice advocacy is also a space affected by inequitable representation issues. The Sierra Club, Wilderness Society, and other groups have tried to launch "outreaches" to majority Melenated communities but their institutional-cultures often limit participation beyond less authoritative activism.[736] Today's pressing environmental debates remain dominated by White activists while African Americans are expected to "sit at the back of the Green Bus."[737]

## HEALTH INEQUITIES

*What kind of society uses medicine as a weapon, keeps it from people needing to heal, all the while continuing to develop the drugs America's prisons use to execute people?*

### —Patricia Khan—Cullors and Asha Bandele

How long will you live? Euro-Americans live about "3.5 additional years over African American lives in the Empire, which is the most glaring of a host of health disparities, starting from infancy where Black infants die at twice the rate of White infants . . . African Americans are 25% more likely to die of cancer than Whites."[738] Other sources say the difference in life-expectancy could be as much as six-years. Black Americans are diagnosed with diabetes at a rate almost double Euro-Americans. Almost half of those infected with HIV-AIDS are Black Americans and 86% of infected children are either Black or Spanish-speakers. More than 80% of Black women will develop fibroids by the age of fifty.[739] "Racism contributes to Blacks getting sick younger and having more severe illnesses; leading to more rapid aging ("weathering")."[740] "Health disparities are the civil [human] rights issue of the twenty-first century."[741]

Health insurance makes a stark difference: In 2017, 28.5 million Americans had no health protections. Compared to other "developed" nations these numbers stagger the imagination. Empire "is the only one of the twenty-five wealthiest nations that doesn't offer our people health care."[742]

The Covid-19 pandemic "laid bare structural racism and inequalities" embodied in the racist dynamics of Covid-1619.[743] Covid-19 underscores: "We live in a country that does not value health care as a human right."[744] This health-disaster may provide opportunities for a "new dawn," but "only new thinking can lead to a new dawn."[745] The "politics of disposability" means some have no value and had to work while others were confined into prisons and nursing homes even as these places became massive virus-spreading contexts.[746] This isn't new: In 2008, the American Medical Association (AMA) apologized for two centuries of relegating Black patients and doctors to "colored" (or charity) wards. The AMA did not officially reject segregation in hospitals until 1968. In 1938, Dr. Louis T. Wright said the "AMA has demonstrated as much interest in the health of the Negro as Hitler had in the health of the Jew."[747]

## BLAXPLOITATION NATION

*One must question the values of a society that tolerates the poverty that exists in America.*

**—Andrew Young**

An African wisdom proverb says: "A boat doesn't go forward if each soul is rowing their own direction." In addition to other obvious benefits "the myth of White superiority is exploded in the presence of equitable social and economic opportunity."[748] After the Civil War, African Americans owned only 0.5% of the Empire's total economic-worth. Understandable, since most former-slaves had just finished being owned. How about today? In 2019, Black households own just 4.2% of the nation's wealth (85.5% White). In 2020, 44% of Black Americans are homeowners compared to 73.7% of Whites — a staggering difference of 29.7%.[749] Since 1865, African Americans have not gained significant economic ownership over very much wealth.

Empire traps Black folks in systematic soul-shaming poverty. This leads into soul-crippling myths "that money can pull you and the people you passionately love out of the feeling of any grief or sadness."[750] Getting a new pair-of-shoes or make-of-automobile become desired out-of-proportion to their actual value. "Unemployment among African Americans is twice that of Whites."[751] More than a third of all Black kids grow-up in poverty and in some places — such as Ohio — numbers increase to more than half.[752] These facts are proof that Empire's racialized capitalism designed by Whites for the benefit of Whites works as intended. Empire racialized-capitalism commodifies segregation and is the engine behind economic segregation.

Today's human rights movements must include economic-justice issues. The rich impoverish the poor. Justice means helping each other when folks are hurting economically. Non- discrimination laws in employment and housing are there — they're just not enforced. The average Black family has less than a dime for every dollar owned by an average White family (1/12th). Only 18% of Black Americans have retirement-accounts compared with over 43% of Whites."[753] The "nest- egg" for the average Black family is a quarter-less than an average White family. No nest-eggs — and not enough regular eggs, either. For many, the issue isn't the color-line but the bottom-line. The main issue isn't Black skin — it's that check-books are in the red.

Recently, there's been an increasing Black middle-class. Economic injustices, however, pose problems to the Black middle (and upper)-class because they live in a space of "fluid identity" between both the "White middle-class and Black lower-classes."[754] Beyond rhetoric about the obligations of wealthy Black folks, the fact is they have to strategically assimilate between both majority White and Black cultures.

Are employees "penalized for being Black?"[755] Some Black corporate managers "serve in personnel functions often administering affirmative-action programs" as "brown-mouthpieces" to show "an illusion of inclusiveness."[756] Some are hired as intermediaries between majority Euro-American businesses and Melenated folks: "Cut off from the corporate mainstream, African American executives often find themselves in dead-end jobs with little job-security."[757]

Whites with a criminal-record have a better chance of getting a job than Blacks with no criminal-record. Studies show "Black names" result in fewer job-chances than identical resumes submitted with "White" names. Looking for work can feel like being stuck on a broken Ferris-wheel. Many 10th to 15th (ca. 1650–1800) generation Black Americans are stuck in "lives of poverty in a sea of prosperity" with one-in-three Black folks below the poverty line.[758]

The first Black millionaire was Madame C.J. Walker (born Sarah Breedlove) who became rich selling hair-care products. The undertaker's business was another success story because Whites refused to bury Black Americans. Insurance-companies fostered Black entrepreneurship since they offered a cushion against economic disaster at a time when Whites wouldn't insure Black folks. Alonzo Herndon (Atlanta Life) was a pioneer in focusing on Black insurance.

The good news is that places like Morgan State University, and many other HBCUs, are supporting Black engineering and collaborating with corporations to empower African American participation in well-paying professions. The shocking news is that, in 2020, only 5% of America's doctors,

4% of engineers, 4% of private-practice lawyers, 2% of architects, and about 7% of construction-tradesmen, and 2% of all senior-managers were African Americans.[759]

## THE COLOR OF MONEY

*All too often when there is mass unemployment in the Black community, it's referred to as a social problem, and when there is mass unemployment in the White community, it's referred to as a depression. But there is no basic difference. The fact is, that the Negro faces a literal depression all over the United States.*

**—Martin Luther King, Jr., 1968**

Today, many Black communities are "banking deserts" where folks rely on pay-day lenders to meet small-loan needs. During neo-slavery, Blacks — often excluded from White banks — relied on their own banks with the first ones forming "less than a decade after slavery ended, in the hostile climate of racism and Jim Crow segregation."[760] These banks were the glue of local communities as economic stability fosters self-respect. Early Black banks often worked with local churches and clients were usually treated as "friends and not as customers or debtors."[761]

Predatory, racialized-capitalism is "baked-into-the-cake" of Empire. Capitalism values and "prioritizes profits over people."[762] Enslavement happened for the "production of cotton, sugar, rice, and tobacco."[763] Today, "there are 400 billionaires . . . and 45 million people living in poverty."[764] The way to gain financial power is to gain financial security through financial control. To be successful in a parasitic capitalist space demands the "mistrust of others [because] greater gain is made possible by hypocrisy and deceit, by emotional control, and detachment."[765] Racist capitalists don't care about your flourishing: They care about you helping their flourishing.

Comedian George Carlin said that to "believe in the American Dream a person has to be asleep!" But we're here, so we've only two choices: change the system or work within the system. Either way, one must guard in the short-term against soul-decay. Poet bell hooks writes: "Capitalism poses a direct threat to the survival of an ethical belief system in Black life."[766]

Advocates of our racialized-capitalistic system resist efforts to overturn structural inequalities: "They define capitalism as the freedom to exploit people into economic ruin, the freedom to assassinate unions, the freedom to prey on unprotected consumers, workers and environments."[767] Dr. King cited "economic exploitation" as one of America's three evils along with militarism and racism. Even tragedies become sources of wealth as "disaster-capitalism."

After the *Maafa*, those who'd owned people-as-property were the same Whites that Blacks had to deal with on unfavorable financial terms for limited resources. Those who had previously- owned them had no desire to share resources or partner in any kind of economically-just relationship. Just as those newly-non-possessed began careers knowing they had no allies and needed to rely entirely on themselves — that same clarifying level of vigilant self-alertness is required today. In Empire, the color of credit is White: Bank credit means wealth. The Empire's economy is based on the "brutal and systemic underdevelopment of Black people."[768]

Ben Carson exemplifies many qualities that Black Americans respect: "He has a strong belief in God, and family, recognized and promoted the importance in education and rising up from very humble beginnings and overcoming such constraints like poverty and racism."[769] His view, however, is that "poverty is really more of a choice than anything else."[770] In fact, poverty is a tightrope-life — an unchosen instability pushing folks into swamps of stress, depression, poor health, substandard-housing, poor education options, crime, catastrophic tearing of the fabrics of society, fractured families, and repetitive cycles of joblessness.[771] Chimamanda Ngozi says poverty is not a willingly-made choice but "the oppressive lethargy of choicelessness."[772] Our self-worth is not a commodity. Fortunately, there are concrete solutions within our communities. The #BlackMoneyMatters movement, in the tradition of Garvey, Minister Malcolm, Madame C. J. Walker, and others, help us see how we can control our own dollars for our mutual support. Self-reinforcing chains can be cut. Poverty is not inevitable: It can be dismantled.

## RESTITUTION MODELS

*Do not think that an integrated cup of coffee is enough payment for 310 years of slave labor.*

### —Minister el—Hajj Malik el—Shabazz Malcolm X

*As Malcolm X said: "if you have had a knife in my back for 400 years, am I supposed to thank you for pulling it out?" The very least of your responsibility now is to compensate me, however inadequately, for centuries of degradation and dis-enfranchisement by granting peacefully – before I take them forcefully – the same rights and opportunities for a decent life that you've taken for granted as an American birthright.*

### —Eldridge Cleaver (1971)

Imagine someone steals your car: After they're caught, they apologize for the theft. They claim they want to make reparations and will give you one-years' worth of bus-tokens. Does that sound fair? Common-sense mandates that restitution means those robbed should be recompensed — reimbursed — as far as possible, towards the full-value of what's been stolen. The thief cannot determine what is fair-restitution in any definition of equitable economic justice.

Those who say Black Americans shouldn't claim victimization are telling you they don't accept the obvious truths of history. The guilt-remorse of the offender is of no concern to the offended. Reparations is a defining-point in determining the future of Black-White interactions.

Randall Robinson explains: "Despite all our sacrifice we've been handed 'law-book freedom' without 'make-right compensation.'"[773] Obviously, no compensation could ever make amends for all Blacks have suffered: Lost eggs cannot be unscrambled. Some have calculated that since African prisoners labored for 246 years (1619–1865) this would be the appropriate time-frame and would (modestly) result in about 220 million unpaid work-hours. Based on 2020 dollars this would be the equivalent of around four-trillion dollars.[774] Another option, based on the precedent of recompense for Japanese internment survivors, is a modest maximum of $60,000 per family. Such a breadth of variance might lead us back to Minister Malcolm's proposal that the actual amount, content, and appropriate recipients be adjudged by an "independent counsel" (perhaps the U.N.) to moderate between government obligations and the need to settle long-standing, outstanding social-debts.

Who should pay reparations? Logically, the U.S. government, since it legally sanctioned the *Maafa* until 1865. Empire's government is a "trans-generational entity" capable of bridging "the gap between the wrongs done to slaves and the present-day Black population."[775] Ancestors of slaves (ADOS) and those living here before 1965 (Civil Rights Act) should be eligible. The argument that it's too expensive, is compromised by a Space-Race, War-on-Terror, countless wars, and — most dramatically — when the Empire literally found trillions to fight Covid-19.

One of the first advocates for Black reparations was Ms. Callie House, an ex-slave who organized a society that promoted each ex-slave being given a modest pension based on the number of years enslaved.[776] James Forman oversaw the "Black Manifesto" (1969) published during the height of the billions-dollars Space-Race. The "Black Manifesto" called for economic reparations in the amount of $500 million dollars. Compare that amount with the $400 million settlement Canada paid to a much smaller First Nations population (1998) and the reparations settlement (1988) Ronald Reagan arranged for the 60,000 Japanese-Americans (alive at the time) in recognition for injustices experienced (about $20,000 per internee with a maximum amount per family) during WWII. Reparations have also been paid by France, England, and the United States to slave-owners at the loss of their property on emancipation.[777]

Every year, since 1989, Congress has proposed a bill calling for a commission to consider the possibility of reparations.[778] Economic restitution was appropriate when first proposed in 1865: It's appropriate today. Disbursing economic resources is not an act of charity but a long overdue recognition of fault and a moral obligation that will generate massive social-benefit.

In 2020, the State of California, initiated a process to study providing reparations for Black Californians. Local solutions are appropriate because injustices happen in local contexts. Other models might be modeled after programs for Jewish Holocaust survivors or programs enacted for First Americans. One proposal is that African Americans would be exempted from Federal Income Tax or from public college tuition for a period of years (400?).

Restitution can also happen at the state or local level and even on an individual level. What about an individual "slavery-restitution tax" where participants would voluntarily pay a set-amount of money to descendants of the enslaved? Each family could determine the amount or recipient. Even the poorest could set a modest $4,000 aside; a tiny token gesture of $10 for each year of slavery and Jim Crow. Such a miniscule amount, if paid by 200 million Whites would total, not including interest, $800 million dollars. Imagine asking a young White couple how they will pay their slavery-restitution obligation. Hours spent on working to pay this debt would leave a strong impression on both recipients and those paying this debt. Such programs are not "giveaways" but frail strategies to recompense centuries of labor without compensation.

# Conclusion

*If You Hear the Dogs – Keep Going"*
*Handwriting on the Wall*

*Americans of goodwill, the nice decent church people, the well-meaning liberals, the good-hearted souls who themselves wouldn't lynch anyone, must begin to realize that they have to be more than passively good-hearted, more than church-goingly Christian, and much more than word-of-mouth in their liberalism.*

**— Langston Hughes**

The Armenian Genocide, Rape of Nanjing, Wounded Knee Massacre, and countless other atrocities tied to religion litter the millennia of our world's history. Armenia, for example, became a killing-ground where life was easily discarded by people who claimed to be doing God's Will. The stories of Armenia, Nanjing, and Wounded Knee may not exclusively be our own stories — but they are our stories in a shared humanity. When we are able to fully "face the beast in humanity" we can face the rampaging beasts within ourselves.[779] Alternatively, "when we fail to recognize and forget to cultivate the seed of our shared humanity, we are in danger."[780]

Guru Nanak, the founder of the religion of Sikhism, explained: "I see no stranger. I see no enemy. Wherever I look, God is all I see."[781] Celebrating what we share — in all of its prismatic differences — makes us all emotionally richer. We should see ourselves and our loved ones in the Armenian, Chinese, and Lakota mothers who watched daughters being taken into cages for sex- slavery and rape or who watched as their babies were thrown into the air to be bayoneted by soldiers. The First Nations Lakota unity declaration is *Miya Oyaksin!* We are all interconnected.

Professor DuBois claimed: "Of all the civil rights for which the world has struggled for in 5,000 years, the right to learn is undoubtedly the most fundamental . . . The freedom to learn . . . has been bought by bitter sacrifice."[782] When the Professor first heard about the lynching of Mr.

Samuel Hose, he said "Something died in me that day."[783] When Edward W. Blyden tried to tell a group of Africans about the Samuel Hose lynching they were incredulous because "their imagination had never pictured any tragedy so revolting."[784] "In the face of all this wreckage," art and beauty can help us work stronger with steady action toward individual and social healing.[785]

## CHANGING DEMOGRAPHICS

*Whites will soon be a minority. This new reality carries consequences. White people have been in charge for a long time now but Black and Brown folk are not going to take a back seat anymore. Whiteness aint what it used to be. I'm here to say, it's time for white folks to sue for peace while the getting is still good."*

**—D.L. Hugley**

*Guess Who's Coming to Dinner?* was a 1967 movie about a White woman who falls in love with a Black man. When the couple goes to meet her White parents, all hell breaks loose. That intercultural meeting is happening again today writ large: "America is at a precarious juncture" as more White Americans "prefer boundaries around the nation's identity that maintain it in their image."[786] Around 2040, Whites will become a minority: "Between 2000 and 2050, America's Black population is projected to grow 71%, the Spanish-speaking heritage population 188%, the Asian population 213% and the White population 7%.[787] One Fox News anchor pleaded to his majority White audience: "Please do your duty! Make more babies!"[788]

White xenophobia will continue obstructing immigration to keep the dominant culture as White as possible. In one survey, "54% of [White] Americans say they prefer living in a community with a small immigration population."[789] Because America's diversity will continue to increase, Whites are running away into the spaces they control, such as Utah or Idaho or similar places where they are not in the minority. When many Whites think of the "Real America," Rev. Dr. Jeremiah Wright, Jr., Colin Kaepernick, or others, are not always included in their vision. The "Real America" they worship is evaporating like the melting Wicked-Witch-of-the-West. Now's the time for all of us to prepare bunker-sanctuaries before the coming storm because Whites are not giving up their fantasies of exploitation and mechanisms of control willingly. Their truths are being called myths, and their gods are being called false. All they've been taught is under threat and some of them are beginning to feel painted into a corner. For some, this is their "Live-Free-or-Die," "Give-Me-Liberty-or-Give-Me-Death!" moment. When they see you, Black man, or White-ally, they see an enemy. The contract they signed when they put their hand on their heart pledging to Red, White, and Blue has no room for Black. Remember the analysis of extremist conservatives offered by President Obama: "All that they have is God and Guns."[790]

Here's a positive thought : In our future, nothing is "written" (*Maktub*) or pre-determined. As happened before (for example, in response to Senator Joseph McCarthy) new alliances can emerge based on shared mutual respect. The Civil War and Civil Rights Movement were unresolved revolutions and a transition to a truer democracy will not appear easily. Extremists are now wearing less camouflage about what they want. Their world is imploding and they've no answers to complicated problems except simplistic assertiveness. The battle is about control. Those who hold a White-is-right mentality will flee into harbors of ignorance instead of accepting power-sharing complexities.

The problem we face is not "race" but the problem of oppression hiding behind "race." Can you imagine an America where those now shouting "White-power!" will one day shout "Black Lives Matter!?" Whites are being asked to give up economic privilege completely fused to their narrow views of the only true God and the world's best country. Remember this Ignatiev quote: "So long as the White race exists; all movements against racism are doomed to fail."[791] Of course, what Ignatiev is encouraging is for Euro-Americans to reject "Whiteness." James Baldwin claimed racist-oppression leads Whites into a "death of the heart" because "whoever is debasing others is debasing himself."[792]

## PEDAGOGY FOR THE CHILDREN OF THE OPPRESSORS

*Alas! And am I born for this? To wear the slavish chain.*

**—George Horton**

Brazilian Paulo Freire wrote *Pedagogy of the Oppressed*, which unpacked how the "privileged" often control those who are "oppressed." Freire claimed oppression thrives when the oppressed internalize their own marginalization. It is vital that we do not give any oxygen to our own self-destruction. Oppressors will try to use levers of control such as education, religion, politics, and business, to uphold their cherished status-quo. Oppressors sow cultural confusion and a false consciousness that undermines any will to resist their oppressive deceptions.

According to Freire, all of the socio-cultural institutions in Empire are interdependent on each other in a spider's-web of support that preaches the goodness of the oppressors and their righteous mission of oppression.

Instead of social levers such as education, religion, politics, the arts, and business, being spaces that encourage interdependence and mutual appreciation they can often become coopted by oppressors who want to blind others from seeing injustice and force those oppressed to accept passive conformity. One potent way to challenge this is through artistic expression which can facilitate liberation-making. Albert Camus wrote: "Perhaps there's no other peace for the artist than what is found in the heat of combat. 'Every wall is a door.'"[793]

Freire taught oppressors often express themselves with self-righteous paternalism. Those who oppress don't want to engage in self-reflection, which might lead them away from confidence and towards the freedom to acknowledge their guilt. Freire writes: "concern for humanization leads at once to the recognition of dehumanization."[794] Oppressors can only free themselves through rejecting privilege and, in a sense, rely on the agency of those oppressed. This rejects any "false form of generosity" that excludes reparations such as those often expressed through our social-services or ministries that claim to help "the poor."[795] The oppressed must build their own base-organizations around shared visions for change and then expand those bases. Political education — organizing step-by-step for change — leads to power.

Freire warned the privileged "will not gain liberation by chance, but through the praxis of their quest for it, through their recognition of the necessity to fight for it."[796] Any sense of "solidarity" with the oppressed, however, won't come independent of a majority of Euro-Americans abandoning their defensiveness. Those who opt to remain "White" cannot bring freedom for others or find freedom for themselves. Freire writes: "Discovering themselves to be an oppressor may cause considerable anguish, but it doesn't necessarily lead to solidarity with the oppressed. Rationalizing guilt through paternalistic treatment of the oppressed is an empty sham. True solidarity with the oppressed means fighting beside them to transform the notion that they exist as 'beings for another.'"[797] James Baldwin asked: "Why do they want to be White? Because it's the only way to justify the slaughter, they're trapped."[798]

When one domino falls others will also fall: Clay Cane writes: "The truth is all forms of oppression – sexism, racism, homophobia, anti-Semitism have a link. You cannot advocate for an end to racism but still be a proponent of homophobia."[799] This is why we need to forge partnerships that "link up with one another across every dividing line and become a movement to challenge slaveholder's religions distorted moral narrative."[800] While we build alliances with communities of those oppressed we must also expose every distorted narrative.[801]

## GOOD TROUBLE

*I knew someone had to take the first step and I made up my mind not to move.*

### —Ms. Rosa Parks

Civil-rights activist John Lewis was an anointed disrupter, a discomfort-generator. He taught that sometimes; we have to get into some "good trouble" and start some rebellions. Sometimes, we have to be demanding so we don't have demands made on us that shouldn't be made. The more that's tolerated – the more that's imposed until resistance is given. In this constant battle, "old inequalities persist, and new varieties of un-freedom emerge."[802]

Remember, the system isn't failing: It's working perfectly as designed to ensure parasitic White supremacy. The healing wisdom of Mother Africa celebrates humanity, inclusion, and mutual respect, even in an Empire wilderness. Being born Black in Empire means you have to clear your name in the cradle. It means that some of the babies in the crib next to yours think they're the only babies in the room and that they're entitled to Mamma's milk before you.

Yes, we'll fight — but there'll always be time for Coltrane and coffee, smiles or kisses from kids and sweethearts. Even Dr. King, after winning the Nobel Prize, went straight into Big Mama's kitchen to get her famous dessert.[803] Yes, we'll need a lot of energy for the fight, but we also need to sip some wine from time to time. Life's a journey without a map. You can map your own course; always remaining open to course corrections and new discoveries.

Bob Marley tells us: "The day you stop racing is the day you win the race."[804] When no one else is for us, we can take our own side. You're fiercely loved by folks who "love you simply because of who you are, not in spite of it, not with condition, not loved in parts."[805] Some in this global Melenated family will be mumblers and stammerers and some will be like Ida B. Wells speaking truth to power against deep pain just below the surface. As one Irish proverb reminds us: There's plenty of sky for plenty of birds. Those once inspired by Minister Malcolm or Dr. King's confrontational truth-telling will resonate with Black Lives Matter today. Those favoring Zora or Maya's lyrical poetry will resonate today with Ms. Amanda Gorman or Common. As a Yoruba wisdom truth reminds: "We cannot dwell in a house together without speaking together."

David Greenburg — in the article "*Why Last Chapters Disappoint*" — says many calls for justice end up as quixotic and flaccid cannonades of utopian idealism — even though optimism is the last thing we need to bring change. Greenburg writes: "solutions seem to be what our natural temper demands."[806] We don't need any more theoretical or impractical blueprints. History already has plenty of examples of strong change-agents who made a lasting difference.

Unified action is threatened by manipulative "hope-peddlers" who are "charlatan-like, blinding, obscuring."[807] Yet, paralyzing despair is also not an option. Either "America will begin healing their long-held drama around racist Whiteness and begin to evolve from race to culture and then to community" or "White body-supremacy will continue to be reinforced as the dominant-structure form of energy in American culture in much the same way Aryan supremacy dominated [Nazi] Germany."[808] False comfort is like the misleading euphoria of a victim dying slowly in an idling car, asleep in a sealed garage, or in the arctic-cold as their body goes numb.

Langston Hughes said liberals need to "realize that they have to be more than passively good-hearted, more than church-goingly Christian, and much more than word-of-mouth in their liberalism." If Martin or Malcolm had wanted, they'd still be living as a respectable Imam or beloved Pastor. South Africa's Archbishop Tutu could've embraced the safety of exile after witnessing Stephen Biko (and others) murdered. Fannie Lou Hamer or Medgar Evers, and many others, loved us more than they loved the isolating harbors of their own comfort and security.

The arrogant think they've everything to teach and nothing to learn.[809] African wisdom spirituality helps us to learn, grow, and listen to truths that make us more mature, humble, and able to take control of situations with balance and right-action. Italian astronomer Galileo Galilei (b.1564) was persecuted for proving that the world revolved around the Sun — not the other way around. In spite of evidence, some still think that everything revolves around them. Theirs is a flat-world and if they travel too far in one direction, they'll probably fall off the world's edge.

Everyone seems to ask the same question: What can be done? The short answer is we can all do something — figure it out! Future generations are coming up fast behind us, and we need to work so that their lives are better and their problems are different from our present problems. We don't get to choose when and where we are born, but we do get to choose where and how we live. In World War II, Pope Pius XII (Eugenio Maria Giuseppe Giovanni Pacelli) held beautiful church services in lofty shrines. History, however, will remember Pope Pius for one thing — what he didn't do: He was silent about Hitler at a time when speaking up would've meant all the difference in the world for millions of Jews and others about to die.

Dr. King wrote: "Evil must be attacked by the day-to-day assault of the battering rams of justice."[810] If you're a person of faith, do you really have a choice about confronting racist-oppression? My Dad (Tait) said: "Nothing beats a failure but a try." Justice — what love looks like in public — is a slumbering volcano waking-up.[811] Passive apathy is not an option.[812]

"To be Black and still alive in America is to know urgency."[813] We must avoid both the "tranquilizing drug of gradualism" and a haphazard (often angry) aimlessness which keeps us from long-term justice. Dr. Angela Davis, aware of the lure of quick solutions writes: "Advocacy of revolutionary transformation is not primarily about violence but about substantive issues like better life-conditions for poor people and people of color."[814] Dr. Davis thought the fresh views youth provided non-formulaic energy in the face of cosmetic-deceptions. Work shouldn't be wasted on temporary "solutions" that only rearrange the deck-chairs of a sinking Titanic.

Gandhi in India, Mandela in South Africa, Begnino Aquino in the Philippines – led grass-roots efforts. In Iowa in 2008, Barack Obama went door-to-door building a grassroots-campaign. After decades of inertia, the 1964 Civil Rights Act and 1965 Voting Rights Act, came through grass-roots activism.[815] Locals launched the Civil Rights Movement already struggling "before the arrival of national groups."[816] Momentum for progress in Empire has happened, not because of liberal White kindness, and in spite of conservative White intolerance.[817] As Ta-Nehishi Coates said of Empire-builders: "They made us into a race. We made ourselves into a people."[818]

America began as an experiment in a monocultural White control. Time now to see if it can become a pluralistic, multiethnic, and multicultural democracy. Instead, cross-burning terror, intimidation, and ethno-violence have our vulnerable democracy on "life-support." During slavery (the Maafa), folks found ways to imagine freedom and speak it into reality through deep faith and abiding hope. As Manning Marable wrote: "freedom is a fragile flower that must constantly be protected."[819] Dr. Angela Davis tells us that "optimism is an absolute necessity."[820]

## MOVIE NIGHT

*"Evil must be attacked by the day-to day assault of the battering rams of justice. . . . No social advance rolls on the wheels of inevitability. Each and every step toward the goal of justice requires sacrifice, suffering and struggle; the tireless exertions and passionate concern of dedicated individuals."*

**—Rev. Dr. Martin Luther King, Jr.**

September 15, 2023: Tonight's movie night and my (CVG) four little girls are waiting for Daddy: Tati, 15, Gretchen, 14, Clare and Gracey, 4½. Being

Daddy for four sweet girls is never boring — but tonight's extra-special: we're going to watch Disney's Mulan with popcorn.

In Birmingham, Alabama, sixty-years ago today, four little girls were midstream in their weekend. Later that day, Daddy might take them to a park for ice-cream. Now, however, it was church time. Parents dropped-off their girls at Ms. Effie McCaw's Sunday-school class and went upstairs for worship. The lesson that Sunday was from Matthew's Gospel: "Love your enemies."

September 15, 1963: Earlier, the KKK had placed 15 sticks of dynamite in the Sixteenth Street Baptist Church basement. At 10:25, it exploded. Dazed and stunned — fathers and mothers — bloodied and covered in white-dust, started sifting through the rubble. Fourteen children were wounded; 12-year-old Miss Sarah Collins lost her eye. Then, they found Sarah's sister and three other bodies: Four little girls taken from their Daddies — Miss Addie Mae Collins, Miss Cynthia Wesley, Miss Carole Robertson, all 14, and Miss Denise McNair, 11, my Gretchen's age.

A month later, a KKK'er responsible was given six-months and fined $100: Southern justice.[821] Earlier, 8,000 mourners came to the girl's funeral, where Dr. King said of the four sweet victims: "They say to each of us, Black and White alike, that we must substitute courage for caution. They say to us that we must be concerned, not merely about who murdered them, but about the system, way of life, and philosophy which produced the murders. Their deaths say to us that we must work passionately and unrelentingly for the realization of the American dream."

September 1963, James Baldwin compared German silence during Jewish suffering with White silence during centuries of Black suffering. September 15th, 1935, in Germany, Hitler announced the Nuremberg Race Laws, designed to strip Jews of all civil-rights. The Nazis claimed inspiration from American Southern "Race Laws" but had to adjust them because, even for Nazis, our Race Laws were too harsh. One cannot appeal to America's moral conscience because there is none that survives. After the Holocaust, one German said: "Evil is what other people do."

The bombing of a church and the infanticide of four little girls should never happen again. No more lives should be lost for no reason. And yet, here we are with more lives being lost: Ms. Breonna Taylor, Mr. Dijon Kizzee, Mr. Deon Kay, Mr. Ahmaud Arberry, Mr. Trayvon Martin, Ms. Sandra Bland, Mr. George Floyd, and so, so many others. Normalcy Never Again!

The bombed church was reopened in 1964. A new stain-glass window, donated by the citizens of Wales, was added (1965) with a Black Christ "with one hand flung wide in protest, the other in acceptance – remembering the sight of a Black figure twisting under the assault of fire-hoses, his arms up-flung. The jets of water transfixing the figure became the bar of a cross symbolizing all violence."[822] Above the chaos of everything is a hopeful, heaven-sent rainbow.

The popcorn's popped now: Time to skedaddle. My four little African American girls are waiting for me in the living-room. Movie's about to start. I cherish my girls — their big grins, the lilt of their laughs, the crinkle of their noses, even their rebellions. They matter so much to me, my little four. But not only them: Rest, sweet Miss Addie Mae, Miss Carolyn, Miss Cynthia, and eleven-year-old Denise. Watching in the dark tonight, beside my own, I will whisper your names.

## "RESPECT BLACK!"

*There's no quick fix to systemic racism but White people need to change. . . . Dear White people, we are the ones that need to change . . . we need to find a way to change what we do.*

**—Mark Cuban**

Our ancestors are our guiding North Star out of cold rivers of cynicism and resignation. Ancient wisdom, healing art, and spiritual movements of song and dance are empowering inheritances. Our ancestors have a message for us: We can turn this boiling cacophony of chaos into a soothing symphony of joy. We can live on the other side of confusion and embody health. When we "keep in contact with our ancestors," Sonia Sanchez wrote, "we can spread truth to our people."[823] No one can defeat us if we know who we are and where we are from.

"It isn't hard to sell people on optimism, but it's hard to keep them sold on it, especially in cynical times."[824] A Chinese proverb says that to move a huge mountain, we have to carry away one stone at a time. Righteous *Sankofa* bulldozes away fear: There is life beyond oppression.

Our motive has been to share our perspectives while helping you focus on the "fierce urgency of now." We're not writing to vent with a cathartic rant. Our communities need us to build highways of healing instead of rehearsing intractable problems. We need to guard against feeling overwhelmed — an acute, "learned helplessness" — which leads to paralysis of justice activism.[825] Sylvia Federici writes: "In a country where private property is defended by the largest arsenal of weaponry in the world, and where three centuries of slavery have produced profound divisions in the social body, the recreation of the commons appears a formidable task that can only be accomplished through a long-term process of experimentation, coalition building, and reparations. Though this task may seem more difficult than passing through the eye of a needle, it is also the only possibility we have."[826]

In Empire, racist-oppression is actually becoming more entrenched among both extremist White conservatives and entitled White liberals. Things will have to change, and it may take a while, so don't lose focus. We need to take possession of clear focus even as oppressors wallow in fantasies about their control. What is needed are radical transformations instead of incremental reforms. Afrocentric wisdom-confidence is not mythical idealism but a path towards the inner transformations we need to bring social justice. Bishop Henry McNeal Turner explained: We have to believe we are somebody. We need to know that nobody else will do for us what we can do for ourselves — and, most of all, we need to respect ourselves and others: "Respect Black!"[827]

Each one of us is a reason that all of us can be hopeful: Every day we survive offers all of us "a widening sky of possibility."[828] General Harriet Tubman has the final word for us: "If you hear the dogs, keep going! If you see the torches in the woods, keep going! If there's shouting after you, keep going! Don't ever stop: Keep going! If you want a taste of freedom, keep going!"[829] Because we are determined that evil injustices that have been assumed to be normal will never again be accepted as normal, our path forward is clearly lit by the enduring wisdom of our healing *Sankofa* heritage. Ashe: Normalcy never again!

# Endnotes

1  During 1890s Alabama, turpentine-worker "Railroad Bill," killed a police-officer, escaped, and proceeded to rob trains. Another desperado, John Hardy's last prayer before dying was: "Just give me time to kill another man, Lord." Litwack, *Trouble in Mind*, 439.

2  "Turpentine camps were rife throughout the South in the early and mid-twentieth century. . . . African Americans made up the majority of those working in this industry before and after the Civil War. . . . Turpentining was brutal, dangerous, and back-breaking work. . . . If "found" loitering, an African American man could be shipped to a turpentine camp and forced into labor." Finney, *Black Faces, White Spaces*, 120.

3  Cane, *Live Through This*, 29.

4  Wilkerson, *Caste: The Origins of our Discontents*, 68.

5  Ward, *America's Racial Karma*, 37.

6  Kendi, *Stamped from the Beginning*, 3.

7  Glaude, *Begin Again*, 7.

8  Fields and Fields, *Racecraft*, 1.

9  Ward, *America's Racial Karma*, 10.

10  Williams, "What Does He Mean by 'They Believe He is White?'" 79.

11  Smith, *Intimations: Six Essays*, 79.

12  Wilkerson, *Caste: The Origins of our Discontents*, 18–19.

13  Rev. Barber II. and Rev. Theoharis, "Normalcy - Never Again!" Https://www.thenation.com/article/society/king-rosa-parks-coronavirus/.

14  Owens et al., *Radical Dharma*, 78.

15  Hill and Taylor, *We Still Here*, 3.

16  Ward, *America's Racial Karma*, 9.

17  Glaude, *Begin Again*, 213.

18    Garza, *The Purpose of Power*, 285.

19    Kendi, *Stamped from the Beginning*, 42– 43. writes a basic idea of rac-
      ist-oppression is "individualizing White negativity and generalizing
      Black negativity. Negative behavior by any Black person became proof
      of what was wrong with Black people, while negative behavior by any
      White person only proved what was wrong with that person."

20    Solomon and Rankin, *How We Fight White Supremacy*, 173.

21    Hughley and Moe, *Surrender White People!*, 3.

22    Breitman, *Malcolm X Speaks*, 46.

23    Glaude, *Begin Again*, 184.

24    Davis and West, *Freedom is a Constant Struggle*, 7.

25    Fields and Fields, *Racecraft*, 118.: The terms "Negro," "Black," "White,"
      "Caucasian," do not appear in the Constitution. The terms that are
      used are "free persons" and the euphemism "other persons." Fields and
      Fields argue: "when well- meaning people affirm, for rhetorical effect,
      that the Constitution declared African Americans to be only three-
      fifth's human, they commit an error for which American historians
      themselves must accept the blame."

26    Finkleman, *Slavery and the Founders*, 1.

27    Glaude, *Begin Again*, 7.

28    Glaude, *Begin Again*, 47.

29    Leary DeGruy, *Post Traumatic Slave Syndrome*, 130.: During slavery
      one of these "roles" was breeder which led to rewards and has now
      "morphed and reemerged as the street/hustler womanizer and the
      more contemporary gangster/pimp."

30    In 1753, Benjamin Franklin stated: "Why increase the sons of Africa
      by planting them in America where they have so far, an opportunity of
      excluding blacks and tawnys, and an increase of the lovely white and
      red."

31    The final word of the anthem (so designated in 1931) "brave" rhymes
      with "slave."

32    Ward, *America's Racial Karma*, 24.

33    Fields and Fields, *Racecraft*, 47.: "The Nixon administration concocted
      the term *Hispanic* for the 1970 census."

34    Ward, *America's Racial Karma*, 93.

35    Glaude, *Begin Again*, 202.

36    Brogdon, *Hope on the Brink*, 2.

37    Magubane, *The Ties That Bind*, 70.

38    The third stanza notes that hirelings (criminals) and slaves will find no refuge in trying to flee: "That the havoc of war and the battle's confusion a home and a Country should leave us no more? Their blood has washed out their foul footsteps pollution No refuge can save the hireling and slave from the terror of flight or the gloom of the grace. And the star-spangled banner in triumph doth wave o'er the land of the free and the home of the brave."

39    Cross, *Say it Louder!*, 30.

40    Cross, *Say it Louder!*, 3.

41    Abdurraqib, *They Can't Kill Us Until they Kill Us*, 175. He continues: "All of us pushed to the margins, trying to fight for ourselves and for one another all at once. Celebrating while still fighting which is perhaps what represents the ethos of this country more than anything else. To bear so much witness to death that could easily be your own is to push toward redefining what it is to be a patriot in this country."

42    Johnson, "The Challenge of Black Patriotism," 31.

43    Cross, *Say it Louder!*, 237.

44    Magubane, *The Ties That Bind*, 3.

45    Ward, *America's Racial Karma*, 9.

46    Owens et al., *Radical Dharma*, 87.

47    Smith, *W.E.B. DuBois, Felix von Luschan and Racial Reform at the Fin de Siècle*, volume 47, number 1.

48    Finney, *Black Faces, White Spaces*, 41. describes Ota Benga, a Congolese slave purchased by Samuel P. Verner and exhibited at the 1904 World's Fair and the Museum of Natural History (1906). Benga was sold to the Bronx Zoo; "housed in the primate exhibit which promoted Ota Benga as the evolutionary missing-link." Benga had his teeth filed, had the floor of his cage littered with bones, and was labelled a savage. Crowds jeered and threw things at him daily until Benga tried to knife a visitor entering his cage. A New York Afro-Baptist group arranged for his freedom but Benga never returned to Africa; shooting himself in 1916. Henry Moss, an albino, won his freedom and earned a living displaying himself. Saartjie Baartman was exhibited throughout Europe as a possible "missing-link" She was displayed nude and repeatedly raped. She was taken to parties to stand naked. In America,

P.T. Barnum bought Joice Heth (1835) and was exhibited as General Washington's wet-nurse. When she died (1836), Barnum sold tickets (50 cents) for her public dissection. Barnum had other Africans exhibited such as "Madame Abomah" the 7-foot 9-inch "African Giantess" and many "African wild-men." Thomas Bethune was trained as a musical prodigy but performed as an untaught musical freak. Bethune died penniless in 1906. (Washington, *Medical Apartheid*, 89–90.).

49   Griffin, *The Seeds of Racism in the Soul of America*, 14.

50   Flora Shaw, wife of Lord Lugard, coined the term "Nigeria" in 1897 where claiming a shorter name was needed or Britain's "agglomeration of pagan and Mohammaden States." "Flora (née Shaw), Lady Lugard," *National Portrait Gallery*, https://www.npg.org.uk/collections/search/person/mp65594/flora-nee-shaw-lady-lugard.

51   Magubane, *The Ties That Bind*, 33.

52   Hochschild, *King Leopold's Ghost*, details this history.

53   Ani, *Yurugu*, 410. Ani is quoting poet Ayi Kwei Armah.

54   Marcus, *Haile Selassie I*, 48.

55   On the topic of African Americans owning slaves see Woodson, *Free Negro Owners of Slaves in the United States in 1830*, Westport,

56   Solomon and Rankin, *How We Fight White Supremacy*, 26.: "The police also murdered 21-year-old Mark Clark and sexually assaulted Hampton's pregnant wife."

57   Kendi, *How to Be an Anti-Racist*, 146. cites William Hannibal Thomas who authored a book entitled *The American Negro* where he claims, "Blacks are an intrinsically inferior type of humanity . . . [and] Black history is a record of lawless existence."

58   Leary DeGruy, *Post Traumatic Slave Syndrome*, 116.

59   Cross, *Say it Louder!*, 160–161.: "Owens was the CEO of Degree 180, an anti-Trump liberal-leaning website, which in 2015 featured such takes as 'good news' that the Republican Tea Party will eventually die off (peacefully in their sleep we hope),' according to Buzzfeed. Back then, Owens talked about Trump being a racist with an immigrant wife."

60   Wilson, Amos. *The Falsification of African Consciousness*. New York: Afrikan World Information, 1993. 3.

61   Kendi, *How to Be an Anti-Racist*, 141.: "The powerless defense says that more than 154 African Americans who have served in Congress

from 1870 to 2018 had no legislative power. It says none of the thousands of state and local Black politicians have any lawmaking power . . . The powerlessness defense says that more than 700 Black judges on state courts and more than 200 Black judges on federal courts have had no power during the trials and sentencing processes that built our system of mass incarceration. It says the more than 57,000 Black police-officers do not have the power to brutalize and kill the Black body. It says the 3,000 Black police chiefs, assistant chiefs, and commanders have no power over the officers under their command. The powerless defense says the more than 40,000 full time Black faculty at U.S. colleges and universities in 2016 did not have the power to pass and fail Black students or shape the minds of Black people. It says the worlds 11 Black billionaires and the 380,000 Black millionaire families in the United States have no economic power to use in racist or anti-racist ways. It says the 16 Black CEOs who've run Fortune 500 companies since 1999 have no power to diversify their workforces."

62  Bryant, *The Heritage*, 74.

63  Ward, *America's Racial Karma*, 35.

64  Bryant, *The Heritage*, 89.

65  Bryant, *The Heritage*, 95.

66  Williams, "What does He Mean by 'They Believe He is White?'" 72–83.

67  Mullen and Ho, *Afro Asia*, 7.

68  Lawson, *Running for Freedom*, 267.

69  Ford, *The Race Card*, 12.: "When the chips-were down, Thomas, whose career before that moment had shown little regard for cultural memory played the Race-Card: "It was racial politics jujitsu: use the enemy's strength against him. We have to pick a Black nominee. Fine. We'll give you a Black nominee so conservative that he makes Edmund Burke look like Che Guevara . . . Clarence Thomas hit the Liberals right between the eyes."

70  Franklin, *Another Day's Journey*, 15.

71  Cobb, *The Devil and Dave Chappelle*, 242.

72  Prisock, *African Americans in Conservative Movements*, 263.

73  Taylor, *From #Blacklivesmatter to Black Liberation*, 78.

74  Bryant, *The Heritage*, 84.

75   "African Diaspora Series, Part 1: History," *Gwinnett County Public Library*, February 8, 2022. https://www.youtube.com/watch?v=oSkeO1I2yjo.

76   Okpewho, Davies and Mazrui, *The African Diaspora*, 374.

77   Lincoln, *Coming through the Fire*, 87.

78   Bay, *The White Image in the Black Mind*, 220.

79   Sussman, *The Myth of Race*, 12.: "The Spanish Inquisition did not focus on religion alone but expanded to include ethnicity or race, introducing the notion of *limpieza de sangre*, or impurity of blood. It was about classes of people rather than just categories of belief." Sussman claims that less-gradual travel experiences also shifted the notion of neighbors.

80   Ward, *America's Racial Karma*, 33.

81   Linnaeus coined the term *homo sapiens* for the human species divided hierarchically into sub-categories. Kendi, *Stamped from the Beginning*, 82.: "He (Linnaeus) relegated humanity's nadir, *H. sapiens afer*, the bottom calling this group 'sluggish, lazy . . . crafty, slow, careless. Covered by grease. Ruled by caprice,' describing, in particular, the females with genital flap and elongated breasts.'"

82   Ward, *America's Racial Karma*, 52.

83   Sussman, *The Myth of Race*, 19. "Caucasian" was random because a favorite skull he had was from the Caucasus Mountains.

84   Hood, *Must God Remain Greek?*, 10.

85   Washington, *Medical Apartheid*, 37.

86   Garza, *The Purpose of Power*, 49.

87   Glaude, *Begin Again*, 113.

88   Wilkerson, *Caste: The Origins of our Discontents*, 52– 53.

89   In 2010 there are at least 1.6 foreign-born African descendants (half of which are Afro-Caribbean) in the US.

90   One of the earliest Black scholars of White behavior was John Russwurm from West India who graduated from Bowdoin College in 1827.

91   Hill and Taylor, *We Still Here*, 96.: "Whites could have interrupted the lynch mobs and stopped the extradical killing of innocent Black people by saying, 'Do not hang these people from trees because all lives matter.'"

92    Bay, *The White Image in the Black Mind*, 123.: "The most persistent single image the slave-songs contain is that of a chosen people."

93    Solomon and Rankin, *How We Fight White Supremacy*, 167.

94    Glaude, *Begin Again*, 17.: This is a reference to the quote from James Baldwin in *No Name in the Street*: "There are no clear vistas: the road that seems to pull one forward into the future is also pulling one backward into the past."

95    Wilkerson, *Caste: The Origins of our Discontents*, 54. Linda and Harold (a Civil Rights activist) Hale were their parents.

96    Kendi, *Stamped from the Beginning*, 118.: "Hemings gave birth to at least five and possibly as many as seven children from Jefferson, a paternity confirmed by DNA tests and documents proving they were together nine months prior to the birth of each of Sally's children." Kendi states that, altogether, Jefferson owned over six hundred people in his lifetime. Another article, from the Washington Post (7/7/2017) mentions the excavation of her basement-room underneath the house.

97    Stephens, *Skin Acts*, 163. Bob Marley's 1999 "Exodus" may be the world's most widely distributed album.

98    Garza, *The Purpose of Power*, 112.

99    Khan-Cullors and Bandele, *When They Call You a Terrorist*, 140.

100   Loretta Mary Maken (b. 1894, Brevard, NC) had a childhood where she was raped twice; resulting in two children being born which were given for adoption. She had two other children. Maken developed the character of "Moms Mabley" while performing at Harlem's Cotton Club and, later, the Apollo. She died in 1975 and was buried (plot #655) at the Ferncliff Cemetery in White Plains, NY. Also buried here are Malcolm X, Whitney Young, Paul Robeson, Betty Shabazz, James Baldwin, Ossie Davis, Ruby Dee, Thelonious Monk, and Aaliyah.

101   Solomon and Rankin, *How We Fight White Supremacy*, 240.

102   Bay, *The White Image in the Black Mind*, 167.

103   Solomon and Rankin, *How We Fight White Supremacy*, 83.

104   Youngblood, "Celebrating the 22nd Year of the Maafa Acknowledgment," https://issuu.com/thebrownsvillecollective/docs/maafa_newspaper 15__2_.

105   Glaude, *Begin Again*, 92.

106   Neil de Grasse-Tyson talks about how we are part of the universe; not apart from the universe.

107   Spencer, *The Rhythms of Black Folk*, 66.

108   Epps, *The Speeches of Malcolm X at Harvard*, 168.

109   Glaude, *Democracy in Black*, 6.

110   Stewart, *Black Spirituality and Black Consciousness*, 15.

111   When the blues became popular, many church-folk saw them as blas-
      phemous and the "devil's music." But they helped ease the pain of life.
      One Blues song from Texas said: "There's a lotta trouble here and more
      down the road. You'll always find trouble no matter where you go"
      (Litwack, *Trouble in Mind*, 454.). Another song about Blacks segregat-
      ing Whites sang: "Well, I'm gonna buy me a railroad of my own / Aint
      gonna let nobody ride it but chocolate to the bone" (456.). Dr. Dred
      "Perky" Scott of Harrisburg related: "The I aint got no woman blues
      is good if the woman you lost aint your wife. The I aint got no money
      blues is good if you are about to be robbed."

112   Browder, *Survival Strategies for African-Americans*, 3.

113   Tucker, *Black Reflections on White Power*, 116.

114   Vespucci (died 2/22/1512) wrote in his will (1511) he'd leave his estate,
      with five household slaves, to his wife. He was active in the slave-trade.
      Alsatian (German) scholars Matthias Ringmann and Martin Wald-
      seemuller named the continents. Ringmann wrote (1507): "I see no
      reason why anyone could properly disapprove of a name derived from
      that of Amerigo, the discoverer, a man of sagacious genius. A suitable
      form would be Amerige, meaning Land of Amerigo, or America, since
      Europe and Asia have received women's names."

115   Ani, *Yurugu*, 311. Ani is quoting the poet Ayi Kwei Armah.

116   Taylor, *From #Blacklivesmatter to Black Liberation*, 50.

117   "Friends of Pine Ridge Reservation," https://friendsofpineridgereser-
      vation.org/.

118   The pejorative sexual insult "squ*w" remains in over one thousand
      place-names in North America. First Nations women are ten times
      more likely to be murdered than non-Indigenous women. Four in
      five Indigenous women have experienced sexual violence accord-
      ing to the Indian Law Resource Centre. They also report that 96%
      of all reported sexual violence against Indigenous women is com-
      mitted by non-Natives. The sexualization of First Nations women
      in the Euro-American imagination was bolstered by the myth of
      Pocahontas ("playful-one") whose real name was Matoaka, meaning

"flower-between-two-streams." She was from the Algonquin nation and was a 10-year-old when John Smith landed in Virginia. She was kidnapped and brought to England where she was 20 when she converted to Christianity, changed her name to "Rebecca" and married John Rolfe. She died at age 21 in London and was buried in England.

119  Taylor, *From #Blacklivesmatter to Black Liberation*, 61.

120  "Religious Studies – The Final Colonization Of American Indians, Part 1 (Tink Tinker, wazhazhe udsethe)," *Religious Theory: E-Supplement to the Journal for Cultural and Religious Theory*, June 1, 2020.

121  Baradaran, *The Color of Money*, 69.

122  According to the 2000 census, about 54% of all African Americans live in 10 Southern states, 19% live in the Midwest and 18% live in the Northeast. New York, with over 3 million Afro-Americans (2.3 in New York City) has the largest number of African Americans. By percentage (2000), Gary, Indiana (85%) and Detroit (83%) have the largest Black population. By 2010 the numbers were closer to 58% with Louisiana (37%) and Mississippi (32%) having the largest Black populations by percentage. Vermont (96%) and New Hampshire (95%) are the "whitest." Of the South D.L. Hughley says (Hughley and Moe, *Surrender White People!*, 175.): "You can live for less in the South. But the chance to live is lower. It doesn't cost you money, it costs you years. In California, your life expectancy is 81 years but in Mississippi it's 74.5 years." He also writes (Hughley and Moe, *Surrender White People!*, 177.): "The South is still a mess for Black people. . . . Republicans are in charge all across the South."

123  Mazel, *And Don't Call Me a Racist*, 48.

124  Loewen, *Lies My Teacher Told Me*, 142.

125  Initially, there were White (mostly Irish) as well as Black indentured servants and all indentured servants could gain their freedom. This changed after the failed revolt by a young frontier Virginia planter named Nathaniel Bacon in 1676 who tried to lead a rebellion on behalf of indentured servants – Black and White. Kendi, *Stamped from the Beginning*, 53. writes: "Rich planters learned from Bacon's Rebellion that poor Whites had to be forever separated from enslaved Blacks."

126  Griffin, *The Seeds of Racism in the Soul of America*, 11.

127  Griffin, *The Seeds of Racism in the Soul of America*, 41.

128  Leary DeGruy, *Post Traumatic Slave Syndrome*, 72.

129  Litwack, *Trouble in Mind*, 487.

130    "It's impossible to reconcile that sense of gentleness with the knowledge more people were lynched here than anywhere else. Lynch is a
word that hides more than it shows."

McKinney-Whitaker, "Travel Notes from Pastor Stephen: Learning from Germans," https://www.derrypres.org/news/travel-notes-from-pastor-
stephen-learning-from-germans/.

131    Litwack, *Trouble in Mind*, 493. Even if it were only a little less stressful
it would be better. White Southerners had been telling Black Southerners to "know their place" and they concluded this was not their
place. It was only a place to rebel. Whites feared a drain of their workforce and did everything they could to stop the Great Migration North
in the only way that they knew how – not by making it better – but
by making it more oppressive. Police arrested Blacks at railroad stations as vagrants even if they had tickets and even if they were already
on trains. Those that got North found two things: A vastly different
America and also an America that was very much the same.

132    Wilson, *Judgment and Grace in Dixie*, 25. Wilson is quoting Walker
Percy from 1961.

133    Bay, *The White Image in the Black Mind*, 175.: Confederates were
known as "Secesh" and uniforms were called "Secsesh clothes."

134    When the Governor gave his speech, Carolyn Bryant, age-86, the
woman who claimed she was whistled at by 14-year-old Emmitt Till,
subsequently lynched, still lives in the state; without ever apologizing.
While in college, Governor Tate Reeves put on "blackface" and posed
beside Confederate flags. Fields and Fields, *Racecraft*, 163.: The present "Confederate Flag" is actually Lee's Battle Flag and not the "Bonny
Blue Flag" of the Confederacy. "Only in the 1890s did the Confederacy
become an emotional symbol" in the "cult of racism."

135    Hughley and Moe, *Surrender White People!*, 215.

136    Viola Liuzzo, a Michigan housewife, and mother of five, had come to
help fight for Civil Rights in Alabama and was driving 19-year-old Leroy Moton down a lonely stretch of Highway 80 (3/25/1965). A carload
of KKK members saw a White woman and a Black man together and
tried to pull over her Oldsmobile. Liuzzo sped away but they reached
her car and shot into the window. Liuzzo died but Moton, covered
in her blood, played dead and was left alone. In the trial against her
killers, Liuzzo's character was attacked. At one point when a prosecut-
ing attorney mentioned that Liuzzo was White, Klan attorney Matt

H. Murphy said: "White woman? Hah! Where's that NAACP card?" He then proceeded to display Liuzzo's bloodied membership card. McGuire, *At the Dark End of the Street*, 226. Murphy also claimed in defaming her that Liuzzo often did not wear a bra.

137 Elijah P. Lovejoy, from Alton, Illinois, was an anti-slavery advocate who was murdered.

138 In 2017, Jefferson Davis Elementary in Jackson, Mississippi was re-named Barack Obama Elementary. In 2020, how many Southern public schools are named after Confederate Generals? In June 2020 (Washington Post), the Southern Poverty Law Center claims that there were still at least 110 schools named after Confederates.

139 Litwack, *Trouble in Mind*, 196. Litwack records countless daily "micro-aggressions" that wore down Blacks at the expense of spiteful Whites on a daily basis. Usually, in any context, such as a bank or post office or store, a Black person would need to wait until all Whites had been served. Black women were not allowed to try on dresses or hats before purchasing them. Workplaces usually had separate spaces for Blacks and Whites with some exceptions such as during emergencies. Some Southern laundries posted signs "We Wash for White People Only" (234) while Blacks were expected not to pass Whites when driving or to be careful on dusty roads to avoid kicking up a cloud of dust on White walkers. Even after integration Black and White schoolchildren used different textbooks and the Bibles in courts used for witnesses to share on were separated for Blacks and Whites. Cemeteries were seg-regated and, when some became full some undertakers simply buried Whites on top of Blacks – "still another unique expression of White supremacy" (236). Sometimes Black folks used these realities to their advantage. One elderly Black man avoided a traffic citation by explain-ing to the judge: "Lord, boss. I sho' thought them green lights was for the White folks and the red lights was for us cullud folk" (240).

140 Because the goal was survival, many had to play dumb, wear masks, or play "possum": "For Black Southerners, however, experience taught them that misreading or misplaying a role might cost them their lives; they could afford neither garbled lines nor ad-libs" (Litwack, *Trouble in Mind*, 431.).

141 Gutzom Borglum, who went on to carve Mount Rushmore began work on the carvings in 1915. The carving at Stone Mountain is larger than Mount Rushmore. The work was completed, three sculptors later, in 1972. The 90 foot-tall (and 115 feet wide) carvings are cut into the

world's largest exposed piece of granite. The stone is estimated to be over 15 million years-old and was long a religious site for the First Americans. More recently, General Nathaniel Bedford Forrest, in 1867, became the first "Grand Wizard" of the KKK. Descendants of Forrest insist he never accepted the "honor." What is certain is that Forrest allowed the Fort Pillow massacre. The KKK consists of many incarnations, the first of which was December 24, 1865, in Pulaski, TN.

142   Perkins, "John M. Perkins Quotes" https://www.azquotes.com/author/ 44524-John_M_Perkins. In the same source Perkins says: "There is no reconciliation until you recognize the dignity of the other, until you see their view- you have to enter into the pain of the people. You've got to feel their need . . . We live out our call most fully when we are a community of faith with arms wrapped about a community of pain." (Perkins, *Beyond Charity: The Call to Christian Community Development*.).

143   Kendi, *Stamped from the Beginning*, 48.: "As early as 1657, English dissenter George Fox prevailed on his newly founded Religious Society of Friends, or Quakers, to convert the enslaved. Eschewing church hierarchies and preaching that everyone had access to the 'inward light of God,' the Quakers seemed primed to one day produce abolitionists and anti- racists." Kendi notes that other Quakers became slave-holders and supported early American Baptists who, led by Roger Williams, supported slavery. Kendi notes that, in April 1688, Mennonites advocated against slavery in the "Germantown Petition Against Slavery claiming: "In Europe there are many oppressed for their religion and here those are oppressed for their black color" (52.).

144   Bay, *The White Image in the Black Mind*, 177.

145   Kendi, *Stamped from the Beginning*, 44.

146   Magubane, *The Ties That Bind*, 141.

147   1 Corinthians 7:20-24. This passage, and the actions of St. Paul to return the slave Onesimus to his owner instead of granting him his freedom, led Dr. Thurman to vow never to preach from St. Paul's letters. Dr. King was a student of Dr. Thurman and also rarely preached from the writings of St. Paul. Dr. King did often cite 1 Corinthians 13. The "preachments" quote is from Allen, Theodore. (Allen, *The Invention of the White Race*, 36.)

148   Newkirk and Rutstein, *Racial Healing*, 56.; Newmann and Sawyer, *Everybody Say Freedom*, 26.

149  Bay, *The White Image in the Black Mind*, 179.

150  Bay, *The White Image in the Black Mind*, 182.

151  In the Vatican's Sistine Chapel, Michelangelo painted both God and Adam as White as was customary.

152  Bay, *The White Image in the Black Mind*, 181.: Some Black preachers imagined if Whites went to heaven, they'd try to make angels work. At funerals for Masters: "The slaves would all stand around and 'tend like they were crying but afterwards they would say that man is going to hell like a damn barrel full of nails." The doctrine of hell offered a great consolation.

153  Kendi, *Stamped from the Beginning*, 50.: John Locke thought "West African women had conceived babies with apes" (50). Locke was a 17$^{th}$ century architect of England's colonial policy towards Africans and First Americans. He was a *monogenecist* who believed in the initial equality described in Genesis is no longer relevant due to human failure. This is why mistreating Africans was allowable. Kendi describes two views: "Assimilationists argued *monogenesis*: that all humans were one species descended from a single human creation in Europe's Garden of Eden. Segregationists argued *polygenesis*: That there were multiple origins of multiple human species."

154  Griffin, *The Seeds of Racism in the Soul of America*, 68. Comedian Hughley notes (134–135.): "There are no White people in the Bible. None, not any White person. Jesus never saw a White person. . . . the only thing that made me think Jesus could be White was that he did turn over all those tables in the temple and didn't go to jail. But I know he's Black because he got convicted and killed for a crime he never committed. And he went around with twelve dudes with him all the time."

155  Spencer, *The Rhythm of Black Folk*, 99.

156  Prisock, *African Americans in Conservative Movements*, 298.

157  Kendi, *Stamped from the Beginning*, 68-69.: "New England churches routinely gifted captives to ministers. Mather named 'it' Onesimus, after St. Paul's adopted son, a converted runaway. Mather kept a close racist eye on Onesimus, constantly suspecting him of thievery." In fact, most Puritans thought that Blacks were even more dangerous than women-witches.

158  Sanneh, *Abolitionists Abroad*, 58.

**159**  Neiman, *Learning from the Germans*, 204.: "I think Southern Whites are very literal minded about the Bible and the Constitution as well because they're always searching for ways to read texts that would support their racial views. It goes beyond race to support a hierarchical worldview where everyone has a place: slaves, children, women. A typical Sunday morning service starts with a biblical text that gives legitimacy to whatever the preacher wants to say." (Charles R. Wilson)

**160**  Nieman, *Learning from the Germans*, 182.

**161**  Wilkerson, *Caste: The Origins of our Discontents*, 54.: [Connor] sought to win "the election of the man he wanted to win by framing the man he wanted to lose. He paid a Black man to shake the opposing candidate's hand in public as a photographer lay in wait."

**162**  Kendi, *How to Be an Anti-Racist*, 15.: " . . .an elite White Jesus Christ who cleaned people up through rules and regulations, a savior who prefigured Richard Nixon's vision of law and order."

**163**  X and Haley, *The Autobiography of Malcolm X*, 241–242.

**164**  Barber, *We are Called to Be a Movement*, 12. Barber wrote: "Jesus puts these same poor people at the center of God's agenda for the world" (15).

**165**  Zamir, *Cambridge Companion to W. E. B. DuBois*, 158. DuBois, positively, said the preacher was "the most unique personality developed by the Negro on American soil" as a "leader, a politician, an orator, a boss, an intriguer, and an idealist" who had a combination of "adroitness with a deep-seated earnestness, of tack with consummate ability" (Litwack, *Trouble in Mind*, 380.). In contrast, Booker T. Washington often joked about how some became pastors. A laborer in a cotton field would pray: "O Lord, de work is so hard, the cotton is so grassy and de sun am so hot. I bleave dis darkey am called to preach" (Litwack, *Trouble in Mind*, 387.). Another theme was that pastors were hustlers. One Southern ballad warned: "I wouldn't trust a preacher out of my sight, because they believes in doin too many things far in de night" (Litwack, *Trouble in Mind*, 410.).

**166**  Owens et al., *Radical Dharma*, 5.

**167**  An early social-justice preacher was Bishop Henry M. Turner (A.M.E.). Once when a congregation sang "Wash Me and I Shall Be Whiter Than Snow" he demanded the organist cease and that folks no longer sing that song: "The time has come when we must be proud that we are Black and proud of our race" (Litwack, *Trouble in Mind*, 392.). The church was also the place to mark the various seasons of life. Reverend Benjamin Mays, speaking of funerals explained: "The church would be crowded if the deceased had been a prominent citizen but it would be overflowing if the deceased had a bad reputation as everyone came eager to hear the preacher's verdict" (Litwack, *Trouble in Mind*, 381.).

168 McGuire, *At the Dark End of the Street*, 217. ABC that night had been showing *Judgment at Nuremberg*, an Academy Award winning TV premier about Nazi War Crimes but stopped the broadcast to report on the brutality at the Edmund Pettus Bridge.

169 Abdurraqib, *They Can't Kill Us Until they Kill Us*, 201.: The Black Church worships "without apology, without the politeness of anxiety."

170 Glaude, *Democracy in Black*, 126. Glaude says some churches have gone from a "prophetic" motive to a "profit motive" (138.).

171 Winters, *Black Fatigue*, 90. Winters claims 78% of Black men and 86% of Black women are certain God exists (116.).

172 Patterson, *Rituals of Blood*, 45.

173 Leary DeGruy, *Post Traumatic Slave Syndrome*, 57.

174 Ani, *Yurugu*, 218.

175 Ani, *Yurugu*, 22.

176 Davidson, *African Civilization Revisited*, 96–97., Finney, *Black Faces, White Spaces*, 57.: "Between 1619 and the early 1800s, approximately 400,000 enslaved Africans were brought to the United States . . . An additional 8 million worked the coffee and sugar slave labor-camps of Brazil, and the Caribbean and the mines of Spanish America."

177 Davidson, *African Civilization Revisited*, 121.

178 van Sertima, *They Came Before Columbus*, 37–49.

179 BBC World Service. "The Story of Africa. West African Kingdoms: Mali." https://www.bbc.co.uk/worldservice/africa/features/storyofafrica/4chapter3.shtml.

180 Feln, "Maya and Egyptian Pyramids: A Hidden Connection?" https://www.psychologytoday.com/us/blog/life-is-a-trip/201110/maya-and-egyptian-pyramids-a-hidden-connection.

181 Wilkerson, *Caste: The Origins of our Discontents*, 44–45.

182 Bay, *The White Image in the Black Mind*, 4.

183 Bay, *The White Image in the Black Mind*, 162.: Olaudah Equiano described first meeting Whites on slave ships with that view. One slave

ballad claimed: "White folks look like monkeys/when dey gets old, old and grey." Bay, *The White Image in the Black Mind*, 164.

184    Hughley and Moe, *Surrender White People!*, 46.

185    Taylor, *From #Blacklivesmatter to Black Liberation*, 44. This is a quote from Huey Newton of the Black Panther Party.

186    Mazel, *And Don't Call Me a Racist*, 27.

187    Baldwin, *Nobody Knows My Name*, 15.

188    Kendi, *Stamped from the Beginning*, 87. Speaking of the hypocrisy of American Christians to enslave Africans, Samuel Johnson said, "I am willing to love all mankind, except an American." (Kendi, *Stamped from the Beginning*, 103.)

189    Sanneh, *Abolitionists Abroad*, 12. Ownership of people became a legal issue from a taxation standpoint in New England's early history. Initially, there were arguments if slaves should be counted as property for taxation purposes and, if so, in what category? One Boston judge, Samuel Sewall, opposed rating slaves with "horses and hogs" (Kendi, *Stamped from the Beginning*, 67.).

190    Sanneh, *Abolitionists Abroad*, 14.

191    McDowell and Deborah, "Slavery as a Sacred Text," 81–91., in Sanders, *Living the Intersection: Womanism and Afrocentrism in Theology*, 83.

192    Pengelly, "Black female editor takes over Alabama paper at center of KKK furore," https://www.theguardian.com/us-news/2019/feb/24/alabama-newspaper-at-centre-of-kkk-outcry-appoints-black-female-editor.

193    Hamad, *White Tears/Brown Scars*, 3.

194    Hamad, *White Tears/Brown Scars*, 194.

195    Hamad, *White Tears/Brown Scars*, 194.

196    Wright, *African Americans in the Colonial Era*, 59. While Franklin later became a strident abolitionist, he once owned slaves. Kendi, *Stamped from the Beginning*, 96. cites Franklin as both an abolitionist and a racist citing his claim that, wile there were some "extraordinary Negroes," most were of "a plotting disposition, dark, sullen, malicious, revengeful, and cruel in the highest Degree." Before the Revolution, Franklin often appealed to his fellow Britishers that their rule made "American Whites Black" (Kendi, *Stamped from the Beginning*, 103.).

197    Magubane, *The Ties That Bind*, 23.

198  Magubane, *The Ties That Bind*, 24.

199  Wilkerson, *Caste: The Origins of our Discontents*, 42.

200  Finkelman, *Slavery and the Founders*, 164. Washington ordered, in 1775, after freed Blacks had fought at Lexington, Concord, and Bunker Hill, that they could no longer serve in the Continental Army. A famous poem about General Washington was written by Phillis Wheatley, a Wolof girl purchased by Wheatley's "as a living reminder" of the child they lost (Kendi, *Stamped from the Beginning*, 93.). The Wheatley's named her "Phillis" after the slave-ship that transported her from Africa.

201  Sally Hemings became the property of Jefferson when she was an infant as part of her wife's inheritance from her father, John Wayles who had six children from Sally's mother Elizabeth. Jefferson was 44 and Hemings was 14 when she came to Paris. Jefferson scorned intercultural sexuality and called for White women who gave birth to children with a Black father to be exiled. Jefferson wrote (Kendi, *Stamped from the Beginning*,118.): "Amalgamation with the other color, produces degradation to which no lover of his country, no lover of excellence in the human character can innocently consent" Kendi notes that Jefferson wrote this comment "in 1814 after he had fathered several biracial children."

202  Finkelman, *Slavery and the Founders*, 107.

203  Mazel, *And Don't Call Me a Racist*, 30.

204  Kaminski, *A Necessary Evil?*, 277.

205  Kendi, *Stamped from the Beginning*, 109-110., notes Jefferson never mentioned "the innumerable enslaved Africans who learned to be highly intelligent blacksmiths, shoemakers, bricklayers, coopers, carpenters, engineers, manufacturers, artisans, musicians, farmers, midwives, physicians, overseers, house-managers, cooks, and bi- and trilingual translators – all of the workers who made his Virginia plantation, and many others almost entirely self-sufficient."

206  Fields and Fields, *Racecraft*, 98.: "Knowing with equal profoundness two irreconcilable truths – that slavery was vital to the nation and, at the same time, likely to destroy it – Jefferson could not sustain . . .his self-deceiving transformation of racism into race." The authors are talking about the "cosmetic" "sleight-of-hand" that such a thing as "race" exists.

207  Finkelman, *Slavery and the Founders*, 152.

208 Franklin, *Another Day's Journey*, 18.

209 Ripon Wisconsin claims this term was first used in a Whig rally there (7/6/1854). Glasco (116) disagrees: "Followers of this party [Whigs], beginning in Pittsburgh in June of 1854 began to call themselves 'Republicans.'"

210 Sorin, *Abolitionism*, 102.

211 Bay (Bay, *The White Image in the Black Mind*,159.): Slaves spoke of "joining the Northerners or abolitionists to kill White folks." One ex-slave explained his reason for joining the Union Army: "I will join them too to help them kill the white folks." Another said he wanted to "be a soldier. Kill all the damn White people."

212 Magubane, *The Ties That Bind*, 72.

213 Kendi, *Stamped from the Beginning*, 219. The quote continued: "and if I could save it by freeing all the slaves, I would do that. What I do about slavery, and the colored race, I do because I believe it helps to save the Union." When about 220 Black prisoners were brought into Fort Pillow, they were massacred without mercy by General Nathaniel Bedford Forrest.

214 A cotton-farmer in Eastern Oklahoma, Charles Sam, convinced a number of fellow-farmers to go with him to British West Africa.

215 Franklin, *Another Day's Journey*, 58.

216 Loewen, *Lies My Teacher Told Me*, 174. Loewen notes that Chinese protestors in Beijing 1989 often carried images of Lincoln.

217 Tillet, "When Culture Really Began to Reckon With White Privilege," https://www.nytimes.com/2020/12/09/arts/black-artists-open-letters.html.

218 Neiman, *Learning from the Germans*, 136.: In the Civil War, of the 78,000 troops from Mississippi fighting for the Confederacy only 28,000 returned alive. A third of those who did survive lost at least one limb.

219 The movie *Glory* featured the first Black company in the Civil War, the 54th Massachusetts Regiment. Half of the soldiers in their first battle to capture Fort Wagner were killed in battle.

220 Berlin, *Freedom: A Documentary History of Emancipation*, 733.: When the Civil War ended the Northern occupying army "had shrunk to 227,000 men, Blacks made up roughly 36% of the total. Generally, Southern Black soldiers remained close to where they enlisted."

221 Franklin, *Another Day's Journey*, 86.

222 "(1867) Thaddeus Stevens," https://www.blackpast.org/african-american-history/1867-thaddeus-stevens-reconstruction/.

223 Darby, *Sisters in Hate*, 54.

224 Perry, *"Race" and Racism*, 159.

225 The infantilization of Black adults is what's behind the use of "boy" and "girl." Whites demanded to be called "Sir, Mr., Miss," etc. while calling Blacks "Uncle" or "Auntie." Litwack (Litwack, *Trouble in Mind*, 332.): "In Bolivar County, MS as late as the 1930s, postal workers made a point of deleting the term "Mr." on the envelopes of mail sent to Black residents."

226 An illustration of the pettiness of Whites was in laws in some municipalities: "A Black person was required to step off the sidewalk when a White person approached and, if male, to uncover his head" (Fields and Fields, *Racecraft*, 35.).

227 Leary DeGruy, *Post Traumatic Slave Syndrome*, 73.

228 Wilkerson, *Caste: The Origins of our Discontents*, 156– 157.

229 Convicts often worked 14-hours a day, facing dangerous conditions. Convicts clearing swamps were chained in knee deep pools of muck often filled with snakes, lice, and alligators. Even small cuts would get infected in fetid waters. Litwack (Litwack, *Trouble in Mind*, 273.): If convicts died "employers only had to replenish the supply with fresh bodies. Before the war we owned the Negroes . . .but these convicts we don't own 'em. One dies, get another. When the prison could not fill the demand for laborers, the police simply conducted one of their periodic sweeps, arresting Blacks on a variety of trivial offenses." Most were youth. In 1893 in Savannah GA, juvenile-home convict gangs consisted of 80% children under 15 "and one was only ten years old" (Litwack, *Trouble in Mind*, 274.).

230 Leary DeGruy, *Post Traumatic Slave Syndrome*, 67., Leary DeGruy, *Post Traumatic Slave Syndrome*, 69.: "What the Fourteenth and Fifteenth Amendments gave, Jim Crow took away."

231 This number is wildly below those actually killed. General Philip Sheridan reported that in only ten years (1865- 1875) only in Louisiana: "2.141 Negroes had been killed by Whites and 2,115 wounded." Briggs, William, and Jon Krakauer, "The Legacy of a Racist Massacre." https://www.nytimes.com/issue/todayspaper/2020/08/29/todays-new-york-times.

232 Briggs, William, and Jon Krakauer, "The Legacy of a Racist Massacre." https://www.nytimes.com/issue/todayspaper/2020/08/29/todays-new-york-times.

233 The Holcombe's were tobacco-farmers (Sampson, NC). Willie's father and mother, Charlie and Dillie wanted their boy to "be something" so they sent Willie to a technical college in Greensboro. After Willie graduated, he returned to help his parents. One day, he took their tobacco to the warehouse and never returned. Charlie went to town and found his son dead. Charlie buried Willie under a tall pine near the house. Litwack (Litwack, *Trouble in Mind*, 6.): "Charlie Holcombe was never the same again. The spirit he had once shown in his determination to succeed no longer animated him." The story happened so often and shows an incredible double-bind parents faced.

234 Litwack, *Trouble in Mind*, 307. He continues (307.): "A Texas youth was jailed for writing an insulting letter to a young White woman; a mob broke into the jail and shot him to death. Jeff Brown accidently brushed against a White girl as he was running to catch a train; a mob hanged him for attempted rape. For their 'utter worthlessness,' John Shaw and George Call, two 18-year-old youths (Lynchburg, VA) were shot to death after a mob's attempt to hang them failed." Rufus Moncrief was lynched (Wilkinson Co., MS) because "he did not display the expected humble demeanor and seemed reluctant to pull of his hat to them when they spoke to him" (Litwack, *Trouble in Mind*, 308.). A Black man (Muskogee, OK, 1914) was arrested for complaining when a White made sexual comments to a Black woman on the street-car. Randomness was added to injustice: Anthony P. Crawford was lynched (10/21/1916, Abbeville, SC) because "it was about time to have another lynching" (Litwack, *Trouble in Mind*, 309.). A Black newspaper (1911) called slaughters "The National Pastime" providing Whites a "welcome escape from the endless routine of drab working-hours and drab homelife." (Litwack, *Trouble in Mind*, 308.)

235 Steelwater, *The Hangman's Knot*, 205.: "Get your rope working easily through the knot by rubbing a little mutton tallow on it. Avoid getting any kinks on your noose, as they will cause the body to spin around when you drop it."

236 Litwack, *Trouble in Mind*, 281.: "After stripping Hose of his clothes and chaining him to a tree, the self-appointed executioners stacked kerosene-soaked wood high around him. Before saturating Hose with oil and applying the torch, they cut off his ears, fingers, and genitals,

and skinned his face. While some in the crowd plunged knives into the victim's flesh others watched with unfeigning satisfaction . . .The only sounds that came from the victim's lips even as his blood sizzled in the fire were 'Oh my God! Oh, Jesus! Before Hose's boy had even cooled his heart and liver were removed and cut into several pieces and his bones were crushed into small particles. The crowd fought over these souvenirs and the more fortunate possessors made some handsome profits from the sales. Small pieces of bones went for 25 cents apiece a piece of the liver 'crisply cooked' sold for ten cents." No one hid their faces.

237 Litwack, *Trouble in Mind*, 286.: The grocery store was in Atlanta. A postcard from the slaughter of five Black men (Sabine Co., TX, 6/15/1908) was distributed by the Harkrider Drug Company with the caption: "This is only the branch of a Dogwood tree / An emblem of White supremacy / A lesson once taught in the Pioneer's school / This is a land of White Man's Rule. / The Red Man once in early day /Was told by Whites to mend his ways. / The Negro now by eternal grace / must learn to stand in Negro's place / In the Sunny South, land of the free / Let the White Supreme forever be. / Let this warning to all Negro's be / or they'll suffer the same fate of the Dogwood Tree."

238 Discussions were had by church leaders as to "what constituted a good lynching and a bad lynching (Litwack, *Trouble in Mind*, 292.)." Those that were orderly and not given to signs of "rowdyism" were praised. A mob of about two thousand in Howard Texas offered the victim time to see his family and pray and the crowd voted on the method of death (burning). In Memphis, one enlightened radical spoke out he thought it "wrong to lynch a Negro who refused to be vaccinated" (Litwack, *Trouble in Mind*, 293.). One pre-slaughter prayer (Morgantown, NC, 1889) was criticized for being too long. Few pastors said anything against lynching: A scandal broke out (Bulloch Co. GA) when Rev. Whitley Langston expelled a congregant for organizing a slaughter.

239 Chapman, *Prove It on Me*, 5., claims James Weldon Johnson coined the term.

240 Cross, *Say it Louder!*, 104.: "Blood-drunk, they burned homes with families inside. They savagely tortured any Black person they could get their hands on. They seemed to delight in inhumanity. Those they didn't kill were left maimed, seared, and forever traumatized by the experience." Killings were done by 500 U.S. soldiers with machine-guns and vigilantes.

241   Tulsa, Oklahoma was part of the Louisiana Purchase. The first Black settlers were slaves of White and First American homesteaders. After the Civil War, freed Blacks came and, by 1921, made up 12% of Tulsa. Along with oil-wealth, Black businesses boomed and the Greenwood financial district became America's "Black Wall Street."

242   https://www.history.com/news/1921-tulsa-race-massacre-planes-aerial-attack. For a full account of the Tulsa Race Riots read: Hirsch, *Riot and Remembranc.*

243   Litwack, *Trouble in Mind*, 316.

244   The nine were all eventually released. https://www.zinnedproject.org/news/tdih/scottsboro-nine/

245   McGuire, *At the Dark End of the Street*, 162.

246   McGuire, *At the Dark End of the Street*, 36–37.

247   Ned Cobb said that Whites would meet returning Black soldiers at the train stations whenever they returned home and would "cut off the buttons and armaments off of their clothes, make em pull their uniforms off and if they didn't have another suit of clothes make walk in their underwear" (Litwack, *Trouble in Mind*, 331.).

248   Litwack, *Trouble in Mind*, 468.

249   Glaude, *Democracy in Black*, 160.

250   Franklin, *Another Day's Journey*, 90.

251   Ward, *America's Racial Karma*, 72.

252   Mississippi Senator Thomas Bilbo warned that the NAACP wanted intermarriage between Whites and Blacks. The first state to outlaw Black-White marriages was Virginia in 1691 and the last to allow it was Arkansas in 2000. Even though the law was changed in Alabama in 1967, a poll claimed 40% of Alabamians were against it in 2000.

253   McGuire, *At the Dark End of the Street*, 172.

254   Neiman, *Learning from the Germans*, 214. Of this death William Faulkner said: "If we in America have reached that point in our desperate culture when we must murder children, no matter for what reason or what color, we don't deserve to survive" (215.).

255   The "Emmett Till Interpretive Center" in Sumner, MS, does not display a picture of Emmett's face. Nearby, the "Emmett Till Historic Intrepid Center" run by John Thomas displays a photo of Till's face. Explaining why Sumner does not show the image Frank Mitchener

says: "In the South, courtesy is more important than truth" (Neiman, *Learning from the Germans*, 212.).

256 Till's grand-uncle, Mose Wright, courageously identified Milam and Bryant but the all-White jury pronounced their innocence. Gleefully, a few months later the two men took $4,000 from *Look Magazine* to tell of their murder.

257 McGuire, *At the Dark End of the Street*, 169.

258 Leary DeGruy, *Post Traumatic Slave Syndrome*, 85.

259 A recording showed King hit with 56 baton blows, 6 kicks, and 2 taser shots (each with 50,000 volts). King survived the beating but was found dead at the bottom of a swimming pool (6/2012).

260 Abdurraqib, *They Can't Kill Us Until they Kill Us*, 141.

261 Bryant, *The Heritage*, 120.

262 Glaude, *Begin Again*, 45.

263 Abu-Jamal, *Have Black Lives Ever Mattered?*, 65.

264 At the time, Trayvon was on a cell-phone call to Rachel, a girl at school being bullied he was trying to encourage.

265 Davis and West, *Freedom is a Constant Struggle*, 16. "Over an 8-year period, the killer made more than 45 unsubstantiated calls to the Sanford, Florida police department about people he termed as 'suspicious Black males'" (Khan-Cullors and Bandele, *When They Call You a Terrorist*, 168.).

266 Cross, *Say it Louder!*, 85.

267 Abdurraqib, *They Can't Kill Us Until they Kill Us*, 21.

268 Taylor, *From #Blacklivesmatter to Black Liberation*, 153.: "Dictators leave bodies in the streets. Petty local satraps leave bodies in the streets. Warlords leave bodies in the streets. Those are the places where they leave bodies in the street as object lessons" (Taylor, *From #Blacklivesmatter to Black Liberation*, 154.).

269 Kendi, *How to Be an Anti-Racist*, 71.

270 Khan-Cullors and Bandele, *When They Call You a Terrorist*, 247. Patrice Khan-Cullors wrote of threats: "What makes me stay is us" (248.).

271 Abdurraqib, *They Can't Kill Us Until they Kill Us*, 86.

272 Khan-Cullors and Bandele, *When They Call You a Terrorist*, 250.

273 Taylor, *From #Blacklivesmatter to Black Liberation*, 131.

274  Taylor, *From #Blacklivesmatter to Black Liberation*, 15.

275  Leary DeGruy, *Post Traumatic Slave Syndrome*, 114.

276  Garza, *The Purpose of Power*, 3.

277  Garza, *The Purpose of Power*, 3.

278  Taylor, *From #Blacklivesmatter to Black Liberation*, 171.

279  Davis and West, *Freedom is a Constant Struggle*, 15.

280  Psalm 56:8, David claims tears are stored in God's "bottle." A similar idea is in Revelations.

281  Washington, Harriet. *Medical Apartheid: The Dark History of Black Americans from Colonial Times to the Present*. New York: Anchor, 2006, 2.

282  Kendi, *Stamped from the Beginning*, 185. In 2020, a statue of Dr. J. Marion Sims, America's first Dr. Mengele, was removed from the Capitol Rotunda. Statues are also tributes to their makers values and pride.

283  Washington, *Medical Apartheid*, 62–63.: "He took a sick black baby from its mother, made incisions in its scalp, then wielded a cobbler's tool to pry the skull bones into new positions . . . Sims attempt to open the skull was based upon a scientific myth that the bones of black infants, unlike white infants, grew together quickly leaving the brain no space to grow."

284  Washington, *Medical Apartheid*, 55. In addition to slaves, sometimes freed persons were kidnapped and used as human guinea-pigs.

285  Washington, *Medical Apartheid*, 43.: "Kidnapped Africans en route to the America's were cursorily examined by ship-surgeons in an attempt to cut losses by immediately jettisoning those with such stigmata as Winterbottom's signs, a swelling of the lymph nodes found in those who harbored trypanosomiasis, or sleeping-sickness. Those who would not survive the Atlantic journey were thrown overboard." Southern physicians at auction-blocks were paid from \$2-\$10 for "soundness practice" [fitness for work] with judgments being challenged if a slave suddenly died.

286  Slave-masters would dye any greying hair, mask marks of small-pox or cuts, and add oil to skin while people being sold would hunch their heads or shuffle or put calomel on their gums or tongue to cause them to swell.

287  Smelling salts were often over-used which could lead to an epileptic fit. Owners "also blurred the therapeutic line by referring jocularly to whipping as 'medicine' for slaves. . . . [one doctor] prescribed 9 drops of essence of rawhide or 'oil of hickory' to a sick slave" (Washington, *Medical Apartheid*, 31.).

288  Washington, *Medical Apartheid*, 71. American plants were distinct than those in Africa.

289  Washington, *Medical Apartheid*, 107.: There was an "open desire for Black bodies to fill wards, surgical suites, operating theatres, autopsy tables, and pathology jars" but all of these "simply reflected the social realities of the slaveholding South." Georgian W.H. Robert performed amputations in school of maimed slaves, many who may not have needed surgery. Body-snatchers unearthed Black cadavers from cemeteries for dissections was common North and South. Entire shipments of Southern cadavers were sent to Northern medical schools (Washington, *Medical Apartheid*, 131–139.).

290  Washington, "The Organ Thieves," https://www.nytimes.com/2020/08/18/books/review/the-organ-thieves-chip-jones.html.

291  Perry, *"Race" and Racism*, 175. By 1922 there were 3,200 forced sterilization of prisoners, insane-asylum patients, the poor, and epileptics; 80% of these were in California. Laws changed in 1922, making it more widespread. Public health data was often manipulated to further a "racial agenda" such as the idea that most insane patients were Black.

292  Washington, *Medical Apartheid*, 204. Black women, once forced to procreate, became the focus of efforts trying to limit procreation. The use of Norplant was banned by 2002 but was prominently featured for tests in Black communities (1990-2002). The main reason it was taken off the market were severe medical side-effects including liver damage and cancer.

Another issue is that "there is no such medical entity as a crack baby," while fetal-alcohol syndrome is far more dangerous for pregnant mothers (Washington, *Medical Apartheid*, 214.). The "bad-mother story" has ramifications: In 1993, Black and Spanish-speaking heritage women were 72% more likely to have children removed by Child Protective Services.

293  Washington, *Medical Apartheid*, 217. At least 18 other people, not all Black, were injected with plutonium in tests. Elmer Allen, a train-porter, was injected with plutonium in 1947 after he was misdiagnosed as having cancer. He died in Italy, TX. Many of these tests took place in

prisons were "volunteers" were offered money or privileges for participation. Dr. Albert Kligman at the University of Pennsylvania became a
millionaire after developing a treatment for acne after years of experiments on prisoners at the Holmsberg Prison. Eugene Saenger oversaw
another radiation case, at the University of Cincinnati who conducted
200 radiation experiments on patients of which 150 were Black (1973-
1974). A five-million-dollar settlement (1999) included the agreement
of a permanent memorial which was placed "behind a dumpster and
nestled between the kitchen and a parking garage (Washington, 236).

294  Washington, *Medical Apartheid*, 271–283. These fenfluramine trials
resulted in serious long-term, damaging mental side-effects. Washington, *Medical Apartheid*, 284–289. also notes that a large number of the
50,000 lobotomies in the United States (1936-1960) were performed
on Black children. University of Mississippi Orlando Andy did many
of these lobotomies to "control emotions" of "African American children as young as 6 who he decided were aggressive and hyperactive.

295  Washington, *Medical Apartheid*, 357. Bailey later explained: "In New
Orleans, where it was cheaper to use N@#* than cats, because they
were everywhere and cheap experimental animals too there wasn't
much working there and the people we have been picking for the operation have really been at the bottom of the can. Nothing is going to
help them – shoot them is the only thing – so they started to use them,
Negroes – patients in hospitals."

296  Washington, *Medical Apartheid*, 359–367.

297  Cross, *Say it Louder!*, 2.

298  Kendi, *Stamped from the Beginning*, 259.

299  Griffin, *The Seeds of Racism in the Soul of America*, 22.

300  Abdurraqib, *They Can't Kill Us Until they Kill Us*, 15.

301  Ward, *America's Racial Karma*, 41.

302  Retica, "Remembering and Forgetting Milan Kundera," https://archive.
nytimes.com/6thfloor.blogs.nytimes.com/2011/04/18/remembering
-and-forgetting-milan-kundera/.

303  Magubane, *The Ties That Bind*, 229.

304  Solomon and Rankin, *How We Fight White Supremacy*, 260.: (of cooperative economics) "My checkbook's like the Bible, full of Black
prophets."

305 Rosa's grandmother, Louisa McCauley lived in Abbeville. Rosa had often visited the town.

306 Leary DeGruy, *Post Traumatic Slave Syndrome*, 198.

307 Washington, *Medical Apartheid*, 44.: "Thomas Jefferson declared, 'I consider a slave woman who breeds once every two years as profitable as the best worker on the farm.'" Pregnant women were worked as long as possible, and in hard labor until the fifth month. Women who were beaten were placed in trenches to protect their bellies. Kendi, *Stamped from the Beginning*, 42.: "In a 1736 exchange of letters on the inextricable sexuality and service of 'African Ladies,' White men were counseled in the South-Carolina Gazette to 'wait for the next shipping from the Coast of Guinny': Those African Ladies are of a strong robust Constitution: not easily jaded out, able to serve them by Night as well as Day.'" (42.): "White men continued to depict African women as sexually aggressive, shifting the responsibility of their own sexual desires to the women." Not one report of a Black woman in the colonies between 1728 and 1776 exists because these "were not considered newsworthy (42.)."

308 Hamad, *White Tears/Brown Scars*, 24.

309 Leary DeGruy, *Post Traumatic Slave Syndrome*, 61.

310 Jensen, *The Heart of Whiteness*, 228.

311 Fogel and Engerman, *Time on the Cross*, 85.: "Women who bore unusually large numbers of children became 'heroes of the plantation and were relieved from all fieldwork."

312 Jensen, *The Heart of Whiteness*, 227.

313 McGuire, *At the Dark End of the Street*, 153.

314 Wells carried a gun: "I'd already determined to sell my life as dearly as possible if attacked. I felt if I could take one lyncher with me this would even up the score a little bit (Litwack, *Trouble in Mind*, 424.).

315 McGuire, *At the Dark End of the Street*, 7. Reporting from Texas, she wrote about how the circus in small towns would segregate crowds as either "Caucasian" or "African."

316 Solomon and Rankin, *How We Fight White Supremacy*, 182.

317 Douglas, *Stand Your Ground: Black Bodies and the Justice of God*, 111.

318 Glaude, *Democracy in Black*, 76. Glaude writes: "White fear can be understood as anticipatory, a fear waiting to be expressed."

319 Douglas, *Stand Your Ground: Black Bodies and the Justice of God*, 115.

320   Hamad, *White Tears/Brown Scars*, 191. Hamad explores how the fluid-
      ity of Whiteness boundaries is contingent on the needs of capitalism.
      Capitalism "deliberately constructed" classifications "in order to per-
      mit and justify exploitation" of Blacks" (193.).

321   McGuire, *At the Dark End of the Street*, 166.

322   McGuire, *At the Dark End of the Street*, 180–181. One of her attack-
      ers, David Beagles, paroled in 1965, was determined to kill Betty Jean
      Owens. In 1969, he thought he'd tracked her down and he killed Betty
      Jean Robinson of Houston, a different person.

323   Their names were Officers Carl R. Burleson and Leonard Davis.

324   Their names were Herschel Gasque and Charles Berryhill. South Car-
      olina Governor Cole Blease often pardoned Whites when convicted: "I
      am of the opinion and always have been and have very serious doubt
      as to whether the crime of rape can be committed upon a Negro" (Lit-
      wack, *Trouble in Mind*, 269.)

325   McGuire, *At the Dark End of the Street*, 204. In Mississippi between
      1940 and 1965 only ten Whites were convicted for raping Black
      women or girls. The first White sentenced (1960) to the electric-chair
      was L.J. Loden who raped a 16-year-old. Judge Henry Lee Rogers
      recalled the jurors; insisting they modify the verdict and Loden was
      resentenced as "guilty with a recommendation for mercy" meaning
      he'd avoid execution (he was paroled ten years later). Laverne Yar-
      brough raped a 7-year-old, was sentenced to life, then immediately
      paroled. Ernest Wilson received 20-years after confessing to raping a
      Black woman the eve of her wedding day. Litwack (Litwack, *Trouble in
      Mind*, 247.): "Guilt and innocence were meaningless words: the Negro
      always blamed, always punished." One judge explained: "All the men
      are thieves, and all the women are prostitutes. It's their natur' to be
      that way and they'll never be no other way" (Litwack, *Trouble in Mind*,
      248.). Popular stories in Black communities joked about a White con-
      vertible-driver who hit two Black pedestrians. One was knocked into
      the backseat of the car and was charged with illegal-entry; the other
      was dragged down the road and was arrested for leaving the scene of a
      crime (Litwack, *Trouble in Mind*, 261.).

326   Solomon and Rankin, *How We Fight White Supremacy*, 47.

327   McGuire, *At the Dark End of the Street*, 275.

328   McGuire, *At the Dark End of the Street*, 174.

329   McGuire, *At the Dark End of the Street*, 62.

330 McGuire, *At the Dark End of the Street*, 104.

331 I Peter 3:7

332 Hamad, *White Tears/Brown Scars*, 50.

333 Cross, *Say it Louder!*, 54., Kendi, *How to Be an Anti-Racist*, 114–115.: "Slaveholders more often worked Light people in the house and Dark people in the fields. . . . A body will be all the more animalistic the darker it is. . . . Slaveholders paid much more for enslaved Light females than for their Dark counterparts." This was a form of 'Light Privilege' and it was said that, in Courts, 'the lighter the skin, the lighter the sentence.' Skin-bleaching, as practiced by Michael Jackson, Sammy Sosa, and Lil' Kim is still an issue with "fairness creams in India" and "skin lighteners used by 70% of women in Nigeria, 35% in South Africa, 59% in Togo and 40% in China." (Kendi, *How to Be an Anti-Racist*, 119.).

334 Joseph, *The Black Friend*, 174.

335 Garza, *The Purpose of Power*, 7.

336 Wallace, *Black Macho and the Myth of the Superwoman*, 13.

337 Jensen, *The Heart of Whiteness*, 307.

338 Dodson, *We Refuse to Be Silent*, 186.

339 Jordan-Zachery, *Black Women, Cultural Images, and Social Policy*, 149.

340 Solomon and Rankin, *How We Fight White Supremacy*, 232.

341 Murphy, *Jim Crow Capital*, 204.

342 Before this boycott, in June 20-24, 1953, there was also a successful bus-boycott in Baton Rouge, Louisiana.

343 Owens et al., *Radical Dharma*, 155.

344 Davis and West, *Freedom is a Constant Struggle*, 67.

345 Taylor, *From #Blacklivesmatter to Black Liberation*, 11.

346 Solomon and Rankin, *How We Fight White Supremacy*, 210.

347 McGuire, *At the Dark End of the Street*, 192.

348 Solomon and Rankin, *How We Fight White Supremacy*, 174.

349 Opie, *Southern Food and Civil Rights*, 119.: "The Big Apple had two signature sandwiches – pig ear sandwiches and hot smoked sausage sandwiches (called smokes) dressed in slaw and mustard which cost $1 each."

350 McGuire, *At the Dark End of the Street*, 193.

351   Neiman, *Learning from the Germans*, 138. The entire quote reads: "The Ole Miss of the plantation was by far the most important person in Mississippi. She held the keys to every lock on the plantation. She was the monitor of culture, the developer of Christian virtue, the matchmaker and the director of education and training." The WKKK was formed in 1923.

352   Hamad, *White Tears/Brown Scars*, 134. The term "Sambo" comes from the Spanish "Zambo" – a derogatory term for a mixed person.

353   Kendi, *Stamped from the Beginning*, 241. Sadly, Sojourner Truth rose in support of this misguided statement against the Fourteenth Amendment: "White women are a great deal smarter, while colored women do not know scarcely anything" (Kendi, *Stamped from the Beginning*, 242.).

354   Garza, *The Purpose of Power*, 188.

355   Griffin, *The Seeds of Racism in the Soul of America*, 100.

356   Griffin, *The Seeds of Racism in the Soul of America*, 111.

357   Morris, *Black Stats*, 147.

358   Hamad, *White Tears/Brown Scars*, 8.

359   Hamad, *White Tears/Brown Scars*, 92–93.: Harper concluded, "While there exists this brutal element in society. . . . If there is any class of people who need to be lifted out of their airy nothings and selfishness, it is the White women of America."

360   Jensen, *The Heart of Whiteness*, 23.

361   Jensen, *The Heart of Whiteness*, 25.

362   Jensen, *The Heart of Whiteness*, 25.

363   Garza, *The Purpose of Power*, 190.

364   Banks, *Race, Rhetoric and Technology*, 1.

365   Hamad, *White Tears/Brown Scars*, 250.

366   Kendi, *Stamped from the Beginning*, 192.

367   Hughley and Moe, *Surrender White People!*, 219.: "It was announced that she'd be put on the back, but Andrew Jackson would stay on the front. It was too much to get rid of Andrew Jackson. Never mind how weird it was that a woman who helped hundreds of people escape slavery would be sharing a bill with a man who owned hundreds of slaves."

368   Glaude, *Democracy in Black*, 63.

369 "Dr. Bethune's Last Will & Testament." *Bethune-Cookman University.* https://www.cookman.edu/history/last-will-testament.html.

370 Bird, *The Healing Power of African-American Spirituality*, 15.

371 Kendi, *Stamped from the Beginning*, 429.

372 Hill and Taylor, *We Still Here*, 82.

373 Cross, *Say it Louder!*, 175. They also have "significant economic power" spending "an estimated \$1.5 trillion annually" (Cross, *Say it Louder!*, 176.).

374 Solomon and Rankin, *How We Fight White Supremacy*, 261. note that abolitionist John Swett Rock used the term in 1858.

375 Solomon and Rankin, *How We Fight White Supremacy*, 260.: "To get to the place of feeling beautiful we must first resist."

376 Abdurraqib, *They Can't Kill Us Until they Kill Us*, 187.

377 Khan-Cullors and Bandele, *When They Call You a Terrorist*,124.

378 Bay, *The White Image in the Black Mind*, 156. Ex-slave Bibb assumed "that abolitionists could not belong to the White race" (161.).

379 Bay, *The White Image in the Black Mind*, 158–159.: Prosser exempted killing of Frenchmen, Quakers, and Methodists because they were potential allies.

380 Hughley and Moe, *Surrender White People!*, 59.

381 Bay, *The White Image in the Black Mind*, 138. A voice told him: "Such are you called to see and let it come rough or smooth you must surely bear it."

382 Chisholm, "Speech at Howard University, Washington, D.C.-April 21, 1969," https://americanradioworks.publicradio.org/features/black-speech/schisholm-2.html.

383 Fields and Fields, *Racecraft*, 279.

384 Litwack, *Trouble in Mind*, 147.

385 Reed, *Renewing Black Intellectual History*, 36.

386 Baradaran, *The Color of Money*, 63.

387 Booker T. Washington defies a simplistic caricature. He said things that can easily be understood as anti-Black. To a White audience he lamented Blacks after the Civil War being able to vote because they didn't have "experience, preparation, and ordinary intelligence" to succeed (Litwack, *Trouble in Mind*, 368.). At the same time, he also

"covertly helped to finance the appeals to the courts, and ultimately the legal strategies [that] would attract the support of black activists particularly the newly organized NAACP" (Litwack, *Trouble in Mind*, 370.).

388   Booker T. Washington died (11/1915) of hypertension related to astronomically high blood pressure. Washington worked with Julius Rosenwald, the Chicago-based President of Sears Roebuck to raise almost $2 million dollars for the Tuskegee Institute. Inspired by Washington's passion for Black education, Rosenwald went on to fund the building of over 5,000 Black schools across the rural South. Finally, people have replaced the accurate – but unfair – appellation "the Great Accommodator" to appreciate the tangible results he accomplished.

389   After completing his BA at Fisk, DuBois was the first Black American at the University of Berlin. After his Ph.D. (Harvard), he taught classics at Wilberforce College (OH) before teaching at the University of Pennsylvania. His research at the latter focused on the social causes of pathology in Philadelphia's Seventh Ward. From 1910 until 1934, he was the founder and the editor-in-chief of the Crisis Magazine (NAACP).

390   Owens et al., *Radical Dharma*, 195.

391   The term "Marxist" can refer to an economic critique of capitalism or a political solution.

392   Watson, *The Souls of White Folk*, 81. "Mulatto" is a Spanish word that refers to breeding a donkey and a horse.

393   Watson, *The Souls of White Folk*, 81. The phrase refers to one defined by an oppressor with assigned stereotypes.

394   DuBois challenged HBCU leadership to consider new ways to educate and not depend solely on models, methods, approaches, and curricula of the White academy. He rejected any concepts of assimilation and cooperation with structures rooted in oppressive assumptions.

395   Magubane, *The Ties That Bind*, 147. In 1951, DuBois (82) was arrested as an 'agent of a foreign principal' (presumably the USSR).

396   Dodson, *We Refuse to Be Silent*, 2.

397   DuBois uses the German word *Bildung* (self-education). Williams, "W. E. B. Du Bois and the Socio-Political Structures of Education,", 2004.

398   Zamir, *Cambridge Companion to W. E. B. DuBois*, 151.

399   Glaude, *Democracy in Black*, 6.

400  Watson, *The Souls of White Folk*, 77.

401  Owens et al., *Radical Dharma*, 192.

402  Kendi, *Stamped from the Beginning*, 309. Woodson lived at a time where academic racism was "mainstream." In 1916, the eugenics movement was growing through the work of Margaret Sanger and Madison Grant, a New York lawyer, who published *The Passing of the Great Race* that claimed that Nordics were superior to all others. Adolf Hitler studied the book and later wrote to Grant calling his book "my Bible" (Kendi, *Stamped from the Beginning*, 311.). Another American that Hitler adored was Henry Ford who was the only non-German (the other was Mussolini) who received the Grand Service Cross of the Supreme Order of the German Eagle (1938). Madison Grant's views on Black Americans were insidious: "As long as the dominant imposes its will on the servient race and as long as they remain in the same relation to the Whites as in the past, the Negroes will be a valuable element in the community but once raised to social equality their influence will be destructive to themselves and to the Whites" (Sussman, 89).

403  Akbar, *Know Thyself*, 5. We should never cooperate in our own exploitation.

404  Fields and Fields, *Racecraft*, 189.: Education is "what schoolbook lessons and non-schoolbook lessons they should receive, about where they stand in the world and what the world is made of."

405  Leary DeGruy, *Post Traumatic Slave Syndrome*, 150.

406  Teaching the holocaust in modern Germany focuses on helping society avoid future barbarities.

407  Magubane, *The Ties That Bind*, 27.

408  "Woodson in Words and Images," *Carter G. Woodson Home.*
https://www.nps.gov/cawo/learn/historyculture/woodson-in-words-and-images.htm

409  Hunter, *I Hate People who Hate Black People*, 122.

410  Lewis, *Marcus Garvey*, 77.

411  Watson, *The Souls of White Folk*, 34.

412  Bay, *The White Image in the Black Mind*, 211. Garvey stated that, while Europeans lived in caves, Africans lived in palaces (213.).

413  Williams, *Anatomy of Four Race Riots*, 13.

414   Watson, *The Souls of White Folk*, 54. Garvey noted that Moorfield
      Storey, a White lawyer was chosen as the first President of the newly
      launched NAACP. Storey held the position for twenty years, until
      1929.

415   Watson, *The Souls of White Folk*, 45.

416   Bantum, *Redeeming Mulatto*, 45. The quote continues: "pointing back
      to the falsity of the claims concerning purity. Their lives are sheer
      performativity. Mulattos/as are constantly negotiating their relation-
      ship and realities because their lives are negotiating the lines (and
      practices) that constitute racial lives (either White or Black) as well
      as seeking to live into racial space despite the impossibility. Attempts
      to live into such entrenched and powerful modes of identification are
      vital aspects of what is the inherently political body of the interracial
      person." (45–46.) The modern version of this term is "multiracial: "A
      ridiculous term because all humans are "multiracial" and there's no
      such thing as a 'race.' The term "mulatto" first appeared on an 1850
      census. Data from the 1970 census reports "24% of Americans listed
      as 'White' probably had African ancestors while more than 80% of
      those listed as 'Black' had non-White ones (Fields and Fields, *Race-
      craft*, 3.). These concepts relate to the extremely bio-racist concept of
      "racial purity."

417   Cane, *Live Through This*, 137. Jean Toomer, Anatole Broyard, Barack
      Obama, Kamala Harris, W.E.B. DuBois, Fredrick Douglass, and Colin
      Kaepernick are just a few of the many individuals who expose "the
      deeper understanding that these categories are too restrictive to fit
      anyone" (Fields and Fields, *Racecraft*, 109.). Another resource on this
      topic is *Fade to Black and White: Interracial Images in Popular Culture*
      by Erica Chito Childs. Toronto: Rowman and Littlefield, 2009.

418   "Though pardoned by Coolidge in 1927, he was deported as an unde-
      sirable alien." Bell, *Faces at the Bottom of the Well*, 46.

419   The Afro-American Cooking School (AACS) in the mid-1930s was
      inspired by Garvey. In 1919, he organized the "Negro Factories As-
      sociation" (NFC) to ran groceries and restaurants.

420   In Cleveland (1921) Garvey formed the *United Negro Improvement
      Association* (UNIA).

421   Beckham, *Garvey Lives!*,

422   Snyder, *On Tyranny*, 51.

423 Opie, *Southern Food and Civil Rights*, 61.: "In order to keep the car-
pools running and make the boycott a success, Gilmore and other
Black women who supported the boycott organized a baking club on
the east and west sides of the city named "the club from nowhere"
(TCN). The club name allowed them to earn money for the movement
without raising suspicions of White officials and members of the Klan.
Many White citizens of Montgomery purchased baked goods from
club members not knowing that they had inadvertently supported the
MIA's boycott."

424 Snyder, *On Tyranny*, 54. The quote, attributed to Winston Churchill,
refers to the determination of the British. Churchill famously said history would be kind to him because he would write it himself.

425 Owens et al., *Radical Dharma*, 197.

426 Watson, *The Souls of White Folk*, 75.

427 Joseph, *Neighborhood Rebels*, 21.

428 Malcolm argued that if he had never moved to Boston he would have
become a "brainwashed-Black Christian."

429 Cobb, *The Devil and Dave Chappelle*, 217.

430 Kendi, *How to Be an Anti-Racist*, 125.: Elijah Muhammad wrote in
*Message to the Blackman in America* (1965) "Six thousand years ago in
an all-Black world, a wicked Black scientist named Yakub was exiled
alongside his 59,999 followers to an island in the Aegean Sea. Yakub
plotted his revenge against his enemies: to create upon the earth a devil race.' . . . He (Yakub) killed all Dark babies and forced Light people
to breed. Bay, *The White Image in the Black Mind*, 212.: "The story of
Yakub clearly goes back at least to Prophet W. D. Fard, who rose to
prominence in the 1930s."

431 Karim, *The End of White World Supremacy*, 79.

432 Glaude, *Democracy in Black*, 91. Minister Malcolm advocated for
"frank and fearless speech" (95.).

433 Malcolm X, "A Summing Up: Louis Lomax interviews Malcolm X (1963),"
https://teachingamericanhistory.org/document/a-summing-up-
louis-lomax interviews-malcolm-x/.

434 West, *Beyond Eurocentrism and Multiculturalism*, 83.

435 King, Jr., "Chapter 13: Pilgrimage to Nonviolence," https://kinginsti-
tute.stanford.edu/chapter-13-pilgrimage-nonviolence.

436   After his father visited Germany in 1934, he changed his name (also
      Michael Luther) to Martin Luther and changed his son's name at the
      same time. King's official birth-certificate was not amended legally
      until 1957.

437   Abdurraqib, *They Can't Kill Us Until they Kill Us*, 15. The quote contin-
      ues: "No matter how far your wings strength, they were still born from
      a single place. For those of us with an eye always facing toward home
      Chance [the Rapper] inspires."

438   Paschal's Restaurant (opened, 1947) was where MLK and his team
      reserved a meeting room to plan the March on Washington and the
      Mississippi Freedom Summer while eating Robert Paschal's amazing
      fried chicken.

439   Carson and Holloran, "A Knock at Midnight,"

440   Jones, *Beyond the Messy Truth*, 5.

441   Genesis 37:19-20.

442   Alexander, *The New Jim Crow*, 246.

443   Davis and West, *Freedom is a Constant Struggle*, 64.

444   The March on Washington was organized in its myriad practical details
      by Bayard Rustin and A. Philip Randolph with an operating budget of
      only $175,000. Four church organizations also helped in the planning
      including the NCC, the UPC, the NCC, and the AJC. Churches aided
      in making two bag lunches for each marcher containing, according to
      Opie (*Southern Food and Civil Rights*, 125.), a peanut-butter and jelly
      sandwich, an apple or another fruit, a brownie, and a soft-drink.

445   Glaude, *Democracy in Black*, 107.: "Reagan put the final nail in the
      coffin for King that conservatives had been building since his death,
      part of a deliberate pattern that defined modern conservative ap-
      proaches to the issue of race in America." Glaude continues (115.):
      "Like vultures we have picked clean his bones, such that his powerful
      dream confirms the illusion of our national innocence and keeps us
      sleepwalking while Black America withers."

446   Barber, *We are Called to Be a Movement*, 87. The entire quote reads:
      A nation that continues year after year to spend more money on mili-
      tary defense than on programs of social uplift is approaching spiri-
      tual death. The bombs in Vietnam explode at home. They destroy the
      hopes and possibilities of a decent America. I am disappointed with
      our failure to deal positively with the triple evils of racism, extreme
      materialism, and militarism.

447 After his death, five more collections of his papers and sermons were also published.

448 Dorrien, *Breaking White Supremacy*, 376.

449 Glaude, *Begin Again*, 159.

450 Colley, *Ain't Scared of Your Jail*, 17. King, released on bail the same day, later said he regretted posting bail.

451 Hodgson, *Martin Luther King*, 10.

452 Watson, *The Souls of White Folk*, 138.

453 Minister Malcolm was shot around 3:30. The ballroom was reopened at 7 for a scheduled dance event. Although initial police records report five assailants only three were charged and two were dubiously charged.

454 Boesak, *Black theology, black power*, 170.

455 Williams, "What Does He Mean By, They Believe They are White?" 72-83, in *Between the World of Ta- Nehishi Coates and Christianity*, Evans, David, and Peter Dula, eds, Eugene, OR: Cascade, 2018, 75–76.

456 Litwack, *Trouble in Mind*, 205.

457 Thandeka explains Whiteness is necessary for oppression: "It's not merely that whiteness is oppressive or false; it is that Whiteness is both oppressive and false." Thandeka, *Learning to be White*, 169. https://journals.sfu.ca/rpfs/index.php/rpfs/article/viewFile/247/246.

458 Garza, *The Purpose of Power*, 166.

459 In 1890, Black politician Isaiah Montgomery suggested a Faustian "truce" that Blacks would surrender the right to vote in exchange for an end to racial conflict: "There was simply no way to win when dealing with White folks. If they acted too obsequiously, they sometimes aroused suspicion and if they readily agreed to vote the way Whites told them to vote, they sometimes aroused suspicion" (Litwack, *Trouble in Mind*, 367.).

460 Litwack, *Trouble in Mind*, 225. In 1904 there were 1,342 Black voters in Mississippi. By 1910, that number had fallen further.

461 Litwack, *Trouble in Mind*, 226. Local Whites told James Plunkett of Virginia: "We don't stop Colored from voting if he wants to vote, but a bullet would follow him out the door" (Litwack, *Trouble in Mind*, 228.). Those who voted were seen as "uppity."

462 Litwack, *Trouble in Mind*, 225. Also used were poll-taxes, property ownership, and "grandfather" clauses for the non-registered.

463 DiAngelo, *White Fragility*, 91.

464 Solomon and Rankin, *How We Fight White Supremacy*, 225.

465 Bryant, *The Heritage*, 20.

466 Thoreau scholars argue whether or not he ever voted.

467 Bryant, *The Heritage*, 21.

468 Davis and West, *Freedom is a Constant Struggle*, 4.

469 Cross, *Say it Louder!*, 67. Certainly, the majority of courtroom decisions for Blacks are made by Whites.

470 Irish Central Staff, "On his birthday" https://www.irishcentral.com/roots/history/robert-f-kennedy-quotes.

471 Wilkerson, *Caste: The Origins of our Discontents*, 25. LBJ said poor Southerners were proud as long as someone was beneath them.

472 Dixiecrat and anti-integrationist Strom Thurmond fathered a Black daughter, Essie Mae.

473 Kendi, *Stamped from the Beginning*, 389.

474 Taylor, *From #Blacklivesmatter to Black Liberation*, 56. The quote is from H. R. Haldeman. Taylor writes (Taylor, *From #Blacklivesmatter to Black Liberation*, 63.): "Nixon officials worked to narrow the definition of racism to the intentions of individual actors while countering the idea of institutional racism by focusing on 'freedom of choice' as a way to explain differential outcomes." To illustrate this, George Romney, Nixon's HUD Director talked about "crisis problem people" saying "Housing itself cannot solve the problems of people who may be suffering from bad habits, lawlessness, laziness, unemployment, inadequate education . . . (Taylor, *From #Blacklivesmatter to Black Liberation*, 71.)."

475 Prisock, *African Americans in Conservative Movements*, 27.

476 George Wallace won a victory when he spoke at Harvard University. Wallace's role is vital because he offered "Conservatives an avenue to recreate themselves" (Prisock, *African Americans in Conservative Movements*, 40.).

477 Prisock, *African Americans in Conservative Movements*, 83.: "I tried hard to win friendship among Blacks [but] I couldn't do it. I talked

with Black leaders after my election in 1980 and they went out and criticized me in horrible ways … so I said to hell with 'em."

478 DiAngelo, *White Fragility*, 154.

479 Lipsitz, *The Possessive Investment in Whiteness*, 75. The quote continues on the same page: "The intersecting identity he offered gave new meanings to white male patriarchal and heterosexual identities by establishing patriotism as the site where class antagonisms between men could be reconciled by in patriotic antagonisms against foreign foes and internal enemies."

480 Cross, *Say it Louder!*, 12. Taylor says the "swinging axe of Reagan destroyed the Johnson Welfare State (71).

481 The lone African American in Reagan's two terms was Housing and Urban Development Director Samuel Riley Pierce, Jr. who was also the only cabinet member to serve for two complete terms. Famously, while serving in his cabinet, Reagan greeted Secretary Pierce at a gathering (at the Roosevelt Room) for the U.S. Conference of Mayors by saying, "Hello, Mr. Mayor!" Brown-Hinds, "Bennett Defiant: Defends Racist Comments," https://blackvoicenews.com/2005/10/07/bennett-defiant-defends-racist-comments/.

482 Herbert, "A Failure of Leadership." https://www.nytimes.com/2005/09/05/opinion/a-failure-of-leadership.html.

483 Garza, *The Purpose of Power*, 17.

484 Ansell, *Race and Ethnicity*, 222.

485 Glaude, *Begin Again*, 166.

486 Ansell, *Race and Ethnicity*, 222.

487 Ansell, *Race and Ethnicity*, 109.

488 Kendi, *Stamped from the Beginning*, 424.

489 Alexander, *The New Jim Crow*, 222.: "When people think about crime, especially drug crime, they do not think about suburban housewives violating laws regarding prescription drugs or White frat boys using ecstasy. Drug crime in this country is understood to be Black and Brown, and it is because drug crime is racially defined in the public consciousness." Musician Keith Richards famously said: "I've never had a problem with drugs. I've had problems with police." Another joke says when you see a White man in prison you know he actually committed a crime.

490 Alexander, *The New Jim Crow*, 224.

491  Baradaran, *The Color of Money*, 224., Prisock, *African Americans in Conservative Movements*, 62.: "Appropriation of King's line would be the perfect rhetorical answer to the Liberal Left's justification for government policies . . . on achieving equality of results and supporting group rights."

492  Giovanni. "Is the 'Convention Bounce' a Thing of the Past?" https://www.nytimes.com/2020/08/22/us/politics/joe-biden-dnc-convention.html

493  Shull, *American Civil Rights Policy from Truman to Clinton*, 229.

494  Cross, *Say it Louder!*, 215.

495  Ford, *The Race Card*, 47.: Jesse Jackson compared New Orleans Superdome "to the hull of a slave-ship."

496  Cobb, *The Devil and Dave Chappelle*, 65.

497  Gilroy, *Darker Than Blue*, 13.

498  Perry, *"Race" and Racism*, 208.

499  Rep. Baker (R-LA), "We Finally Cleaned Up Public Housing in New Orleans," https://www.democracynow.org/2005/9/12/headlines/rep_baker_r_la_we_finally_cleaned_up_public_housing_in_new_orleans.

500  Hadjor, *Another America*, 96.

501  Kendi, *Stamped from the Beginning*, 451. Clinton often talked about personal responsibility as a way to avoid sounding racist but there were also times when he made no attempt to hide his feelings. In a speech at the University of Texas in October of 1995 he stated: "Violence for White people too often has a Black face . . .. It's not racist for Whites to assert that a culture of welfare dependency, out of wedlock pregnancy and absent fatherhood cannot be broken by social programs (p. 464)."

502  Baradaran, *The Color of Money*, 218.

503  Taylor, *From #Blacklivesmatter to Black Liberation*, 101. The 1995 Crime Bill led to Black incarceration rates tripling under the Clinton presidency. California Governors Pete Wilson, and Ronald Reagan (as well as Nelson Rockefeller, R-NY) also launched statewide policies of mass incarceration.

504  DiAngelo, *White Fragility*, 152.

505  Hillary Clinton (3/27/2008) said that the comments from Reverend Wright that caused the most consternation was: "The government gives them drugs, builds bigger prisons, passes a three-strike law, and

then wants us to sing 'God Bless America.' No, no, no . . . God damn America for treating our citizens as less than human (Kendi, *Stamped from the Beginning*, 490.).

506   Garza, *The Purpose of Power*, 169., Garza, *The Purpose of Power*, 170.: "The Clinton's used Black America to advance their agenda . . . The more they could be seen as a friend of the Black community, the better. But, in truth, the Clintons did little for the Black community."

507   Davis and West and West, *Freedom is a Constant Struggle*, 87.

508   Garza, *The Purpose of Power*, 58.

509   Wise, *Colorblind*, 9., Glaude, *Democracy in Black*, 145.) writes: "Black critics, like my friend Cornel West, have been obsessed with President Obama's failures. Much of that anger is rooted in profound disappointment and righteous outrage at the state of Black America and the country. 'We ended up with a Rockefeller Republican in Blackface' West said."

510   Some referred to Obama as "half-White" while others only referred to him as "half-Black."

511   ABC News, "State of the Union," https://abcnews.go.com/Politics/State_of_the_Union/president-obama-state-of-the-union-address/story?id=9678571.

512   ABC News, "State of the Union," https://abcnews.go.com/Politics/State_of_the_Union/president-obama-state-of-the-union-address/story?id=9678571.

513   ABC News, "State of the Union," https://abcnews.go.com/Politics/State_of_the_Union/president-obama-state-of-the-union-address/story?id=9678571.

514   Writer, "DePass suggests gorilla is related to Michelle Obama." https://www.blueridgenow.com/story/news/2009/06/14/depass-suggests-gorilla-is-related-to-michelle-obama/28187595007/.

515   Goodman, "While Gingrich Says Obama Acts" https://www.democracynow.org/2010/9/13/while_gingrich_says_obama_acts_kenyan.

516   Starkman, "Investors vs. the Public," https://www.cjr.org/the_audit/investors_vs_the_public.php.

517   Baradaran, *The Color of Money*, 247.

518   Fouhy and Pickler, "Obama: Changes May Take Some Time," A3.

519   D'Oro, "Anti-Government Militias Popping Up Across the U.S.," 5B.

520 Wypijewski, "Red Scare, Black Scare." https://www.thenation.com/article/archive/red-scare-black-scare/.

521 Dyson, Michael Eric. "Whose President Was He?" https://www.politico.com/magazine/story/2016/01/barack-obama-race-relations-213493/.

522 Garner, "What Drives Social Progress?" C6.

523 Glaude, *Democracy in Black*, 8.

524 Abdurraqib, *They Can't Kill Us Until they Kill Us*, 255. He writes: "It was always here, the promise of 'The Obama Moment'" where we saw ourselves.

525 Trump does not merit an extensive evaluation here.

526 Cross, *Say it Louder!*, 10. Of the Republican party Cross writes (Cross, *Say it Louder!*, 181.): "the party morphed into a modern-day Klan championed by racists, cheered on by idiots, normalized by the media, celebrated by foreign adversaries and taken over by conspiracy theorists."

527 Hill and Taylor, *We Still Here*, 79.

528 Hamad, *White Tears/Brown Scars*, 98.: Men see women as "a receptacle for sins so that they may claim innocence for themselves (101.)."

529 Glaude, *Begin Again*, 139.

530 The Trump family came from Germany and Trump's father was arrested, and then released from a KKK rally in 1927. Trump's grandfather was born in Germany (and is a distant relation to the Heinz family) who came to America at age 16 and made his living running a bar, hotel, and brothel for Gold Rush participants in Washington. The grandfather tried to return to Germany but his application was denied because he had eluded military service.

531 Pilkington, "Truth isn't truth" https://www.theguardian.com/us-news/2018/aug/19/truth-isnt-truth-rudy-giuliani-trump-alternative-facts-orwellian.

532 Caroline Randall Williams says that every Black person who is light skinned serves as a "monument" to racist Confederate miscegenation. Williams, "You Want a Confederate Monument?" https://www.nytimes.com/2020/06/26/opinion/confederate-monuments-racism.html.

533 Leary DeGruy, *Post Traumatic Slave Syndrome*, 212.: [Speaking of the Statue of Liberty] "The artist Bartholdi wanted to build a colossal monument to liberty holding chains in protest of the political repression

in his own country and in recognition of the end of the Civil War and with it the official end of slavery in America. But Bartholdi was met with opposition by American leadership who complained that the presence of chains placed too much emphasis on slavery and were a reminder to the Southerners of their loss, therefore, the chains needed to be removed." They are now at her feet.

534   Ani, *Yurugu*, 299.

535   Graham, Green, Murphy and Richards, "An Oral History of Trump's Bigotry" https://www.theatlantic.com/magazine/archive/2019/06/trump-racism-comments/588067/.

536   Kendi, *How to Be an Anti-Racist*, 62.

537   Williams, "What Does He Mean By, They Believe They are White?" 72–83, in *Between the World of Ta-Nehishi Coates and Christianity*, Evans, David, and Peter Dula, eds, Eugene, OR: Cascade, 2018, 75.

538   Baron, "Joe Biden's Obama moment," https://blogs.illinois.edu/view/25/1441.

539   Wright, *African Americans in the Colonial Era*, 9.

540   Cross, *Say it Louder!*, 41.

541   Abdurraqib, *They Can't Kill Us Until they Kill Us*, 5.

542   Gottlieb, *Making Their Own Way*, 9.

543   Pittsburghers are less proud of Newt Gingrich, Ron, and Rand Paul, and the White-rapper "Pittsburgh Slim."

544   Earl Johnson (born in Baltimore), DeHart Hubbard, who had been a redcap at Pittsburgh's Union Station, and Charley West, a student from Washington and Jefferson College all trained at the Morgan Community Athletic Club and all went on to represent the United States in the Olympics (Paris, 1924). Hubbard became the first Black American to win an Olympic championship when he earned a gold medal in the long-jump competition.

545   Glasco, *WPA History of the Negro in Pittsburgh*, 37.

546   Glasco, *WPA History of the Negro in Pittsburgh*, 169.

547   Glasco, *WPA History of the Negro in Pittsburgh*, 44. Glasco reports no slaves were reported in Western Pennsylvania after that year.

548   Glasco, *WPA History of the Negro in Pittsburgh*, 34. The largest KKK chapter in Pittsburgh was in Carnegie but when they tried to stage a rally there (1923) they were refused a permit and one of their leaders,

Thomas Abbott was shot dead when they tried to march anyway. It is claimed that the largest Klavern represented at the 1925 Washington D.C. rally was from Pittsburgh: Jackson, *The Ku Klux Klan in the City*, 172.

549   There was also a secretive "underground railway" from Texas into Mexico for enslaved people in the South seeking freedom. Harsh deserts and few landmarks were major obstacles, but Mexicans, Texicans, and German Americans along the border often helped enslaved people trying to get to Mexico. Contreras, "Story of Underground Railroad to Mexico Gains Attention," A3.

550   A famous Underground Railway stop was 1408 Reedsdale Street which held 15 people at a time. On the Oakdale Road another station (near Raccoon State Park) was the Glen Gormley Inn. Rev. Andrew McDonald hosted escapees in Aliquippa, and the Hazel Street home of steam-boater Rev. Thomas Arthur Brown was another station. Whenever the "Pioneer Bishop" William Paul Quinn visited Pittsburgh he'd stay with Rev. Brown.

551   Glasco, *WPA History of the Negro in Pittsburgh*, 114. Once freedom-seekers reached Pittsburgh, there safety was mostly guaranteed.

552   Delaney came to Pittsburgh (1831) and lived there except for three years in Chatham, Ontario. Delaney was a physician, publisher of the abolitionist paper *The Mystic* and opened one of the nation's first anti-slavery bookstores on St. Clair Street (Sixth Street). Delaney was friends with John Brown, Fredrick Douglass, W.L. Garrison, and John Vashon. One of his grandfather's was an African Gullah and another traced her lineage to Mandingo royalty.

553   Bay, *The White Image in the Black Mind*, 64. Delaney said Whites were "driven by avarice and love of lucre" (94.); rich only at Africa's expense (93.).

554   Glasco, *WPA History of the Negro in Pittsburgh*, 87. Delaney was most proud of being the father of eleven children. All of his children were given Afrocentric names such as his first, Toussaint L'Overture Delaney, the third Alexander Dumas, the fourth Saint Cyprian, the fifth Faustin Soluque, emperor of Haiti, the sixth Ramses Placido, and the seventh Ethiopia Amelia.

555   Ruck, *Sandlot Seasons*, 9.

556  Unions that welcomed Black men included Lathers Local #33, Hoisting Engineers Union, and Cement Finishers Union. Black unionists became pillars in the local Black community.

557  Gottlieb, *Making Their Own Way*, 136.

558  Gottlieb, *Making Their Own Way*, 104.

559  Henry Clay Frick was one of the first to recruit Blacks in the South to break strikes. Glasco, *WPA History of the Negro in Pittsburgh*, 224.: In response to Southern states passing "laws forbidding agents to enter the state, a new tactic was employed. A Northern Black was sent into a Southern town apparently to visit relatives and friends. Inconspicuous and cautions, he moved about drawing men into casual talk in the barber shops and on street corners or by feeding them in restaurants. He was well-supplied with bills of large denomination. These he flashed at stores, at churches, at socials. The surprise they caused and the questions assured were the effect calculated upon. The explanation was simple: the visitor worked in the steel mills for $10.00 a day. He worked six and seven days a week. When the astonished listeners asked what their chances were of earning such wealth, they were told to see the Rev. So-and-So: he could tell them. And shortly afterwards groups of men and women surreptitiously left for the Northern mills."

560  Gottlieb, *Making Their Own Way*, 158.

561  Robert Vann was, along with A. Philip Randolph, Mary McLeod Bethune, and others one of FDR's "Black Cabinet" that he consulted on Black issues. The *Pittsburgh Courier* was the world's largest Black-owned newspaper (reaching 450,000 subscribers). When Vann died, his wife Jesse Vann became the publisher. The paper closed (1966) for a few months until it was reopened in its present incarnation. Another force for Black Labor Union participation was the *Greater Pittsburgh Improvement League*. The GPIL was central in a number of boycotting efforts that opened doors of inclusion. They were also involved, in the 1950s, in desegregating Pittsburgh's public pools. A leading politician against "tokenism" in hiring was K. Leroy Irvis, a local NAACP representative who went on to be a force in Pennsylvania state politics.

562  Jasiri X runs the Pittsburgh based 1Hood Media focused on empowerment and media-control.

563  Glasco, *WPA History of the Negro in Pittsburgh*, 324. Pittsburgh clubs hosted trumpet-piano pioneer Earl Hines, born in the shadow of the Duquesne mills. Pittsburgh was home to composer Billy Eckstine,

Billy Strayhorn, pianist Ahmad Jamal (East Liberty) and Lena Horne (raised on the Hill). Phyllis Hyman went to Carrick High and recorded in Beltzhoover. The corner of Center and Herron was the home of WHOD (WAMO) that launched the Hill's George Benson.

564　Glasco, *WPA History of the Negro in Pittsburgh*, 260.: "In these groups a man may become a Grand Patriarch, a Grand Sword Bearer, a Noble Grand, or a Grand Pursuivant, and in the auxiliaries a woman may be a Daughter Worth Councilor. To talk and to deal with Grand Special Communications, Decorations of Chivalry, Royal Purple Degrees, is to touch glamour and achieve exaltation."

565　Glasco, *WPA History of the Negro in Pittsburgh*, 233.: "In the early days of Bethel, Father Collins, an elder, walked twice to Philadelphia and back to report and get aid for his church." Bethel became the pride of OP wealth. By contrast, Southerners felt they were more ambitious, tougher, and God-fearing than their Northern hosts. Ebenezer Baptist welcomed Southerners with open arms. In Homestead, Clark Memorial Church, founded in the 1890s, and the Second Baptist Church, led by millworker Pastor J.D. Morton both served as leading forces in slowly ending Pittsburgh's Black class-wars.

566　In East Liberty, the "Lexington," a segregated skating-rink. Black Pittsburghers had to build their own parks and playgrounds. The first YMCA was built on Center Avenue opposite the Pittsburgh Courier in 1928. Robert Vann led fundraising efforts for the "Y" along with Chicagoan Julius Rosenwald. Carnegie also paid for clubs and libraries.

567　The writings of John Edgar Wideman also brought the everyday life of Homewood-Brushton to his readers.

568　Glasco, *WPA History of the Negro in Pittsburgh*, 265. Herbert Spencer visited Pittsburgh in the 1870s.

569　Brewer, *African Americans in Pittsburgh*, 44. The editor's father was the first (1954) Black principal in Pittsburgh's Public Schools, John M. Brewer, Sr.

570　Gibson's father had come to work in the Carnegie-Illinois Steel Mill from Buena Vista, GA (1921). In 1924, he'd earned enough to send for his wife and children. Josh was 13 when he moved into the Pleasant Valley section of the Northside. Josh left school after ninth grade to work for Westinghouse Airbrake (steel mill) and he also stocked-shelves at the Gimbels department store. He first played for the Gimbel Brothers Athletic Club before he was scouted by the Crawfords. Pittsburgh baseball stars Lefty Burton was a mailman, Harold Tinker a janitor, Bus Christian a sanitation worker, Wyatt Turner a chauffeur, and the rest of the Crawfords worked in the mills. Josh Gibson died (1/27/1947) after excessive drinking and a series of mental setbacks after being passed over by the majors after integration. One story relates: "He went to the ballpark one day and saw Joe Garagiola on a major's team and the whole horrible meaning of prejudice came over him" (Ruck, *Sandlot Seasons*, 159.). When one New York Yankee saw Gibson play he said: "Too bad this Gibson is a colored fellow" (Ruck, *Sandlot Seasons*,159.).

571   The game was held against the Phillies on September 1, 1971, at Three Rivers Stadium. The Bucs won 10-7.

572   Ruck, *Sandlot Seasons*, 12.

573   Gottlieb, *Making Their Own Way*, 174.

574   Lindqvist, *The Skull-Measurer's Mistake*, 12.

575   Recent reports from Far-Right rallies in Germany are also showing QAnon, Russian and the First Reich flag.

576   Snyder, *On Tyranny*, 25.

577   Wilkerson, *Caste: The Origins of our Discontents*, 78. The term *Untermensch* (subhuman) was a label based on American eugenicist Lothrop Stoddard. When Stoddard heard of the Nazi laws he said: "If anything, their judgments were almost too conservative" (80.).

578   Wilkerson, *Caste: The Origins of our Discontents*, 81.

579   Neiman, *Learning from the Germans*, 264.

580   Neiman, *Learning from the Germans*, 191. Of course, there are many former slave-labor camps that retell the story of slavery and many other museums that include some exhibit or component that focuses on slavery. The "Great Blacks in Wax" Museum in Baltimore has an immensely powerful re-creation of a slave ship. A noted Plantation, called "America's Auschwitz" by Smithsonian Magazine is the Whitney Plantation about an hour north of New Orleans. Visitors are given a tag of a name of a slave when they arrive and see the entire property through the eyes of that particular slave. Only at the end of the tour does one enter the main house and then only through the back door and servants' quarters.

581   Wilkerson, *Caste: The Origins of our Discontents*, 378– 380.: Einstein was a member of the NAACP and found other ways to support the Civil Rights Movement. He rarely accepted honorary doctorates but did so when invited to receive one at Lincoln University (1946) where

he met the young Julian Bond. Einstein explained: "The more I feel an American, the more this situation pains me. I can escape the feelings of complicity in it only by speaking out" (379.).

582   Glaude, *Begin Again*, 206.

583   "The Shoah and Southern History," 35–42, Nell Irvin Painter, Conyers, *Afrocentric Traditions*, 35.

584   Between 1945 and the reunification of Germany, the West German government paid 80 billion German Marks (around 100 billion dollars US) to individual Jews and Jewish families in addition to extensive monies to Israel.

585   Neiman, *Learning from the Germans*, 383.

586   Bays, *The White Image in the Black Mind*, 167.

587   Mechanic, "Why Are Successful Black Men" https://www.mother-jones.com/politics/2021/10/why-white-americans-assume-success-ful-black-people-athletes-entertainers/.

588   Griffin, *The Seeds of Racism in the Soul of America*, 6.

589   Bryant, *The Heritage*, 52.

590   Joseph, *The Black Friend*, 25.

591   Kendi, *How to Be an Anti-Racist*, 10.: "The language of color-blind-ness – like the language of 'not racist' – is a mask to hide racism. 'Our Constitution is color-blind,' U.S. Supreme Court Justice John Harlan proclaimed in his dissent to Plessy v. Ferguson, the case that legalized Jim Crow segregation in 1896. 'The White race deems itself to be the dominant race in this country . . . I doubt not, it will continue to be for all time if it remains true to its great heritage.'"

592   A good book on this topic is Tran, Jonathan. *Asian Americans and the Spirit of Racial Capitalism. Reflection and Theory in the Study of Religion*. New York: Oxford University, 2022. Tran argues that identarian concepts of race provide ways for capitalism to avoid complicity in the intersections of economic injustices and economic oppression.

593   Cross, *Say it Louder!*, 236.: "I love being part of this secret society existing before their very eyes. We speak a language in which they recognize the words, presume to understand them. But the duality of our kind is hard to capture. There is something so ingrained in the souls of Black folk that it can't be taught or absorbed by osmosis. It's empowering."

594  One Black Southerner said: "By long and close association with the White man, the Negro has learned all of his ways, and can read at a glance his innermost thoughts, and can now size him up and classify him just as accurate as a cotton buyer does the different grades of cotton and can do it much quicker" (Litwack, *Trouble in Mind*, 413.). This was contrasted by Whites who "have only the faintest comprehension of the inner lives of Negroes which remain forever secret and alien to them . . .Whatever Whites said about their unique gifts of comprehending Negroes many came to realize they knew only what Blacks chose to reveal and that was remarkably little" (Litwack, *Trouble in Mind*, 412.). A song clarified: "White folk think they so fine / But their dirty linen stinks just like mine!' (Litwack, *Trouble in Mind*, 414.).

595  Hill and Taylor, *We Still Here*, 1.

596  Ani, *Yurugu*, 379.

597  Ani, *Yurugu*, 354.

598  Garza, *The Purpose of Power*, 12.

599  Prisock, *African Americans in Conservative Movements*, 103. Shirley Chisolm said: "To label family planning and legal abortion programs 'genocide' is male-rhetoric for male ears. It falls flat to female listeners and to thoughtful male ones (124.)."

600  Ansell, *Race and Ethnicity*, 115.

601  Glaude, *Democracy in Black*, 88.

602  "James Baldwin vs William F Buckley: A legendary debate from 1965." *Aeon Video*. Video Accessed: October 26, 2024. https://www.youtube.com/watch?v=5Tek9h3a5wQ.

603  Mazel, *And Don't Call Me a Racist*, 98.

604  Bass, *Blessed Are the Peacemakers*, 91.

605  Mills College, Oakland, CA, June 15, 2007. There is no longer any archive available for this website.

606  Tucker, *Black Reflections on White Power*, 138.

607  Solomon and Rankin, *How We Fight White Supremacy*, 194. "Imposter-syndrome" is a term from Dr. Joy Harden Bradford.

608  Joseph, *The Black Friend*, 192. Joseph wrote this in reference to a flippant response to the movie *Moonlight*.

609  Glaude, *Democracy in Black*, 65.

610   Kendi, *How to Be an Anti-Racist*, 210.: "We arrive at demonstrations excited, as if our favorite musician is playing on the speaker's stage. We convince ourselves we are doing something to solve the racial problem when we are really doing something to satisfy our feelings. We go home fulfilled like we dined at our favorite restaurant."

611   Cross, *Say it Louder!*, 63. Cross said: "You call that victimization, but I call that reality for a lot of people."

612   Glaude, *Democracy in Black*, 198.

613   Fields and Fields, *Racecraft*, 222.

614   Glaude, *Begin Again*, 97.

615   Abdurraqib, *They Can't Kill Us Until They Kill Us*, 149.

616   Lambert and Klineberg, *Children's Views of Foreign People*, 208.

617   Shipler, *A Country of Strangers*, 278. Shipler writes (243.): "Another researcher underwent the intriguing assignment of analyzing Victoria Secret catalogues. Only 25 people of color appeared among the 2,198 Euro-American models. Most of the 25 had lighter skin which is "intentionally ambiguous."

618   Cane, *Live Through This*, 178.

619   Nye, *William Lloyd Garrison, and the Humanitarian Reformers*, 206.

620   Klunder was a Presbyterian pastor who was run-over by a bulldozer at a rally (4/7/1965). His death was ruled an accident. Reeb was born in Wichita, KS but spent his youth in Casper, WY. He died (Selma, AL, 3/11/1965) two days after being clubbed on the head. Three men were arrested but were acquitted. Reeb, a Presbyterian, became a Unitarian because of their social justice focus. A father of four, Reeb's family lived in a Black neighborhood in Philadelphia while working at the West Branch YMCA. He then became pastor at the All Souls Church (Washington, D.C.) Later, Reeb worked for the American Friends (Quaker) Service Committee.

621   Yancey, *Beyond Racial Gridlock*, 19.

622   "Integration," *Vocabulary.com*, https://www.vocabulary.com/dictionary/integration.

623   Griffin, *The Seeds of Racism in the Soul of America*, 96.

624   Waters, *Maria W. Stewart and the Roots of Black Political Thought*, 71. The quote continues: "This especially happens in churches: We write the prayer in Spanish, do a responsive reading in Cherokee or Korean, and throw in a 'Negro' spiritual and have someone perform a Japanese

dance. But when it is all said and done, all we have is a White worship service with ethnic trappings."

625 Kendi, *Stamped from the Beginning*, 488.

626 Shipler, *A Country of Strangers*, 236.

627 Hinton et al., *The Sun Does Shine*, 238.

628 Smith, *Stolen Heart*, 207.

629 Mazel, *And Don't Call Me a Racist*, 100.

630 Ignatiev, *Race Traitor*, 9.

631 Ignatiev, *Race Traitor*, 10.

632 Solomon and Rankin, *How We Fight White Supremacy*, 118.

633 Owens et al., *Radical Dharma*, 144.

634 Griffin, *The Seeds of Racism in the Soul of America*, 6.

635 Glaude, *Democracy in Black*, 201. Glade states: "Moments of democratic awakening are fugitive. They happen in fits and starts, are rarely sustained by extended periods of time. Democratic awakenings can, however, switch the tracks." (220.).

636 Joseph, *The Black Friend*, 2. Joseph wrote (27.): "I've realized that a fear of accountability is why White people say things like, 'I don't see color' and 'why does everything have to be about race.' Because to see my color, to see my culture, to see my race, would also mean taking responsibility for how White people have historically treated people, my color, with my culture, from my race."

637 Hamad, *White Tears/Brown Scars*, 4.

638 Devega, "Cornel West on this moment of 'escalating consciousness' and the need for radical democracy." https://www.salon.com/2020/06/26/cornel-west-on-this-moment-of-escalating-consciousness-and-the-need-for-radical-democracy/.

639 Loewen, *Lies My Teacher Told Me*, 139.

640 Zirin, *What's My Name, Fool?*, 17.

641 Even the name "Harlem" was a contrivance since Saperstein was from northern Chicago and all of the original players were from Chicago. The team had its headquarters in Chicago until 1972. The name "Harlem" was chosen because it was considered a center of Black culture. The Trotters have played in over 122 countries and were ambassadors for Black sports prowess. They often performed two games a day, one

for an all-Black audience and another for an all-White audience. In many cities, White audiences that cheered refused any aid after games.

642 Ruck, *Sandlot Seasons*, 121.

643 The first Black Canadian in the NHL was Willie O'Ree (Fredericton, NB) with Boston (1958). Today, there are 43 non-White NHLers – out of 700. The first Black hockey league was in Nova Scotia (1895) with the Africville Seasides, Dartmouth Jubilees and teams from Halifax, Truro, PEI, and Amherst. The first Black Canadian in a pro league was Hippo Galloway (Central Ontario Hockey) who played for Woodstock (1899). Val James was the first Black American in the NHL joining Buffalo (1980). Grant Fuhr was the first Black elected to the Hall of Fame.

644 Shipler, *A Country of Strangers*, 180. notes some positions were "White" (QB) while others were "Black" (WR).

645 Jack Roosevelt Robinson (JR), born in Georgia (1919), grew up in Pasadena, CA. JR played in the majors for ten years compiling a .311 lifetime batting-average. His first minor-league coach was Clay Hooper who asked: "Mr. Rickey, do you REALLY think a N@#* is a human being?" (Zirin, *What's My Name, Fool?*, 43.). Of his family, JR said: "My father's will and spirit were slowly broken down by the economic slavery imposed upon him" (Zirin, *What's My Name, Fool?*, 41.). After retirement JR failed to find a front-office position because "baseball couldn't wait to get rid of him" (Bryant, *The Heritage*, 59.). Speaking of his defamation of Robeson, JR said his participation in the "House un-American Activities Commission" was "the greatest regret of my life" (Zirin, *What's My Name, Fool?*, 47.). His comments against Robeson angered many Civil Rights activists. Dr. King, however, was a personal friend. When King was sentenced to work four-months on a Georgian prison work-gang, JR appealed to Nixon but his request was ignored. Afterwards, Robinson vowed never again to stand for the National Anthem.

646 Bryant, *The Heritage*, 51. Wilson was traded to Detroit after standing-up for himself after a racist incident.

647 Even though these were technically called the "Summer Olympics," this protest took place on October 16, 1968. The third athlete on the dais was Silver medalist, a White Australian - Peter Norman. When Norman noticed that Carlos (from Harlem) and Smith (from Clarksville, TX) were wearing black gloves and had no shoes and about to make a protest he ran into the crowd and asked for an OPHR (Olympic

Project for Human Rights) patch to show solidarity. When Norman died (10/9/2006) both Smith and Carlos served as pall-bearers at his funeral.

648  Zirin, *What's My Name, Fool?*, 54. The quote concludes: "After the abolition of slavery boxing was unique among sports because it was desegregated. This was not because the people who ran the sport were progressive . . . Promoters simply wanted to make a buck off the rampant racism in American society by pitting Black vs. White for public spectacle. Jack Johnson became the first Black Heavyweight champion in 1908 and was then asked to fight Jim Jeffries, called the "Great White Hope." Jeffries said: 'I am going into this fight for the sole purpose of proving that a White man is better than a Negro.' At ringside (1910) the band played "All Coons Look Alike to Me" and promoters led the nearly all-White crowd in the chant 'Kill the N@#*!' But Johnson was faster, stronger, and smarter than Jeffries, knocking him out with ease" (Zirin, *What's My Name, Fool?*, 54–55.). The next Black champion, Joe Louis had an all-White management team. Louis fought German boxer Max Schmeling in 1936 and 1938. After Schmeling won in 1936 a Southern newspaper explained "I guess this proves who really is the Master Race" (Zirin, *What's My Name, Fool?*, 56.). When Nazi propaganda efforts led to a live-broadcast in 1938, the broadcast abruptly went silent when Louis knocked out Schmeling.

649  Zirin, *What's My Name, Fool?*, 58–59.: "Clay loved his gold medal . . . He slept with it. . . . He never took it off. After returning from the Olympics, Clay went with his medal swinging around his neck to eat a cheeseburger in a Louisville restaurant and was denied service. He threw his beloved medal into the Ohio River. This started the 18-year-old on a political journey that would define his era."

650  Zirin, *What's My Name, Fool?*, 60. Before Ali fought Sonny Liston Malcolm X said: "Clay will be our hero . . . few people know the quality of mind he has in there. One forgets that although a clown never imitates a wise man, a wise man can imitate the clown (Zirin, *What's My Name, Fool?*, 60.)." Clay changed his name to Cassius X until Elijah Muhammad renamed him Muhammad Ali. Bryant Gumbel said: "One of the reasons the Civil Rights Movement went forward was that Black people were able to overcome their fear. And I honestly believe that for many Black Americans, that came from watching Muhammad Ali. He refused to be afraid and being that way, he gave other people courage" (Zirin, *What's My Name, Fool?*, 63.). Floyd Patterson, speaking of Ali's Islam and evoking Jeffries decades before, said he was fighting Ali to

take the title away from a Muslim and return it to a Christian. In his thrashing of Patterson, Ali shouted: "Come on, America! Come on White America . . .What's my name? Is my name Clay? What's my name, fool?" (Zirin, *What's My Name, Fool?*, 64.).

651   Bryant, *The Heritage*, 2.

652   Ali actually said: "Man, I aint got no quarrel with them Vietcong" (Zirin, *What's My Name, Fool?*, 64.). Later, he turned these words into a poem: "Keep asking me, no matter how long, On the war in Vietnam, I sing this song, I aint got no quarrel with the Vietnam." Dr. King said: "Like Muhammad Ali puts it, we are all – Black and Brown and poor – victims of the same system of oppression" (Zirin, *What's My Name, Fool?*, 65.). When asked about jail, Ali responded: "So, I'll go to jail, so what? We've been put in jail for 400 years (Zirin, *What's My Name, Fool?*, 66.). Ali stated: "I was determined to be the one Nigger that the White man didn't get" (Zirin, *What's My Name, Fool?*, 69.).

653   Bryant, *The Heritage*, 9. In response to his critics, Kaepernick wore a t-shirt saying: "We march – Y'all mad. We sit down – Y'all mad. We speak up – Y'all mad. We die – Y'all silent" (14).

654   Owens et al., *Radical Dharma*, 185.

655   Solomon and Rankin, *How We Fight White Supremacy*, 138.

656   Davis, *Women, Culture & Politics*, 21.

657   Abdurraqib, *They Can't Kill Us Until they Kill Us*, 9.

658   Abdurraqib, *They Can't Kill Us Until they Kill Us*, 166. He continues: "Heartbreak is one of the many emotions that sits inside the long arms of sadness, a mother with many children. I suppose it isn't all bad either. For example, I am heartbroken at the state of the world, so I take to the streets again. But the real work of the emotion . . . happens beneath the surface."

659   In 2020, two "Simpsons" Black characters, Dr. Hibbert and Carl Carlson, voiced-over by White actors will now be voiced-over by Black voices. Moreau, "Harry Shearer No Longer Voicing Black 'Simpsons' Character Dr. Hibbert, Kevin Michael Richardson to Take Over," https://variety.com/2021/tv/news/the-simpsons-dr-hibbert-recast-harry-shearer-kevin-michael-richardson-1234912612/.

Most networks have discontinued showing "Gone With the Wind," a glorification of anti-bellum virtue. Other recent films are also under scrutiny such as "Green Book" (2018), and "The Help" (2012). Spike Lee speaking of the "magical negro" portrayal of Wil Smith's character in the "Legend of Bagger Vance" commented: "Blacks getting lynched right and left and Bagger Vance is more concerned about improving Matt Damon's golf swing." France, "These films don't help the racism conversation,"

660 Abdurraqib, *They Can't Kill Us Until they Kill Us*, 166.

661 Patterson, *Rituals of Blood*, 4.

662 Kendi, *How to Be an Anti-Racist*, 183.

663 Solomon and Rankin, *How We Fight White Supremacy*, 97.

664 Abdurraqib, *They Can't Kill Us Until they Kill Us*, 61.

665 Patterson, *Rituals of Blood*, 5.

666 Hill and Taylor, *We Still Here*, 100.

667 Early Black Pittsburgh police officers were known for community-involvement. One was known as "Big Blue" because of his uniform color and size. Vagrants knew he was nearby because he would tap on metal-poles blocks away. He loved kids and "was known to stop by playgrounds and help kids assemble their bikes which had been broken (Brewer, *African Americans in Pittsburgh*, 105.)."

668 Owens et al., *Radical Dharma*, 183.

669 Khan-Cullors and Bandele, *When They Call You a Terrorist*, 61.: "American prisons house an estimated 356,268 with severe mental illness."

670 Hughley and Moe, *Surrender White People!*, 185.

671 Khan-Cullors and Bandele, *When They Call You a Terrorist*, 131. "Prisoners are literally an enslaved workforce" (Khan-Cullors and Bandele, *When They Call You a Terrorist*, 131.).

672 Owens et al., *Radical Dharma*, 181.

673 Obama, *Dreams from my Father*, 259.

674 John Ehrlichman wrote: "We knew we couldn't make it illegal to be Black but by getting the public to associate Blacks with heroin and then criminalizing them heavily, we could disrupt their communities. We know we were lying. Of course, we did (Khan-Cullors and Bandele, *When They Call You a Terrorist*, 9.).

675 White people often commit crimes for which they were never suspected. See: Khan, "Racial and Ethnic Disparities,"

676 Leary DeGruy, *Post Traumatic Slave Syndrome*, 88.

677 Davis and West, *Freedom is a Constant Struggle*, 107.

678   Leary DeGruy, *Post Traumatic Slave Syndrome*, 55.

679   Conyers, *Afrocentric Traditions*, 67.

680   Ignatiev, *Race Traitor*, 60.

681   Ward, *America's Racial Karma*, 97.

682   Leary DeGruy, *Post Traumatic Slave Syndrome*, 72.

683   Darby, *Sisters in Hate*, 197.

684   Cross, *Say it Louder!*, 174.

685   Taylor, *From #Blacklivesmatter to Black Liberation*, 108. "Police also reflect and reinforce the dominant ideology of the state" (108.).

686   Owens et al., *Radical Dharma*, 137.

687   Darby, *Sisters in Hate*, 35., cites stages of hatred: "Animus is justified, incentivized, learned, and performed."

688   Mazel, *And Don't Call Me a Racist*, 68.

689   Solomon and Rankin, *How We Fight White Supremacy*, 245.

690   Hunter, 111

691   Leary DeGruy, *Post Traumatic Slave Syndrome*, 31.

692   Khan-Cullors and Bandele, *When They Call You a Terrorist*, 68.

693   Khan-Cullors and Bandele, *When They Call You a Terrorist*, 91.

694   Morris, *Pushout*, 92.

695   Garza, *The Purpose of Power*, 117.

696   Kendi, *How to Be an Anti-Racist*, 177.

697   Davis and West, *Freedom is a Constant Struggle*, 56.

698   Taylor, *From #Blacklivesmatter to Black Liberation*, 128.

699   Khan-Cullors and Bandele, 26: From Morris's *Pushout: The Criminalization of Black Girls in Schools* (2015). Morris tells of one 12-year (Detroit) threatened with expulsion and criminal charges for writing "Hi" on her locker. Students are often suspended, leading to educational alienation, for minor offenses such as "being disrespectful."

700   Letters to the Editor, "Closing the Racial Gap in Education" https:// www.nytimes.com/2010/08/22/opinion/l22schools.html.

701   Stolberg, "Obama Pledges Expanded Ties With Muslim Nations" https://www.nytimes.com/2010/11/10/world/asia/10prexy.html.

702   Krugman, "Leaving Children Behind" https://www.nytimes. com/2011/02/28/opinion/28krugman.html.

703  Patterson, *Rituals of Blood*, 17.

704  "Academic Fields Where Blacks Earn Few or No Doctoral Degrees in 2017," *The Journal of Blacks in Higher Education*. https://jbhe.com/2018/12/academic-fields-where-blacks-earn-few-or-no-doctoral-degrees-in-2017/.

705  Shipler, *A Country of Strangers*, 27.

706  Garza, *The Purpose of Power*, 187.

707  Hughley and Moe, *Surrender White People!*, 146.: "Despite constituting only 3% of four-year colleges in the country, HBCUs have produced 80% of the Black judges, 50% of the Black lawyers, 50% of the Black doctors, 40% of Black engineers, 40% of the Black members of Congress and 13% of the Black CEOs."

708  Students at Georgetown voted to increase their tuition in order to pay reparations to the descendants of the 272 sales who were owned by the University before the Civil War. These slaves were sold by the Jesuits in 1838. The Virginia Theological Seminary also set up a reparations fund for the descendants of slaves at their institution.

709  Students at North Carolina State were caught writing graffiti on campus (reading "Let's shoot the N@*# in the head!"). One high-school in Rexburg, Iowa had to discipline students on a bus chanting "assassinate Obama." Woodward, "Racial Incidents Follow Obama Win," 4A.

710  Fields and Fields, *Racecraft*, 115.: "In the United States there are scholars and *Black* scholars, women and *Black* women . . ."

711  In World Literature classes, folks of Black heritage, such as the Russian Alexander Pushkin or the Frenchman Alexander Dumas, are rarely presented as of being of African ancestry.

712  Shipler, *A Country of Strangers*, 76.

713  Epps, *The Speeches of Malcolm X at Harvard*, 65.

714  Taylor, *From #Blacklivesmatter to Black Liberation*, 113.

715  Hamad, *White Tears/Brown Scars*, 43.

716  Leary DeGruy, *Post Traumatic Slave Syndrome*, 122.

717  Hamad, *White Tears/Brown Scars*, 59.

718  Glasco, *WPA History of the Negro in Pittsburgh*, 313.

719  Wright, *African Americans in the Colonial Era*, 123.

720  Taylor, *Toxic Communities*, 226.

721  Taylor, *Toxic Communities*, 226.

722  Inequitable distributions were also in New York and New Jersey where "fewer than 100 of the 67,000 mortgages insured by the GI Bill were for Black people's homes" (Hughley and Moe, *Surrender White People!*, 150.). Numerous housing estates, such as Levittown, were not open to "non-Caucasians" in their original charter: "The original homes in Levittown only cost you $7,990, but the median price today is $400,000. That's what building wealth in real estate gets you" (Hughley and Moe, *Surrender White People!*, 155.).

723  Taylor, *Toxic Communities*, 248.

724  Benjamin, *Whitopia*, 5. Benjamin claims "White flight" happens most often either when Whites first have children or when they retire. In both instances the goal of their departure is a search for physical safety and emotional security.

725  Hughley and Moe, *Surrender White People!*, 162.: "It's 17 miles on average before Black people can access fresh produce or fresh meat. Grocery stores just don't open in our neighborhoods the way that dollar-stores and liquor-stores do. The Greenwood section of Tulsa, former home of Black Wall Street, went from having dozens of grocery-stores to having none. It does have 8 dollar-stores. Dollar-stores are replacing grocery-stores in poor communities of color throughout the country."

726  Cross, *Say it Louder!*, 222. Another 15% live in small metropolitan areas and 10% live in rural America.

727  Solomon and Rankin, *How We Fight White Supremacy*, 267.

728  Barber, *We are Called to Be a Movement*, 46. The water-crisis began in Flint in 2014 when a money-saving effort turned toxic.

729  Cross, *Say it Louder!*, 119. Led-poisoning led some pregnant women to miscarry while others lost their hair.

730  Kendi, *How to Be an Anti-Racist*, 21.

731  Hughley and Moe, *Surrender White People!*, 167.

732  Winsboro, *Old South, New South, or Down South?*, 237.

733  Some "sundown towns" even had the word "White" in their name which served as a warning to avoid at night.

734  Thurman, *Jesus and the Disinherited*, 37.

735  Finney, *Black Faces, White Spaces*, 118.

736   Finney, *Black Faces, White Spaces*, 29.: Naturalist John Muir spoke of Blacks as "largely lazy and easy-going and unable to pick as much cotton as a White man."

737   Finney, *Black Faces, White Spaces*, 31.

738   Kendi, *How to Be an Anti-Racist*, 22.

739   Hill and Taylor, *We Still Here*, 94.

740   Winters, *Black Fatigue*, 75. Winters cites specifics (2019, Families USA): Blacks are 44% more likely to die from a stroke, 20% more likely to have asthma, 25% more likely to die from heart disease than Whites. Black women are 40% more likely to die from breast cancer, 52% more likely to die from cervical cancer, and 243% more likely to die from pregnancy or child-birth related causes than Whites. Black women represent 66% of all new HIV/AIDS cases (71.).

741   Washington, *Medical Apartheid*, 3.

742   Barber, *We are Called to Be a Movement*, 43.

743   Ellis, „COVID-19: Structural Racism and Black Health" https://newpittsburghcourier.com/2020/11/11/covid-19-structural-racism-and-black-health/.

744   Hill and Taylor, *We Still Here*, 25.

745   Smith, *Intimations: Six Essays*, 10.

746   Hill and Taylor, *We Still Here*, 43.

747   Washington, "Apology Shines Light on Racial Schism in America," 20.

748   Welsing, *The Isis Papers*, 8.

749   USAFacts Team, "White People Own 86% of Wealth and Make up 60% of the Population," https://usafacts.org/articles/white-people-own-86-wealth-despite-making-60-population.

750   Abdurraqib, *They Can't Kill Us Until they Kill Us*, 158.

751   Leary DeGruy, *Post Traumatic Slave Syndrome*, 81.

752   Columbia University Center on Poverty and Social Policy, "The Black-White child poverty gap persists. Can we close it?" March 10, 2022. https://www.povertycenter.columbia.edu/news-internal/2022/black-white-child-poverty-gap.

753   Norris, "The Return of the Misery Index" https://www.nytimes.com/2008/09/13/business/economy/13charts.html.

754   Lacy, *Blue-Chip Black*, 200.

755  Glasco, *WPA History of the Negro in Pittsburgh*, 225. The quote is from A. Philip Randolph from a speech presented at the A.F. of L. convention (Atlantic City, NJ, 1935). The C.I.O. had a much better relationship with the Black labor community at that time.

756  Cane, *Live Through This*, 141.

757  Steinberg, *The Ethnic Myth*, 196.

758  Glaude, *Democracy in Black*, 19. Speaking of America's economy Glaude says there are "corruptorations" and "banksters" (21.).

759  A notable Black physician was Dr. Charles Drew who was the country's leading expert on blood storage from his base at Howard University. Inaccurate myths of denials of a blood-transfusion at his death are rife.

760  Baradaran, *The Color of Money*, 2.

761  Baradaran, *The Color of Money*, 43.

762  Garza, *The Purpose of Power*, 250., Garza, *The Purpose of Power*, 251.: "Capitalism monetizes everything, creating a dynamic in which absolutely everything, including movements, can be bought or sold." Garza ties this to placing a primacy on individualism.

763  Taylor, *Toxic Communities*, 25., Fields and Fields, *Racecraft*, 122.: "Virginia was a profit-seeking venture, and no one stood to make a profit growing tobacco by democratic methods. Only those who could force large numbers of people to work tobacco for them stood to get rich during the tobacco boom."

764  Taylor, *Toxic Communities*, 194.: "These are not parallel facts; they are intersecting facts. There are 400 American billionaires because there are 45 million people living in poverty. Poverty comes at the expense of the living wage."

765  Ani, *Yurugu*, 386.

766  Hooks and West, *Breaking Bread*, 95.

767  Kendi, *How to Be an Anti-Racist*,161. Kendi said Elizabeth Warren offered a different definition of capitalism that sought to disentangle "capitalism from theft, and racism, and imperialism . . . however, history does not affirm this definition of capitalism . . . What capitalism introduced to this mix was global theft, racially uneven playing fields, unidirectional wealth that rushes upward in unprecedented amounts . . . to love capitalism is to end up loving racism." (162–163.)

768  Baradaran, *The Color of Money*, 9.

769  Prisock, *African Americans in Conservative Movements*, 1.

770 Baradaran, *The Color of Money*, 255.

771 The "stress hormone" (cortisol) when out of balance can blur reason as well as shortening life.

772 Baradaran, *The Color of Money*, 262.

773 Robinson, *The Debt*, 414.

774 Robinson, *The Debt*, 428.

775 Wolfe, *The Politics of Reparations and Apologies*, 54.

776 Callie Guy House, born a slave in Tennessee (1861-1928), saw a pamphlet entitled *Freedmen's Pension Bill: A Plea for American Freedmen* (1891) that advocated for reparations for slavery which inspired her to organize the *National Ex-Slave Mutual Relief, Bounty and Pension Society*. She lectured in every former slave-state and raised a membership of 300,000 by 1900. In 1916, she was imprisoned for a year for taking money from ex- slaves under false pretenses. Curry, "Callie Guy House" https://www.blackpast.org/african-american-history/callie-house-c-1861-1928/.

777 In 1825, France forced the Haitian government to pay reparations to former slave-owners. In 1833, the British government paid over 3,000 families for the loss of their property after slavery was banned. In 1892, $25,000 was given by the U.S. government to the families of eleven Italian Americans who had been lynched in New Orleans (1891) while they were awaiting trial. When Germany paid reparations to Israel, David Ben-Gurion said it was fitting so that "the murderers do not become the heirs as well."

778 Rep. John H. Conyers, Jr., (D, Michigan,13) first proposed H.R.40. Sheila Jackson Lee also sponsored it.

779 Ward, *America's Racial Karma*, 41.

780 Ward, *America's Racial Karma*, 47.

781 Guru Arjan Dev Ji. "Adi Granth." Translation by Dr. Inder Mohan Singh. *World Prayers*. https://www.worldprayers.org/archive/prayers/adorations/i_see_no_stranger_i_see_no.html.

782 "The Freedom to Learn," (1949), in *W.E.B. DuBois Speaks*, P.S. Forner, ed. New York: Pathfinder, 1970, 230.

783 Litwack, *Trouble in Mind*, 405. Booker T. Washington "refused to comment" on the Hose slaughter because he needed "to keep silent and not engage in any controversy that might react on the work to which I am now lending my efforts (404.).

784   Litwack, *Trouble in Mind*, 405. The quote continues: "Nothing in their experience or their traditions could afford any parallel to such hideous barbarities practiced as they were by people supposed to be Christians and highly civilized."

785   Abdurraqib, *They Can't Kill Us Until they Kill Us*, 153. He quotes rapper Foxx: "I pull up at the club VIP/Gas tank on E/But all drinks on me" (157.).

786   Darby, *Sisters in Hate*, 15.

787   Fields and Fields, *Racecraft*, 27.: "'Minority' ranks alongside 'the color of their skin' as a verbal prob for the mental trick that turns racism into race. The word slips its literal meaning as well as its core definition, which is quantative."

788   Benjamin, *Whitopia*, 59.

789   Benjamin, *Whitopia*, 188.

790   Speaking of conservatives, Obama got in "hot-water" for saying in 2008: "They get bitter, they cling to guns or religion or antipathy to people who aren't like them or anti-immigrant sentiment or anti-trade sentiment as a way to explain their frustrations." Pilkington, "Obama angers midwest voters with guns and religion remark," https://www.theguardian.com/world/2008/apr/14/barackobama.uselections2008.

791   Ignatiev, *Race Traitor*, 10.

792   Baradaran, *The Color of Money*, 284.

793   Camus, *Resistance, Rebellion, and Death*, 272.

794   Freire and Macedo, *Pedagogy of the Oppressed*, 43.

795   Freire and Macedo, *Pedagogy of the Oppressed*, 44.

796   Freire and Macedo, *Pedagogy of the Oppressed*, 45.

797   Freire and Macedo, *Pedagogy of the Oppressed*, 49.

798   Glaude, *Begin Again*, 200.

799   Cane, *Live Through This*, 68.

800   Barber, *We are Called to Be a Movement*, 31. Barber continues: "The rejected! The rejected! The rejected! They must lead a revival until lives are changed, until systemic racism is dealt with, and classism is dealt with, and homophobia and Islamophobia and xenophobia are dealt with. . . . And all human beings are loved with equal regard" (76–77.).

801   Nguyen, "Vietnamese Lives, American Imperialist Views," https://www.nytimes.com/2020/06/24/movies/da-5-bloods-vietnam.html.

802   Gilroy, *Darker Than Blue*, 4.

803   Opie, *Southern Food and Civil Rights*, 106.: "Quilly" was "a cool, gentle dessert necessary after King's favorite supper of ribs, collard greens, and baked sweet potatoes. Quilly according to Mrs. King Sr., was the name the children gave this dessert years ago."

804   "Bob Marley," *Quotes of Famous People* (October 1, 2023). https://quotepark.com/quotes/1237495-bob-marley-the-day-you-stop-racing-is-the-day-you-win-the-ra/.

805   Khan-Cullors and Bandele, *When They Call You a Terrorist*, 101. We often seek "a better vision" of ourselves even as we are both "flawed and flawless, as each one of us is" (p. 106). She writes of her father "who got cages instead of compassion" (p. 107).

806   Greenberg, "Why Last Chapters Disappoint," 31.

807   West, *Beyond Eurocentrism and Multiculturalism*, 6.

808   Ward, *America's Racial Karma*, 81.

809   Ward, *America's Racial Karma*, 93.

810   Khazan, "Being Black in America Can Be Hazardous to Your Health," https://www.library.wales/discover-learn/digital-exhibitions/pictures/the-wales-window-in-birmingham-alabama.

811   Owens et al., *Radical Dharma*, 104. The authors are quoting Cornel West.

812   At the Sorbonne in Paris, Theodore Roosevelt said (4/23/1910): "It's not the critic who counts, nor the man who points out how the strong man stumbles or where the doer of deeds cold has done better. The credit belongs to the man who is actually in the arena whose face is marred by dust and sweat and blood; who strives valiantly, who errs, who comes short again and again, because there is no effort without error and shortcoming; but who does actually strive to do the deeds; who knows great enthusiasms, the great devotions; who spends himself in a worthy cause; who at best knows in the end the triumph of high achievement, and who, at worst, if he fails, at least fails while daring greatly, so that his place shall never be with those cold, timid souls who neither know victory nor defeat."

813   Abdurraqib, *They Can't Kill Us Until they Kill Us*, 101. The quote continues: "We have to dance, and fight, and make love, and fight, and live, and fight, all with the same ferocity. There are no half measures to be had. It is true, yes, that joy in a violent world can be a rebellion. Sex

can be rebellion. . . . There is no moment in America where I do not feel like I am fighting."

814   Davis and West, *Freedom is a Constant Struggle*, 7.

815   From 1937-1956 LBJ voted against every single piece of Civil Rights legislation.

816   Gore, Theoharis and Woodard, *Want to Start a Revolution?*, 11.

817   This is a major theme in *Resistance, Rebellion, and Death* by Albert Camus (1961).

818   Baradaran, *The Color of Money*, 40.

819   Henderson, "Democracy a Fragile Flower?," https://anglicanism.org/democracy-a-fragile-flower.

820   Davis and West, *Freedom is a Constant Struggle*, 49.

821   Later, stiffer penalties were imposed when federal agents began to oversee prosecution.

822   Khazan, "Being Black in America Can Be Hazardous to Your Health,"

823   Khan-Cullors and Bandele, *When They Call You a Terrorist*, 3.

824   Abdurraqib, *They Can't Kill Us Until They Kill Us*, 8.

825   Leary DeGruy, *Post Traumatic Slave Syndrome*, 164.

826   Federici and Linebaugh, *Re-Enchanting the World*, 109.

827   Litwack, *Trouble in Mind*, 462.

828   Hill and Taylor, *We Still Here*, 112.

829   Khan-Cullors and Bandele, *When They Call You a Terrorist*, 243.

# Glossary

**African Diaspora** — Dispersion of African peoples around the world, primarily through slavery.

**Afrocentrism** — A belief articulated by Maulana Karenga, Molefi Asante, and others that the worldview of Black Americans should relate to traditional African history and cultural values.

**Assimilationism** — The idea folks should surrender their own values for the values of Whites.

**Black Nationalism** — Movement stressing Blacks should have political, and economic autonomy.

**Black Panther Party** — Formed by Huey Newton and Bobby Seale it was a militant, political organization whose members conducted armed patrols to defend Blacks from police brutality.

**De-facto Segregation** — Segregation that is not enforced by law but exists in practice.

**Double-Consciousness** — A concept that Blacks are required to be both "Black and American."

**Dred Scott Case** — Supreme Court decision (1857) that returned plaintiff Dred Scott to slavery.

**Fugitive Slave Law** — This law (1850) prohibited Blacks from the legal trial rights to a trial by jury. Those aiding runaways were punished and even free African Americans could be captured.

**Integrationism** — The belief all minorities should be incorporated as equals into society.

**Kwanzaa (Kswahili)** — A yearly seven-day festival teaching African values and traditions begun by Maulana Karenga (1966). The Seven Principles are: Umoja (unity), Kujicahagulia (self- determination), Ujima (collective work/

responsibility), Ujamaa (cooperative economics), Nia (purpose), Kuumba (creativity), and Imani (faith).

**Maroons —** A term used to describe the communities of fugitive African enslaved.

**Nation of Islam (NOI) —** A religious group that teaches Black separatism.

**Reconstruction —** Federal policies/legislation for defeated Confederate states (1865–1877).

**Sambo —** A racial slur from Helen Bannerman's 1899 children's story Little Black Sambo.

**Underclass —** The term parallels "underprivileged" which implies some are "over privileged."

## AFRICAN TERMS

*Asante Sana* (Swahili): Thank You

*Baraka* (Swahili/Arabic): merit, grace, blessing

*Danka* (Mandingo): curse, evil spell

*Griot* ("French" West African): storyteller/poet/prophet

*Habari Gani?* (Swahili): What's happening?

*Harambee* (Swahili): togetherness, loyal support

*Jambo* (Swahili): greeting that could mean hello or goodbye

*Kemet/Kemetic* (Ancient Egyptian): pertaining to *Kem* or Egypt

*Maafa* (Swahili): great suffering or deep anguish

*Maat* (Ancient Egyptian): righteousness *Malaika* (Swahili): beautiful one

*Mwalimu* (Swahili): teacher

*Nyancho* (Mandingo): royal warrior clan

*Oluku Mi* (Yoruba): my Friend

*Sankofa* (Akkan): to remember/draw strength from the past

*Teranga* (Wolof): hospitality/care for visitors

*Ubuntu* (Zulu): community

*Windugol* (Fulani): writing

*Yurugu* (Akkan): *White man*/one who is disfigured

# Martyrs Memorial Dates (Partial)

30, January 1885: Ebenezer Fowler, businessman

31, January 1964: Louis Allen, farmer

3, February 1989: John Jackson, student

21, February 1965: el-Hajj Malik el-Shabazz Malcolm X, Minister

26, February 1965: Jimmy Lee Jackson, Deacon

11, March 1965: James J. Reeb, Minister

13, March 2020: Breonna Taylor, Louisville, KY

18, March 2018: Stephon Clark, Sacramento, CA

25, March 1965: Viola Gregg Liuzzo, homemaker

31, March 1914: Marie Scott, Muskogee, OK

4, April 2015: Walter Scott, N. Charleston, SC

8, April 1968: Martin Luther King, Jr., Minister

17, April 1880, James Webster Smith, student at West Point, NY

19, April 2015: Freddie Gray, killed in Baltimore

22, April 1894: Thomas Black, Tuscumbia, AL

23, April 1963: William L. Moore, CORE worker

25, April 1939: Mack Parker, farmer

28, April 1899: Sam Holt, burned alive

7, May 1955: George W. Lee, Minister

15, May 1916: Jesse Washington lynched by 15,000 in Waco, TX

19, May 1918: Mary Turner, pregnant, lynched in Folsom, GA

23, May 1891: Dennis Hampton, Barnsley, PA

25, May 1912: Dan Davis, field-hand

29, May 2020: George Floyd, security-guard.

7, June 1998: James Byrd, itinerant worker

12, June 1963: Medgar Wiley Evers, NAACP worker

14, June 1893: George Williams, Waco, TX

21, June 1964: James Earl Chaney; Andrew Goodman; Michael Henry Schwerner.

22, June 1903: George White, laborer

22, June 1982: Willie Turks, age 34, Gravesend, New York

2, July 1822: Denmark Vescey, revolutionary

5, July 2016: Alton Scott, Baton Rouge, LA

6, July 2016: Philando Castile, St. Paul, MN

14, July 1889: Henry Davis, Waco, TX

16, July 2011 – Kenneth Harding, Oakland, CA

17, July 2014: Eric Garner, New York

7, August 1901: John Pennington, laborer

9, August 2014: Michael Brown, Ferguson, MO

14, August 1911: Zachariah Walker, "Negro Desperado," Coatesville, PA

20, August 1965: Jonathan Myrick Daniels, seminarian

23, August 1989: Yusuf Hawkins, age 16, Bensonhurst, NY

28, August 1955: Emmett Till, age 14, student

15, September 1983: Michael Stewart, 25, artist and model

25, September 1961: Herbert Lee, farmer

7, October 1797: Gabriel Prosser, revolutionary

29, October 1984: Eleanor Bumpers, grandmother, 66

31, October 1899: George Wells, miner

7, November 1837: Elijah P. Lovejoy, printer/journalist

11, November 1831: The Reverend Nat Turner

13, November 1988: Mulugeta Seraw, Ethiopian Exchange-student, killed, Portland, OR

21, November 1895: Unknown in Madisonville, Texas one of tens of thousands of "unknowns."

22, November 2014: Tamir Rice, Cleveland, OH

6, December 1899: Richard Coleman, house-servant

13, December 1899: David Pierce, Dunbar, PA

21, December 1986: Michael Griffith, Howard Beach, New York

22, Dec. 1980: Luis Rodriguez; Antoine Davis; Richard Renner

25, December 1951: Harry T. Moore, NAACP worker

# About the Authors

**Lewis T. Tait, Jr.** is the pastor of the Village Church, Washington, D.C; before founding the New Life United Church of Christ, Stone Mountain, GA and serving as founding pastor of Harambee United Church of Christ, Harrisburg, PA (1993–1999). Tait also served as associate pastor with his father for seven years at the Faith Bible Church, Washington, D.C. Tait received a bachelor's degree (Business Administration) from Hardin-Simmons (TX), a master's degree from Howard University School of Divinity (Washington, D.C.), a master's degree from Washington University (Social Work), and a Doctor of Divinity degree in Afrocentric Pastoring and Preaching from United Theological Seminary (Dayton, OH). Tait also received a certificate in the study of Muslim-Christian relations at the Mansfield College, Oxford University, England. Tait was born in Washington, D. C., where he now lives, and has two children, Essence Ayana, and Lewis Thomas Asante.

**A. Christian van Gorder** is Associate Professor of Islamic Studies and World Religions at Baylor University (since 2005). Before that, van Gorder taught at Messiah College (Grantham, PA, 1997–2004) and Yunnan University, Kunming, China. Van Gorder received a bachelor's degree (English and Theatre) from Oral Roberts University, a master's from Asbury Theological Seminary (Kentucky) and a Doctor of Philosophy degree in Muslim-Christian Studies at the Queen's University of Belfast, Ireland. Van Gorder has also studied at Trinity College, Dublin, the National University of Singapore, and the University of Pittsburgh. Van Gorder was born in Pittsburgh, PA and has eleven children: Patrick Xavier, Brendan Daniel, Keegan Joy, Sean Michael, Tatijiana Erika Ezeife, Gretchen Michele Ngozi, Andrew Christian Ojukwu, and the quadruplets, Eric Timo Rieley, Tristan Markus Peter, Clare Raquel, and Grace Helen Sophia.

# Bibliography

"(1867) Thaddeus Stevens, 'Reconstruction,'" *BlackPast*, August 16, 2010. https://www.blackpast.org/african-american-history/1867-thaddeus-stevens-reconstruction/.

Abdurraqib, Hanif. *They Can't Kill Us Until They Kill Us: Essays*. Columbus, Ohio: Two Dollar Radio, 2017.

Abu-Jamal, Mumia. *Have Black Lives Ever Mattered?* Open Media Series. San Francisco: City Lights Books, 2017.

"Academic Fields Where Blacks Earn Few or No Doctoral Degrees in 2017." *The Journal of Blacks in Higher Education*, December 31, 2018. https://jbhe.com/2018/12/academic-fields-where-blacks-earn-few-or-no-doctoral-degrees-in-2017/.

Akbar, Na'im. *Know Thyself*. Tallahassee, FL: Mind Productions & Associates, 1999.

Alexander, Michelle. *The New Jim Crow: Mass Incarceration in the Age of Colorblindness*. Revised paperback edition. New York: New Press, 2012.

Allen, Theodore W. *The Invention of the White Race, Volume 1: Racial Oppression and Social Control*. Verso; Second Edition, 2012.

Ani, Marimba. *Yurugu: An African-Centered Critique of European Cultural Thought and Behavior*. Trenton, N.J: Africa World Press, 1994.

Ansell, Amy Elizabeth. *Race and Ethnicity: The Key Concepts*. Routledge Key Guides. Abingdon, Oxon New York Routledge, 2013. https://doi.org/10.4324/97802034 48236.

BBC World Service. "The Story of Africa. West African Kingdoms: Mali." https://www.bbc.co.uk/worldservice/africa/features/storyofafrica/4chapter3.shtml.

Baldwin, James. *Nobody Knows My Name: More Notes of a, Native Son*. 1st Vintage International ed. New York: Vintage International, 1993.

Banks, Adam J., ed. *Race, Rhetoric, and Technology: Searching for Higher Ground*. NCTE-LEA Research Series in Literacy and Composition. Mahwah, NJ Urbana, Ill: Lawrence Erlbaum, 2006.

Bantum, Brian. *Redeeming Mulatto: A Theology of Race and Christian Hybridity*. Paperback edition. Waco, TX: Baylor University Press, 2016.

Baradaran, Mehrsa. *The Color of Money Black Banks and the Racial Wealth Gap*. Cambridge, MA: Harvard University Press, 2017.

Barber, William J. *We Are Called to Be a Movement*. New York Workman Publishing Co., Inc, 2020.

Baron, Dennis. "Joe Biden's Obama moment, or, I love it when you talk white to me" *The Web of Language*, February 6, 2007. https://blogs.illinois.edu/view/25/1441.

Bass, S. Jonathan. *Blessed Are the Peacemakers: Martin Luther King Jr., Eight White Religious Leaders, and the "Letter from Birmingham Jail."*. Repr. Baton Rouge: Louisiana State University Press, 2009.

Bay, Mia., *The White Image in the Black Mind: African-American Ideas about White People, 1830-1925*. New York: Oxford University Press, 2000.

Beckham, Barry. *Garvey Lives!: The First Produced Play About Black Moses*. Beckham Publication Group, Inc., 2017.

Bell, Derrick. *Faces at the Bottom of the Well: The Permanence of Racism*. New York : Basic Books, 1992.

Benjamin, Rich. *Whitopia: An Improbable Journey to the Heart of White America*. New York: Hyperion, 2009.

Berlin, Ira. *The Destruction of Slavery*. Freedom, a Documentary History of Emancipation, 1861-1867 1. Cambridge: Cambridge University Press, 1985.

Bird, Stephanie Rose. *The Healing Power of African-American Spirituality: A Celebration of Ancestor Worship, Herbs and Hoodoo, Ritual and Conjure*. Newburyport: Hampton Roads Publishing Company, Incorporated, 2022.

Boesak, Allan. *Black theology, black power*. London Oxford: Mowbrays, 1978.

Breitman, George, ed. *Malcolm X Speaks: Selected Speeches and Statements*. New York: Grove Press, 2024.

Brewer, John M. *African Americans in Pittsburgh*. Black America Series. Charleston, SC: Arcadia Pub, 2006.

Briggs, William and Jon Krakauer. "The Massacre That Emboldened White Supremacists." *The New York Times*, August 29, 2020. https://www.nytimes.com/issue/todayspaper/2020/08/29/todays-new-york-times.

Brogdon, Lewis. *Hope on the Brink: Understanding the Emergence of Nihilism in Black America*. Eugene, Oregon: Cascade Books, 2013.

Browder, Anthony T. *Survival Strategies for Africans in America: 13 Steps to Freedom*. Washington, D.C.: Institute of Karmic Guidance, 1996.

Brown-Hinds, Paulette. "Bennett Defiant: Defends Racist Comments," *Black Voice News*, October 7, 2005. https://blackvoicenews.com/2005/10/07/bennett-defiant-defends-racist-comments/.

Bryant, Howard. *The Heritage: Black Athletes, a Divided America and the Politics of Patriotism*. Erscheinungsort nicht ermittelbar: Beacon Press, 2018.

Camus, Albert. *Resistance, Rebellion, and Death: Essays*. Vintage International Ser. Westminster: Knopf Doubleday Publishing Group, 2012.

Cane, Clay. *Live through This: Surviving the Intersections of Sexuality, God, and Race*. First edition. Jersey City, NJ: Cleis Press, 2017.

Chapman, Erin D. *Prove It on Me: New Negroes, Sex, and Popular Culture in the 1920s*. New York: Oxford University Press, 2012.

Chisholm, Shirley. "Speech at Howard University, Washington, D.C.-April 21, 1969." *American Radio Works*. https://americanradioworks.publicradio.org/features/blackspeech/schisholm-2.html.

Cobb, Jelani. *The Devil & Dave Chappelle & Other Essays*. New York: Thunder's Mouth Press, 2007.

Colley, Zoe A. *Ain't Scared of Your Jail: Arrest, Imprisonment, and the Civil Rights Movement*. 1st pbk. printing. Gainesville: University Press of Florida, 2014.

Contreras, Russell. "Story of Underground Railroad to Mexico Gains Attention." *Waco Tribune-Herald*, September 17, 2020.

Conyers, James L., ed. *Afrocentric Traditions*. Africana Studies v. 1. New Brunswick, N.J: Transaction Publishers, 2005.

Cross, Tiffany. *Say It Louder! Black Voters, White Narratives, and Saving Our Democracy.* New York: HarperCollins Publishers, 2020.

Curry, Andrew. "Callie Guy House (ca. 1861-1928)," *BlackPast*, July 6, 2010. https://www.blackpast.org/african-american-history/callie-house-c-1861-1928/.

Darby, Seyward. *Sisters in Hate: American Women on the Front Lines of White Nationalism.* First edition. New York: Little, Brown and Company, 2020.

Davidson, Basil. *African Civilization Revisited: From Antiquity to Modern Times.* Trenton, N.J: Africa World Press, 1991.

Davis, Angela Y. *Women, Culture & Politics.* Westminster: Knopf Doubleday Publishing Group, 2011.

Davis, Angela Y., and Cornel West. *Freedom Is a Constant Struggle: Ferguson, Palestine, and the Foundations of a Movement.* Edited by Frank Barat. Chicago, Illinois: Haymarket Books, 2016.

Devega, Chauncey. "Cornel West on This Moment of 'Escalating Consciousness' and the Need for Radical Democracy," *Salon*, June 26, 2020. https://www.salon.com/2020/06/26/cornel-west-on-this-moment-of-escalating-consciousness-and-the-need-for-radical-democracy/.

DiAngelo, Robin J. *White Fragility: Why It's so Hard for White People to Talk about Racism.* Boston: Beacon Press, 2018.

Dodson, Angela P., ed. *We Refuse to Be Silent: Women's Voices on Justice for Black Men.* Minneapolis: Broadleaf Books, 2024.

D'Oro, Rachel. "Anti-Government Militias Popping Up Across the U.S." *Waco Tribune-Herald*, November 21, 2009.

Dorrien, Gary J. *Breaking White Supremacy: Martin Luther King Jr. and the Black Social Gospel.* New Haven; London: Yale University Press, 2018.

Douglas, Kelly Brown. *Stand Your Ground: Black Bodies and the Justice of God.* Maryknoll, New York: Orbis Books, 2015.

"Dr. Bethune's Last Will & Testament," *Bethune-Cookman University.* https://www.cookman.edu/history/last-will-testament.html.

Du Bois, William E. B. *W.E.B. DuBois Speaks. 1: 1890 - 1919.* 6. print. New York: Pathfinder, 1988.

Dyson, Michael Eric. "Whose President Was He?" *Politico Magazine*, January/February 2016. https://www.politico.com/magazine/story/2016/01/barack-obama-race-relations-213493/.

Ellis, Glenn. „COVID-19: Structural Racism and Black Health". *New Pittsburgh Courier*, November 11, 2020. https://newpittsburghcourier.com/2020/11/11/covid-19-structural-racism-and-black-health/.

Federici, Silvia, and Peter Linebaugh. *Re-Enchanting the World: Feminism and the Politics of the Commons.* Oakland, California: PM Press, 2019.

Feln, Judith. "Maya and Egyptian Pyramids: A Hidden Connection?" *Psychology Today*, October 31, 2011. https://www.psychologytoday.com/us/blog/life-is-a-trip/201110/maya-and-egyptian-pyramids-a-hidden-connection.

Fields, Karen E., and Barbara Jeanne Fields. *Racecraft: The Soul of Inequality in American Life.* Paperback edition. London: Verso, 2014.

Finkelman, Paul. *Slavery and the Founders: Race and Liberty in the Age of Jefferson.* 2nd ed. Armonk, N.Y: M.E. Sharpe, 2001.

Finney, Carolyn. *Black Faces,, White Spaces: Reimagining the Relationship of African Americans to the Great Outdoors*. Chapel Hill: The University of North Carolina Press, 2014.

Fogel, Robert William, and Stanley L. Engerman. *Time on the Cross: The Economics of American Negro Slavery*. New York London: W.W. Norton, 1989.

Ford, Richard Thompson. *The Race Card*. 1st ed. New York: Farrar, Straus & Giroux, 2008.

Fouhy, Beth, and Nedra Pickler. "Obama: Changes May Take Some Time." *Waco Tribune-Herald*, November 10, 2008.

France, Lisa Respers. "These films don't help the racism conversation." *CNN Entertainment*, 11 June 2020. https://www.cnn.com/2020/06/10/entertainment/racism-movies-conversation/index.html.

Franklin, Robert Michael. *Another Day's Journey: Black Churches Confronting the American Crisis*. Minneapolis: Fortress Press, 1997.

Freire, Paulo, and Donaldo P. Macedo. *Pedagogy of the Oppressed: 30th Anniversary Edition*. Translated by Myra Bergman Ramos. 30th anniversary edition. New York: Bloomsbury Publishing, 2014.

Garner, Dwight. "What Drives Social Progress? An Argument for Honor." *The New York Times*, September 14, 2010. https://www.nytimes.com/2010/09/15/books/15book.html.

Garza, Alicia. *The Purpose of Power: How We Come Together When We Fall Apart*. New York: One World, 2020.

Gilroy, Paul. *Darker than Blue: On the Moral Economies of Black Atlantic Culture*. The W.E.B. Du Bois Lectures. Cambridge, Massachusetts London, England: The Belknap Press of Harvard University Press, 2010.

Glaude, Eddie S. *Begin Again: James Baldwin's America and Its Urgent Lessons for Our Own*. Erscheinungsort nicht ermittelbar: Crown/Archetype, 2020.

———. *Democracy in Black: How Race Still Enslaves the American Soul*. First paperback edition. New York: B\D\W\Y Broadway Books, 2017.

Goodman, Amy. "While Gingrich Says Obama Acts "Kenyan, Anti-Colonial," What Does a Real Kenyan Anti-Colonialist Think? A Conversation with Novelist Ngugi wa Thiong'o." *Democracy Now*, September 13, 2010. https://www.democracynow.org/2010/9/13/while_gingrich_says_obama_acts_kenyan.

Gore, Dayo F., Jeanne Theoharis, and Komozi Woodard, eds. *Want to Start a Revolution? Radical Women in the Black Freedom Struggle*. New York: New York University Press, 2009.

Gottlieb, Peter. *Making Their Own Way: Southern Blacks' Migration to Pittsburgh, 1916-30*. Illini books ed. Urbana: University of Illinois Press, 1997.

Graham, David A., Adrienne Green, Cullen Murphy, and Parker Richards. "An Oral History of Trump's Bigotry." *The Atlantic*, June 2019. https://www.theatlantic.com/magazine/archive/2019/06/trump-racism-comments/588067/.

Greenberg, David. "Why Last Chapters Disappoint." *The New York Times*, March 18, 2011. https://www.nytimes.com/2011/03/20/books/review/why-last-chapters-disappoint-essay.html?pagewanted=all.

Griffin, Paul R. *Seeds of Racism in the Soul of America*. Naperville, Ill.: Sourcebooks, 2000.

Hadjor, Kofi Buenor. *Another America: The Politics of Race and Blame*. Boston, MA: South End Press, 1995.

Hamad, Ruby. *White Tears / Brown Scars: How White Feminism Betrays Women of Color.* New York: Catapult, 2020.

Henderson, The Rev'd Dr. Nicholas. "Democracy a Fragile Flower?" *Anglicanism.org*, July 2024. https://anglicanism.org/democracy-a-fragile-flower.

Herbert, Bob. "A Failure of Leadership." *The New York Times*, May 9, 2005. https://www.nytimes.com/2005/09/05/opinion/a-failure-of-leadership.html.

Hill, Marc Lamont, and Keeanga-Yamahtta Taylor. *We Still Here: Pandemic, Policing, Protest, and Possibility.* Edited by Frank Barat. Chicago, Illinois: Haymarket Books, 2020.

Hinton, Anthony Ray, Lara Love Hardin, and Bryan Stevenson. *The Sun Does Shine: How I Found Life and Freedom on Death Row.* New York: St. Martin's Press, 2018.

Hirsch, James S. *Riot and Remembrance: The Tulsa Race War and Its Legacy.* Boston: Houghton Mifflin, 2002.

Hochschild, Adam. *King Leopold's Ghost: A Story of Greed, Terror, and Heroism in Colonial Africa.* 1st ed. Piraí: HarperCollins Publishers, 1999.

Hodgson, Godfrey. *Martin Luther King.* London: Quercus, 2010.

Hood, Robert E. *Must God Remain Greek? Afro Cultures and God-Talk.* Minneapolis: Fortress Press, 1990.

Hooks, Bell, and Cornel West. *Breaking Bread: Insurgent Black Intellectual Life.* New York: Routledge/Taylor & Francis Group, 2017.

Hughley, D. L., and Doug Moe. *Surrender, White People! Our Unconditional Terms for Peace.* First edition. New York: William Morrow, an imprint of HarperCollins Publishers, 2020.

Hunter, David. *I Hate Black People Who Hate Black People: A Grassroots Analysis of an Untreated Disease in the African American Community.* Charleston, S.C.: Createspace, 2011.

Ignatiev, Noel, ed. *Race Traitor.* New York: Routledge, 1996.

Irish Central Staff. "On His Birthday, the Best Quotes from Robert F. Kennedy," *Irish Central*, November 20, 2023. https://www.irishcentral.com/roots/history/robert-f-kennedy-quotes.

Jackson, Kenneth T. *The Ku Klux Klan in the City, 1915-1930.* 1st Elephant pbk. ed. Chicago: I.R. Dee, 1992.

Jensen, Robert. *The Heart of Whiteness: Confronting Race, Racism, and White Privilege.* San Francisco, CA: City Lights, 2005.

Johnson, R. Theodore. "The Challenge of Black Patriotism." *The New York Times*, November 18, 2020. https://www.nytimes.com/2020/11/18/magazine/black-voters-election-patriotism.html.

Jones, Van. *Beyond the Messy Truth: How We Came Apart, How We Come Together.* First edition. New York: Ballantine Books, 2017.

Jordan-Zachery, Julia S. *Black Women, Cultural Images, and Social Policy.* Routledge Studies in North American Politics 2. New York: Routledge, 2009.

Joseph, Frederick. *The Black Friend: On Being a Better White Person.* First edition. Sommerville, Massachusetts: Candlewick Press, 2020.

Joseph, Peniel E., ed. *Neighborhood Rebels: Black Power at the Local Level.* 1st ed. Contemporary Black History. New York: Palgrave Macmillan, 2010.

Kaminski, John P., ed. *A Necessary Evil? Slavery and the Debate over the Constitution.* 1. ed. Constitutional Heritage Series 2. Madison, Wis: Madison House, 1995.

Kendi, Ibram X. *How to Be an Antiracist.* New York: One World, 2019.

———. *Stamped from the Beginning: The Definitive History of Racist Ideas in America.* First trade paperback edition. History / African American Studies. New York: Bold Type Books, 2017.

Khan-Cullors, Patrisse, and Asha Bandele. *When They Call You a Terrorist: A Black Lives Matter Memoir.* First edition. New York: St. Martin's Press, 2018.

Khan, Maria R., Farzana Kapadia, Amanda Geller, Medha Mazumdar, Joy D. Scheidell, Kristen D. Krause, Richard J. Martino, et al. "Racial and Ethnic Disparities in 'Stop-and-Frisk' Experience among Young Sexual Minority Men in New York City." Edited by Nickolas D. Zaller. *PLOS ONE* 16, no. 8 (August 26, 2021): e0256201. https://doi.org/10.1371/journal.pone.0256201.

Khazan, Olga. "Being Black in America Can Be Hazardous to Your Health." *The Atlantic*, July/August 2018. https://www.library.wales/discover-learn/digital-exhibitions/pictures/the-wales-window-in-birmingham-alabama.

King, Martin Luther, Clayborne Carson, and Peter C. Holloran. *A Knock at Midnight: Inspiration from the Great Sermons of Reverend Martin Luther King, Jr.* New York: Time Warner AudioBooks, 2005.

Krugman, Paul. "Leaving Children Behind." *The New York Times*, February 27, 2011. https://www.nytimes.com/2011/02/28/opinion/28krugman.html.

Lacy, Karyn R. *Blue-Chip Black: Race, Class, and Status in the New Black Middle Class.* Berkeley: University of California Press, 2007.

Lambert, Otto, and Wallace E. Klineberg. *Children's Views of Foreign Peoples: A Cross-National Study.* Appleton-Century-Crofts; First Edition, 1967.

Lawson, Steven F. *Running for Freedom: Civil Rights and Black Politics in America since 1941.* 3rd ed. Chichester, West Sussex, U.K.; Malden, MA: Wiley-Blackwell, 2009.

Leary, Joy DeGruy. *Post Traumatic Slave Syndrome: America's Legacy of Enduring Injury and Healing.* Newly revised and Updated edition. United States: Joy DeGruy Publications Inc., 2018.

Letters to the Editor. "Closing the Racial Gap in Education." *The New York Times*, August 21, 2010. https://www.nytimes.com/2010/08/22/opinion/l22schools.html.

Lewis, Rupert. *Marcus Garvey.* The Caribbean Biography Series. Mona (Jamaïque): the University of the West Indies press, 2018.

Lincoln, C. Eric. *Coming through the Fire: Surviving Race and Place in America.* Duke University Press Books, 1996.

Lindqvist, Sven. *The Skull Measurer's Mistake: And Other Portraits of Men and Women Who Spoke out against Racism.* New York: New Press: Distributed by W.W. Norton, 1997.

Lipsitz, George. *The Possessive Investment in Whiteness: How White People Profit from Identity Politics.* Rev. and Expanded ed. Philadelphia, Pa: Temple University Press, 2006.

Litwack, Leon F. *Trouble in Mind: Black Southerners in the Age of Jim Crow.* Westminster: Knopf Doubleday Publishing Group, 2010.

Loewen, James W. *Lies My Teacher Told Me: Everything Your American History Textbook Got Wrong.* This Touchstone trade paperback edition October 2007. New York London Toronto Sydney: Touchstone, 2007.

Lomax, Louis E. "A Summing Up: Louis Lomax Interviews Malcolm X." *"A Summing Up: Louis Lomax Interviews Malcolm X." When the Word Is Given: A Report on Elijah Muhammad, Malcolm X, and the Black Muslim World.*, 1963. https://

teachingamericanhistory.org/document/a-summing-up-louis-lomax-interviews-malcolm-x/.

Magubane, Bernard. *The Ties That Bind: African-American Consciousness of Africa.* Trenton, N.J: Africa World Press, 1987.

Malcolm X. "A Summing Up: Louis Lomax interviews Malcolm X (1963)." *Teaching American History.* https://teachingamericanhistory.org/document/a-summing-up-louis-lomax interviews-malcolm-x/.

Marcus, Harold G. *Haile Sellassie I.* Berkeley Los Angeles London: University of California press, 1987.

Martin Luther King, Jr. "Chapter 13: Pilgrimage to Nonviolence." In *Autobiography of Martin Luther King Jr,* edited by Clayborne Carson. Warner Books and Time, 1998. *The Martin Luther King, Jr. Research and Education Institute.* https://kinginstitute. stanford.edu/chapter-13-pilgrimage-nonviolence.

Mazel, Ella. *And Don't Call Me a Racist!* Argonaut, 1988.

McDowell, Deborah E., and Arnold Rampersad. *Slavery and the Literary Imagination.* Johns Hopkins Paperbacks. Baltimore London: Johns Hopkins university press, 1989.

McGuire, Danielle L. *At the Dark End of the Street: Black Women, Rape, and Resistance; a New History of the Civil Rights Movement from Rosa Parks to the Rise of Black Power.* 1. ed. New York, NY: Vintage Books, 2010.

McKinney-Whitaker, Rev. Dr. Stephen, "Travel Notes from Pastor Stephen: Learning from Germans," *Derry Church,* April 17, 2023. https://www.derrypres.org/news/travel-notes-from-pastor-stephen-learning-from-germans/.

Morris, Monique W. *Black Stats: African Americans by the Numbers in the Twenty-First Century.* New York: The New Press, 2014.

———. *Pushout: The Criminalization of Black Girls in Schools.* New York London: The New Press, 2016.

Moreau, Jordan. "Harry Shearer No Longer Voicing Black 'Simpsons' Character Dr. Hibbert, Kevin Michael Richardson to Take Over." *Variety,* February 22, 2021. https://variety.com/2021/tv/news/the-simpsons-dr-hibbert-recast-harry-shearer-kevin-michael-richardson-1234912612/.

Mullen, Bill, and Fred Wei-han Ho, eds. *Afro Asia: Revolutionary Political and Cultural Connections between African Americans and Asian Americans.* Durham, NC: Duke University Press, 2008.

Murphy, Mary-Elizabeth B. *Jim Crow Capital: Women and Black Freedom Struggles in Washington, D.C., 1920-1945.* North Carolina Scholarship Online. Chapel Hill: University of North Carolina Press, 2018.

Neiman, Susan. *Learning from the Germans: Race and the Memory of Evil.* First edition. New York: Farrar, Straus and Giroux, 2019.

Newkirk, Reginald, and Nathan Rutstein. *Racial Healing: The Institutes for the Healing of Racism.* Albion, Mich.: National Resource Center for the Healing of Racism, 2000.

Newman, Richard, and Marcia Sawyer. *Everybody Say Freedom: Everything You Need to Know about African-American History.* New York: Plume, 1996.

Nguyen, Viet Thanh. "Vietnamese Lives, American Imperialist Views, Even in 'Da 5 Bloods.'" *The New York Times,* June 24, 2020. https://www.nytimes.com/2020/06/24/movies/da-5-bloods-vietnam.html.

Norris, Floyd. "The Return of the Misery Index." *The New York Times*, September 12, 2008. https://www.nytimes.com/2008/09/13/business/economy/13charts.html.

Nye, Russel B. *William Lloyd Garrison and the Humanitarian Reformers*. Little, Brown & Company; 1st Paperback Edition, 1955.

Obama, Barack. *Dreams from My Father: A Story of Race and Inheritance*. New York, NY: Three Rivers Press, 2004.

Okpewho, Isidore, Carole Boyce Davies, and Ali A. Mazrui, eds. *The African Diaspora: African Origins and New World Identities*. 1st paperback ed. Bloomington, Ind.: Indiana University Press, 2001.

Opie, Frederick Douglass. *Southern Food and Civil Rights: Feeding the Revolution*. Charleston, SC: American Palate, 2017.

Owens, Lama Rod. *Radical Dharma: Talking Race, Love, and Liberation*. Berkeley: North Atlantic Books, 2016.

Patterson, Orlando. *Rituals of Blood: Consequences of Slavery in Two American Centuries*. New York, NY: Basic Civitas, 1998.

Pengelly, Martin. "Black female editor takes over Alabama paper at center of KKK furore," *The Guardian*, September 21, 2019. https://www.theguardian.com/us-news/2019/feb/24/alabama-newspaper-at-centre-of-kkk-outcry-appoints-black-female-editor.

Perkins, John. *Beyond Charity: The Call to Christian Community Development*. Grand Rapids, Mich: Baker Books, 1993.

Perry, Richard John. *"Race" and Racism: The Development of Modern Racism in America*. 1st ed. New York: Palgrave Macmillan, 2007.

Pilkington, Ed. "'Truth isn't truth': Giuliani trumps 'alternative facts' with new Orwellian outburst." *The Guardian*, August 19, 2018. https://www.theguardian.com/us-news/2018/aug/19/truth-isnt-truth-rudy-giuliani-trump-alternative-facts-orwellian.

Prisock, Louis G. *African Americans in Conservative Movements: The Inescapability of Race*. Palgrave Macmillan, 2018.

Reed, Adolph L. *Renewing Black Intellectual History: The Ideological and Material Foundations of African American Thought*. London New York: Routledge, 2016. https://doi.org/10.4324/9781315632414.

"Religious Studies – The Final Colonization Of American Indians, Part 1 (Tink Tinker, wazhazhe udsethe)," *Religious Theory: E-Supplement to the Journal for Cultural and Religious Theory*, June 1, 2020. https://jcrt.org/religioustheory/2020/06/01/religious-studies-the-final-colonization-of-american-indians-part-1-tink-tinker-wazhazhe-udsethe/#:~:text=Religious%20Studies%20%E2%80%93%20The%2-0Final%20Colonization,%2C%20wazhazhe%20oudsethe)%20%E2%80%93%20RELIGIOUS%20THEORY.

"Rep. Baker (R-LA): 'We Finally Cleaned Up Public Housing in New Orleans,'" *Democracy Now*, September 12, 2005. https://www.democracynow.org/2005/9/12/headlines/rep_baker_r_la_we_finally_cleaned_up_public_housing_in_new_orleans.

Retica, Aaron. "Remembering and Forgetting Milan Kundera," *The New York Times*, April 18, 2011. https://archive.nytimes.com/6thfloor.blogs.nytimes.com/2011/04/18/remembering-and-forgetting-milan-kundera/.

Rev. Barber II., William and Rev. Theoharis, Liz. "'Normalcy - Never Again!'" *The Nation*, May 8, 2020. Https://www.thenation.com/article/society/king-rosa-parks-coronavirus/.

Robinson, Randall. *The Debt: What America Owes to Blacks*. East Rutherford: Penguin Publishing Group, 2001.

Ruck, Rob. *Sandlot Seasons: Sport in Black Pittsburgh*. Illini Books ed. Sport and Society. Urbana: University of Illinois Press, 1993.

Sanders, Cheryl J., ed. *Living the Intersection: Womanism and Afrocentrism in Theology*. Minneapolis, Minn: Fortress Pr, 1995.

Sanneh, Lamin O. *Abolitionists Abroad: American Blacks and the Making of Modern West Africa*. 2. print. Cambridge, Mass.: Harvard University Press, 2001.

Shipler, David K. *A Country of Strangers: Blacks and Whites in America*. New York: Vintage Books, 1998.

Shull, Steven A. *American Civil Rights Policy from Truman to Clinton: The Role of Presidential Leadership*. M.E. Sharpe; 2nd ed. edition (July), 1999.

Smith, Barbara Dawson. *Stolen Heart*. New York: Avon Books, 1988.

Smith, John David. *W.E.B. Du Bois, Felix von Luschan, and Racial Reform at the Fin de Siècle*. Vol. 47. Universitätsverlag WINTER Gmbh, 2002. https://www.jstor.org/stable/41157700.

Smith, Zadie. *Intimations: Six Essays*. New York: Penguin Books, 2020.

Snyder, Timothy. *On Tyranny: Twenty Lessons from the Twentieth Century*. 37th printing. New York: Crown, 2017.

Solomon, Akiba, and Kenrya Rankin, eds. *How We Fight White Supremacy: A Field Guide to Black Resistance*. First edition. New York, NY: Bold Type Books, 2019.

Sorin, Gerald. *Abolitionism: A New Perspective*. 3. print. New York: Praeger, 1975.

Spencer, Jon Michael. *The Rhythms of Black Folk: Race, Religion, and Pan-Africanism*. Trenton, N.J: Africa World Press, 1995.

Staff Writer. "DePass suggests gorilla is related to Michelle Obama." *BlueRidgeNow*, June 14, 2009. https://eu.blueridgenow.com/story/news/2009/06/14/depass-suggests-gorilla-is-related-to-michelle-obama/28187595007/.

Starkman, Dean. "Investors vs. the Public: Why the business press should focus on the latter." *Columbia Journalism Review*, September 17, 2009. https://www.cjr.org/the_audit/investors_vs_the_public.php.

"State of the Union: Obama Makes Jobs Top Priority for 2010." *ABC News*, January 27, 2010. https://abcnews.go.com/Politics/State_of_the_Union/president-obama-state-of-the-union-address/story?id=9678571.

Steelwater, Eliza. *The Hangman's Knot: Lynching, Legal Execution, and America's Struggle with the Death Penalty*. Boulder, Colo.: Westview Press, 2003.

Steinberg, Stephen. *The Ethnic Myth: Race, Ethnicity, and Class in America*. 3rd ed. Boston: Beacon Press, 2001.

Stephens, Michelle Ann. *Skin Acts: Race, Psychoanalysis, and the Black Male Performer*. Durham, NC: Duke Univ. Press, 2014.

Stewart, Carlyle Fielding. *Black Spirituality and Black Consciousness: Soul Force, Culture, and Freedom in the African-American Experience*. Trenton, NJ: Africa World Press, 1999.

Stolberg, Sheryl Gay. "Obama Pledges Expanded Ties With Muslim Nations." *The New York Times*, November 9, 2010. https://www.nytimes.com/2010/11/10/world/asia/10prexy.html.

Sussman, Robert W. *The Myth of Race: The Troubling Persistence of an Unscientific Idea.* Fourth printing. Cambridge, Massachusetts: Harvard University Press, 2016.

Taylor, Dorceta E. *Toxic Communities: Environmental Racism, Industrial Pollution, and Residential Mobility.* New York: New York University Press, 2014.

Taylor, Keeanga-Yamahtta. *From #BlackLivesMatter to Black Liberation.* Chicago: Haymarket Books, 2016.

Thurman, Howard. *Jesus and the Disinherited.* Boston: Beacon Press, 2012.

Tillet, Salamishah. "When Culture Really Began to Reckon With White Privilege." *The New York Times*, December 9, 2020. https://www.nytimes.com/2020/12/09/arts/black-artists-open-letters.html.

Tran, Jonathan. *Asian Americans and the Spirit of Racial Capitalism.* New York, NY: Oxford University Press, 2022.

Tucker, Sterling. *Black Reflections on White Power.* W. B. Eerdmans Pub. Co, 1969.

USAFacts Team. "White People Own 86% of Wealth and Make up 60% of the Population," *USAFacts*, October 5, 2023. https://usafacts.org/articles/white-people-own-86-wealth-despite-making-60-population.

Van Sertima, Ivan. *They Came before Columbus: The African Presence in Ancient America.* Random House trade pbk. ed. New York: Random House Trade Paperbacks, 2003.

Wallace, Michele. *Black Macho and the Myth of the Superwoman.* New ed. London: Verso, 2015.

Ward, Larry. *America's Racial Karma: An Invitation to Heal.* Erscheinungsort nicht ermittelbar: Parallax Press, 2020.

Washington, Harriet A. *Medical Apartheid: The Dark History of Medical Experimentation on Black Americans from Colonial Times to the Present.* 1st pbk. ed. New York: Harlem Moon, 2006.

———. "Apology Shines Light on Racial Schism in Medicine." *The New York Times*, July 29, 2008. https://www.nytimes.com/2008/07/29/health/views/29essa.html.

———. "The Organ Thieves. The Shocking Story of the First Heart Transplant in the Segregated South By Chip Jones." *The New York Times*, August 18, 2020. https://www.nytimes.com/2020/08/18/books/review/the-organ-thieves-chip-jones.html.

Waters, Kristin. *Maria W. Stewart and the Roots of Black Political Thought.* Margaret Walker Alexander Series in African American Studies. Jackson: University Press of Mississippi, 2022.

Watson, Veronica T. *The Souls of White Folk: African American Writers Theorize Whiteness.* Margaret Walker Alexander Series in African American Studies. Jackson, Miss: Univ. Press of Mississippi, 2013.

Welsing, Frances Cress. *The Isis Papers: The Keys to the Colors.* Place of publication not identified: C.W. Pub., 1991.

West, Cornel. *Beyond Eurocentrism and Multiculturalism.* Monroe, Me: Common Courage Press, 1993.

Wilkerson, Isabel. *Caste: The Origins of Our Discontents.* First edition. New York: Random House, 2020.

Williams, Lee E. *Anatomy of Four Race Riots. Racial Conflict in Knoxville, Elaine -Arkansas-, Tulsa and Chicago, 1919-1921.* Hattiesburg: Univ. and College Pr, 1972.

Williams, Reggie. "What Does He Mean by 'They Believe He is White?'" In *Between the World of Ta-Nehisi Coates and Christianity*, edited by David Evans and Peter Dula, 72-83. Eugene, Oregon: Cascade Books: an Imprint of Wipf and Stock Publishers, 2018.

Williams, Robert W., Ph.D. "W. E. B. Du Bois and the Socio-Political Structures of Education." *Negro Educational Review Journal* 55, No. 1., January 1, 2004.: 9-26. https://web.p.ebscohost.com/ehost/pdfviewer/pdfviewer?vid=0&sid=cbbb312e-3de3-471e-ae68-5eff84aa5fcf%4oredis.

Williams, Caroline Randall. „You Want a Confederate Monument? My Body Is a Confederate Monument". *The New York Times*, June 26, 2020. https://www.nytimes.com/2020/06/26/opinion/confederate-monuments-racism.html.

Wilson, Charles Reagan. *Judgment & Grace in Dixie: Southern Faiths from Faulkner to Elvis*. Athens, Ga: Univ. of Georgia Press, 1995.

Winsboro, Irvin D. S., ed. *Old South, New South, or down South? Florida and the Modern Civil Rights Movement*. 1st ed. Morgantown: West Virginia University Press, 2009.

Winters, Mary-Frances. *Black Fatigue: How Racism Erodes the Mind, Body, and Spirit*. San Francisco, USA: Berrett-Koehler, 2021.

Wise, Tim J. *Colorblind: The Rise of Post-Racial Politics and the Retreat from Racial Equity*. Open Media Series. San Francisco: City Lights Books, 2010.

Wolfe, Stephanie. *The Politics of Reparations and Apologies*. Springer Series in Transitional Justice volume 7. New York, NY: Springer, 2014.

Woodson, Carter Godwin. *Free Negro Owners of Slaves in the United States in 1830: Together with Absentee Ownership of Slaves in the United States in 1830*. Place of publication not identified: Historic Publishing, 2015.

Woodward, Calvin. "Racial Incidents Follow Obama Win." *Waco Tribune-Herald*, November 16, 2008.

Wright, Donald R. *African Americans in the Colonial Era: From African Origins through the American Revolution*. 2nd ed. American History Series. Wheeling, Ill: Harlan Davidson, 2000.

Wypijewski, Joann. "Red Scare, Black Scare. The birthers, the anticommunist crazies, the "Obama as Witch Doctor" caricatures: they're all of a piece, welded to sex." *The Nation*, November 19, 2009. https://www.thenation.com/article/archive/red-scare-black-scare/.

X, Malcolm. *The End of White World Supremacy: Four Speeches*. Edited by Benjamin Karim. First Arcade edition with audio download. New York: Arcade Publishing, 2020.

X, Malcolm, and Archie C. Epps. *Malcolm X: Speeches at Harvard*. 1st Paragon House ed. New York: Marlowe & Company, 1994.

X, Malcolm, and Alex Haley. *The Autobiography of Malcolm X: As Told to Alex Haley*. 1. Ballantine Books ed., [Nachdr.]. New York: Ballantine Books, 1999.

Yancey, George A. *Beyond Racial Gridlock: Embracing Mutual Responsibility*. Downers Grove, Ill.: InterVarsity Press, 2006.

Youngblood, Rev. Dr. Johnny Ray, "Celebrating the 22nd Year of the Maafa Acknowledgment," *The Brownsville Collective Maafa Edition*, February 2016. https://issuu.com/thebrownsvillecollective/docs/maafa_newspaper15__2_.

Zamir, Shamoon, ed. *The Cambridge Companion to W. E. B. Du Bois*. 1. publ. Cambridge Companions to American Studies. Cambridge, UK: Cambridge Univ. Press, 2008. https://doi.org/10.1017/CCOL9780521871518.

Zirin, Dave. *What's My Name, Fool? Sports and Resistance in the United States*. Chicago: Haymarket Books, 2005.